THE ARAMAIC ORIGIN

OF THE

FOURTH GOSPEL

THE ARAMAIC ORIGIN

OF THE

FOURTH GOSPEL

BY

THE REV. C. F. BURNEY, M.A., D.LITT.

Oriel Professor of the Interpretation of Holy Scripture at Oxford
Fellow of Oriel and St. John's Colleges, Oxford
Canon of Rochester

Wipf & Stock
PUBLISHERS
Eugene, Oregon

Wipf and Stock Publishers
199 West 8th Avenue, Suite 3
Eugene, Oregon 97401

The Aramaic Origin of the Fourth Gospel
By Burney, Charles F.
ISBN: 1-59244-598-5
Publication date 3/17/2004
Previously published by Oxford University Press, 1922

CONTENTS

PRINCIPAL ABBREVIATIONS EMPLOYED

Cur. = The Curetonian Syriac Version of the Gospels (cf. p. 26).

Pal. Syr. = The Palestinian Syriac Lectionary (cf. p. 25).

Pesh. = The Peshiṭtā Syriac Version (cf. p. 25).

Sin. = The Sinaitic Syriac Version of the Gospels (cf. p. 26).

Targ. Jer. = The Jerusalem Targum on the Pentateuch (cf. p. 24).

Targ. Jon. = The Targum of Jonathan on the Prophets (cf. p. 24).

Targ. Onk. = The Targum of Onkelos on the Pentateuch (cf. p. 23).

Targ. Ps.-Jon. = The Targum of Pseudo-Jonathan on the Pentateuch (cf. p. 23).

WH. = The Greek text of Westcott and Hort.

Abbott, *JG.* = Edwin A. Abbott, *Johannine Grammar* (1906).

Dalman, *Gramm.* = G. Dalman, *Grammatik des jüdisch-palästinischen Aramäisch* (1894).

Dalman, *WJ.* = G. Dalman, *The Words of Jesus considered in the light of Post-Biblical Jewish Writings and the Aramaic Language* (Eng. Trans., 1902).

Deissmann, *LAE.* = A. Deissmann, *Light from the Ancient East* (Eng. Trans., 1910).

HS[2]. = Sir John C. Hawkins, *Horae Synopticae* (2nd edition, 1909).

Moulton, *NTG*[3]. = J. H. Moulton, *A Grammar of New Testament Greek* (vol. i, 3rd edition, reprinted 1919).

Schlatter, *Sprache* = A. Schlatter, *Die Sprache und Heimat des vierten Evangelisten* (1902).

Wellhausen, *Einleitung*[2] = J. Wellhausen, *Einleitung in die drei ersten Evangelien* (zweite Ausgabe 1911).

INTRODUCTION

In a sermon preached in June 1920 before the University of Oxford* the present writer made a plea for a closer synthesis of Old Testament learning with the study of the New Testament; and reviewing summarily and generally the kind of New Testament problems which might receive fuller elucidation through the more direct application to them of Semitic learning, he put forward the possibility that in the future a Semitic scholar might arise who, examining the language of the Fourth Gospel in detail, would prove beyond the range of reasonable doubt that it was based upon an Aramaic original.

In venturing upon this somewhat bold prophecy, the writer had not at the time any thought of undertaking the task himself. Absorbed in Old Testament studies, and realizing with ever-growing insistency the task which lies before Semitic scholars of widening and deepening the basis of their learning if they would make any really first-hand contribution to their subject, he had not enjoyed the opportunity of prosecuting his New Testament studies beyond the somewhat superficial stage which ordinarily represents a theological tutor's acquaintance with the wide range of learning in which, in addition to his own special branch of research, he has generally to direct his pupils' reading. The problem of the origin and authorship of the Fourth Gospel had, however, always attracted him. He had been impressed (as every Hebrew scholar must be impressed) with the Semitic character of its diction, and recognizing to the full the importance of Dr. Lightfoot's remarks on the question,† had realized that this was a subject of research fundamental to the problem of authorship which called for closer and more expert attention than it had hitherto received; and he had been amazed at the lightness with which it was dismissed or

* Since published by the Oxford University Press under the title *The Old Testament Conception of Atonement fulfilled by Christ.*

† *Biblical Essays*, pp. 126 ff.

altogether ignored by New Testament scholars who confidently asserted the Hellenistic character of the Gospel. An article by Dr. C. J. Ball, entitled 'Had the Fourth Gospel an Aramaic Archetype?', which appeared in the *Expository Times* for November 1909, explained certain peculiarities in the first chapter of the Gospel by the theory of an Aramaic original; and this, though (to the best of the present writer's knowledge) it stands alone in advocating this theory, yet appealed to him as evidently upon right lines.* The evidence there adduced he had casually supplemented by notice of additional peculiarities pointing in the same direction; notably, the sharing by the Fourth Gospel of many of the peculiarities of diction which Canon Allen and Prof. Wellhausen cite as exhibiting the influence of Aramaic upon the style of St. Mark's Gospel.

This was about the position at which the writer's acquaintance with the subject stood when he wrote the sermon which he has mentioned. He had formed an opinion based on general observation, but he could not claim to have substantiated it by the kind of close study which deserves to be dignified as research. Further reflection, however, convinced him that the matter could not be allowed to rest here. He had suggested in the sermon that both

* The view that the Fourth Gospel was originally written in Aramaic was put forward, though not worked out, by C. Salmasius (*De Hellenistica Commentarius*, 1645, pp. 257 f.), I. A. Bolten (*Der Bericht des Joannes von Jesu dem Messias, übersetzt*; 1797, *Vorbericht*, pp. xiv ff.), H. F. Pfannkuche (*Ueber die palästinische Landessprache in dem Zeitalter Christi*, in Eichhorn's *Allgem. Bibl d.b. Litt.* viii, 1797, p. 367). L. Bertholdt (*Verosimilia de origine evangelii Joannis*, 1805; *Einleitung in . . . Schriften des A. u. N.T.*, iii, 1813, § 342) supposed that St. John wrote down the discourses of our Lord in Aramaic soon after they were spoken, and long subsequently translated them into Greek and incorporated them into his Greek gospel.

Many scholars, from Grotius (*Annotationes*, 1641) onwards, while holding the Gospel to have been written in Greek, have emphasized the Semitic character of its diction. The opinion of so great a Semitic scholar as H. Ewald (*Die johann. Schriften*, 1861, i, p. 44) is worthy of quotation: 'The Greek language of the author bears in itself the plainest and strongest marks of a genuine Hebrew. He is one born among Jews in the Holy Land, one who grew up to manhood in this society, without speaking Greek. Under the Greek mantle that he at a late date learned to throw about himself, he still bears in himself the whole mind and spirit of his mother tongue, and does not hesitate to let himself be led by it.' The discussion by C. E. Luthardt on the language of the Gospel (*St. John's Gospel*, E. T., 1876, i, pp. 15–64) is of considerable value.

Mention should here be made of the highly important work by Prof. A.

Old and New Testament scholars were as a rule content to dwell too much in water-tight compartments, and that more systematic first-hand application of Semitic linguistic knowledge to the New Testament might be expected to shed light upon a variety of problems. It followed that it was not only desirable that professed New Testament scholars should realize the importance to their researches of a first-hand equipment in Hebrew and Aramaic, but that Old Testament scholars equipped with a knowledge of these languages should turn to New Testament research, and endeavour by practical demonstration of the value of such knowledge to substantiate the truth of this thesis.

Thus it was that the writer turned seriously to tackle the question of the original language of the Fourth Gospel; and quickly convincing himself that the theory of an original Aramaic document was no chimera, but a fact which was capable of the fullest verification, set himself to collect and classify the evidence in a form which he trusts may justify the reasonableness of his opinion not merely to other Aramaic scholars, but to all New Testament scholars who will take the pains to follow out his arguments.

Inquiry into the Semitic characteristics of a New Testament book has nowadays to take account of the fact that the great modern discoveries of papyri and ostraka in Egypt have revolu-

Schlatter, *Die Sprache und Heimat des vierten Evangelisten* (1902), with which the writer was unacquainted until he had practically completed the present study. Schlatter has demonstrated the Palestinian origin of the diction of the Fourth Gospel in the fullest possible manner by citing Rabbinic parallels to its phraseology verse by verse, the majority of verses throughout the whole Gospel being thus illustrated (thus e.g. in *ch.* 1 parallels are cited for phrases in 34 out of the total 51 verses), and his work is a marvel of industry and intimate knowledge of the Midrashic sources which he employs. He has drawn, not from Aramaic, but from Rabbinic Hebrew—the Mechilta (commentary on Exodus) and Siphrê (commentary on Numbers and Deuteronomy) which date in substance from the 2nd century A. D., with supplements from the Midrash Rabba (on the Pentateuch and the Five Megilloth). He chooses these Rabbinic Hebrew parallels rather than the Aramaic material which we possess e.g. in the Palestinian Talmud, because the former are nearer in date to the Fourth Gospel and better illustrate the religious thought of Palestinian Judaism in the first century; but, as he remarks (p. 12), any phrase employed in Rabbinic Hebrew (the language of the Schools) could without difficulty be similarly expressed in Aramaic (the popular medium of speech in Palestine). Schlatter's conclusion is that the writer of the Gospel was a Palestinian who thought and spoke in Aramaic, and only acquired his Greek in the course of his missionary work (p. 9).

tionized our conception of Biblical Greek, proving it to be, not a thing apart, but a more or less characteristic representative of the widespread Κοινή dialect. The writer is not unacquainted with the researches of Professors Deissmann and Thumb, Milligan and Moulton, and recognizes the fact that they have proved that many constructions and usages both in the LXX and New Testament which were formerly supposed to reflect Semitic influence, are really nothing more than ordinary phenomena of the Κοινή language. While readily making this acknowledgement to the excellent work of these scholars, he does not stand alone in holding that their reaction against the theory of Semitic influence upon Biblical Greek has been pushed too far. The fact is surely not without significance that practically the whole of the new material upon which we base our knowledge of the Κοινή comes from Egypt, where there existed large colonies of Jews whose knowledge of Greek was undoubtedly influenced by the translation-Greek of the LXX, and who may not unreasonably be suspected of having influenced in some degree the character of Egyptian Κοινή.* A good example of such influence has been unwittingly

* Cf. the judicious remarks of Dr. Swete, *Apocalypse*[2] (1907), p. cxxiv, n. 1: 'The present writer, while welcoming all the light that can be thrown on the vocabulary and syntax of the New Testament by a study of the Graeco-Egyptian papyri, and in particular the researches of Prof Deissmann, Prof. Thumb, and Dr. J. H. Moulton, deprecates the induction which, as it seems to him, is being somewhat hastily based upon them, that the Greek of the New Testament has been but slightly influenced by the familiarity of the writers with Hebrew and Aramaic.... It is precarious to compare a literary document with a collection of personal and business letters, accounts, and other ephemeral writings; slips in word-formation or in syntax which are to be expected in the latter, are phenomenal in the former, and if they find a place there, can only be attributed to lifelong habits of thought. Moreover, it remains to be considered how far the quasi-Semitic colloquialisms of the papyri are themselves due to the influence of the large Greek-speaking Jewish population of the Delta.' Similarly, Mr. G. C. Richards, in reviewing the 2nd edition of Dr. Moulton's *Grammar of New Testament Greek* in the *Journal of Theological Studies*, x (1909), p. 289, remarks: 'The discovery of the Aramaic papyri from Assuan emphasizes this point [the evidence for large Jewish settlements in Egypt from an early date] most strongly, and even Deissmann (*Licht vom Osten*, p. 83, n. 5) is prepared to admit that the adoption of εἰς τὸ ὄνομα as a legal phrase may be due to Semitic influence "in grauer Vorzeit". But this "Vorzeit" can scarcely be earlier than the end of the fourth century B.C. No doubt it is possible, as he says, that if originally a Semiticism, it may not have been felt to be so any longer. Such influence on the language of a population from an influx of settlers is quite common. Dr. Moulton makes

presented to us by Prof. Deissmann (*LAE.* pp. 129 ff.) in one of two passages which he quotes from the papyri for the express purpose of proving that the parataxis so characteristic of the Fourth Gospel, with its '*and . . . and*', is not due to Semitic influence, but belongs to the popular Κοινή style. This is a letter from two pig-merchants (*c.* A.D. 171) in which they complain to the Strategus that they have been attacked by brigands and robbed and beaten: *ἀνερχομένων ἡμῶν ἀπὸ κώμης Θεαδελφείας Θεμίστου μερίδος ὑπὸ τὸν ὄρθρον ἐπῆλθαν ἡμεῖν κακοῦργοί τινες . . . καὶ ἔδησαν ἡμᾶς σὺν καὶ τῷ μαγδωλοφύλακι καὶ πληγαῖς ἡμᾶς πλίσταις ἤκισαν κ[αὶ] τραυματιαῖον ἐποίησαν τὸν [Πασίω]να καὶ εἰσανῆρα[ν ἡμ]ῶν χοιρίδι[ον] α καὶ ἐβάσ[ταξαν τὸν τοῦ Πασίων]ος κιτῶνα . . .* The term here used to describe 'the guard of the tower', *μαγδωλοφύλαξ*, embodies the ordinary Hebrew word for 'tower', *migdôl* (originally *magdôl*), and is thus clear evidence for Jewish influence upon Egyptian Κοινή terminology. Yet Prof. Milligan (*New Testament Documents*, p. 154), referring to this section of Deissmann's work, states that he 'has been able to produce examples of similar [to the Fourth Gospel] paratactic sentences from sources *where no Semitic influence can be predicated*' (the italics are the present writer's); and similarly Prof. Moulton (*Cambridge Biblical Essays*, p. 486) remarks, 'Those who still find Semitism in these plain co-ordinated sentences [of the Fourth Gospel], with their large use of *καί*, may be recommended to study the most instructive parallels which Deissmann has set out,' &c.

We cite this passage merely as suggesting that the theory of Jewish influence upon the Κοινή of Egypt, so far from being false or negligible, may in fact be supported by concrete evidence drawn from the papyri themselves. It does not follow, of course, that the

a point of the case of Wales. South Wales Welsh is regarded by North Wales people as an inferior *patois* because of the Anglicisms, which are to be seen not only in borrowed words but also in turns of expression. In fact we may say that, if the native language of a whole district may be strongly affected by the entry of aliens who learn it and learn it badly, *a fortiori* is a language, which is not the native one, but the medium of communication between natives and strangers, likely to be modified by all who use it.' So also Dr. A. T. Robertson, *A Grammar of the Greek Testament in the light of historical research*[3] (1919), p. 91: 'The LXX,' though "translation Greek", was translated into the vernacular of Alexandria, and one can but wonder if the LXX did not have some slight and resultant influence upon the Alexandrian Κοινή itself. The Jews were very numerous in Alexandria.'

paratactic style of the pig-merchants is due to Semitic influence; for, as Prof. Moulton justly observes (*NTG.*[3] i, p. 12), in speaking of co-ordination of sentences with simple καί, 'in itself the phenomenon proves nothing more than would a string of "ands" in an English rustic's story—elementary culture.' The vice of arguing from the epistolary style of an Egyptian pig-merchant or the speech of an English rustic to the style of the Fourth Gospel lies in the fact that the former are not *in pari materiâ* with the latter. The theory of elementary culture which satisfactorily explains the style of the former is ill applied to a work which in thought, scheme, and execution takes rank as the greatest literary production of the New Testament, and the greatest religious monument of all time.

So with other stylistic peculiarities of the Gospel, such as the frequent use of *Casus pendens.* This, Prof. Moulton tells us, 'is one of the easiest of anacolutha, as much at home in English as in Greek' (*NTG.*[3] i, p. 69). We recognize the truth of this statement as regards colloquial English, especially among the semi-educated. We might be talking to a groom, and it would be natural for him to say, 'The gentleman who used to ride that horse—he lost his arm in the war.' Probably at times we use the same kind of anacoluthon ourselves in ordinary conversation; but we do *not* use it in writing a book or article which we hope may be worthy to rank as literature. Nor, if we take the whole New Testament as a fair specimen of literature written in the Κοινή, do we find as a rule more than very occasional instances of the usage. In the Fourth Gospel, however, it *is* remarkably frequent; and it is reasonable to seek some better reason than the supposition that the writer of the finest piece of literature in the New Testament was more than ordinarily infected with colloquialism. Now there *is* a literature in which both the usages which we have been noticing—parataxis and *Casus pendens*—are not the marks of lack of education but common phenomena of the best writing style, namely, the literature of Semitic-speaking peoples. If, then, these two characteristics of the style of the Fourth Gospel, only selected by way of example, fit in with numerous other characteristics which point to translation from a Semitic language, their evidence as part of our proof that the Gospel is such a translation is not in the slightest degree invalidated by the fact that parallels can be adduced from the non-literary and ephemeral type of document which we find represented in the papyri.

As a matter of fact, we have little cause to quarrel with Prof. Moulton at any rate in the course which is followed in our discussion of the language of the Fourth Gospel, for he lays down a canon which covers a great part of the characteristics which are brought forward. 'If we are seeking', he says, 'for evidences of Semitic birth in a writer whose Greek betrays deficient knowledge of the resources of the language, we must not look only for uses which strain or actually contravene the Greek idiom. We shall find a subtler test in the *over-use* of locutions which can be defended as good Κοινή Greek, but have their motive clearly in their coincidences with locutions of the writer's native tongue. This test of course applies only to Greek which is virtually or actually translated—to the Hebraism of the LXX and the Aramaism of New Testament books which are either translated from Aramaic sources or written by men who thought in Aramaic and moved with little freedom in Greek.' * It is precisely this over-use of locutions coincident with locutions of Aramaic which will repeatedly be found to characterize the Greek of the Fourth Gospel.

From the remarks which are occasionally to be encountered in books and articles dealing with the Gospels it would appear that some amount of vagueness exists in the minds of many non-Semitic scholars as to the existence of a clear distinction between Aramaisms and Hebraisms. By some scholars, in fact, the question of distinction is ignored, and the two terms are used indifferently as though they were synonymous.† A glaring instance of this is to be seen in Prof. Schmiedel's remarks on the original language of St. Mark's Gospel in *Encyc. Bibl.* 1870. 'The language of Mk.', he says, 'Hebraizes still more strongly than does that of Mt. Nevertheless, the combinations of Allen (*Expositor*, 1900, i, pp. 436–43) do not prove that the evangelist wrote Aramaic, but only that he wrote a kind of Jewish Greek

* *Cambridge Biblical Essays*, p. 474.

† Cf. Dalman, *WJ.* pp. 18 f.

that he had derived from a reading of the LXX. Lk. also has Hebraisms, not only in chaps. 1 f. but elsewhere as well, and not only where he is dependent on Mk. or Mt. but also where he had no exemplar before him (as, for example, often "and it came to pass", καὶ ἐγένετο; see *HS.*[2] p. 37), and yet no one holds Lk.'s writing to be a translation of a Semitic original.'

It is something of a feat to have crowded so many misconceptions into the space of a few lines. Mk. does not Hebraize at all in the proper sense of the term; but the fact that his Greek exhibits a strong Aramaic colouring is admitted by all Semitic scholars who have studied the subject, though they differ as to whether this colouring implies actual translation from an original Aramaic document, or is merely due to the fact that the author was ill versed in Greek and accustomed to think and speak in Aramaic. Mk.'s 'Jewish Greek' cannot have been 'derived from a reading of the LXX', for it exhibits peculiarities (those which connect it with Aramaic) which are not found there, while at the same time the most striking Hebraisms of the LXX are absent from it. The fact that Lk. has Hebraisms is the first accurate statement which Prof. Schmiedel makes; but he goes on at once to confuse the issue again by equating the supposed 'Hebraisms' which are the result of dependence upon Mk. or Mt. with those which are found in passages in which the author 'had no exemplar before him'. The fact as regards the Marcan source in Lk. is that the third evangelist has made some attempt to smooth away the most palpable solecisms, but has by no means carried this out thoroughly or consistently; consequently a number of Marcan Aramaisms (not 'Hebraisms') remain in Lk.* The parts of Lk.

* As regards Mt., which Schmiedel also mentions as a source containing 'Hebraisms' employed by Lk., i.e. of course the Q document which is used in common by Mt. and Lk., the present writer cannot claim to have examined in detail into the question of its original language (Greek or Aramaic). No Semitic scholar can, however, study such a passage as Mt. 10^{26-33} = Lk. 12^{2-9} without arriving at the clear conviction that we either have in it the literal translation of an Aramaic original, or that the *ipsissima verba* of our Lord in Aramaic were branded on the hearts of His hearers and reproduced with a reverential exactitude amounting to virtual translation. Cf. especially the phrases μὴ φοβηθῆτε ἀπό (Semitic מן *of aversion* after a verb of fearing), ὁμολογήσει ἐν ἐμοί (cf. on this expression even Moulton, *NTG.*[3] i, p. 104), ἀκολουθεῖ ὀπίσω μου (Mt. 10^{38}). Mistranslation of an

which may be taken to be due to the author himself (such as the setting of narratives, to which the phrase cited, *καὶ ἐγένετο*, belongs) *do* contain Hebraisms, and these so striking as to make this Gospel stand out as stylistically the most Hebraic Gospel of the four. Yet, as Schmiedel states, 'no one holds Lk.'s writing to be a translation of a Semitic original', for, paradoxical as it may seem, the very existence of this Hebraic colouring in his style

Aramaic original seems clearly to the indicated by comparison of the following passages:

Mt. $23^{25.26}$	Lk. 11^{39-41}
25 Οὐαὶ ὑμῖν, γραμματεῖς καὶ Φαρισαῖοι, ὑποκριταί, ὅτι καθαρίζετε τὸ ἔξωθεν τοῦ ποτηρίου καὶ τῆς παροψίδος,	39 Νῦν ὑμεῖς οἱ Φαρισαῖοι τὸ ἔξωθεν τοῦ ποτηρίου καὶ τοῦ πίνακος καθαρίζετε,
ἔσωθεν δὲ γέμουσιν ἐξ ἁρπαγῆς καὶ ἀκρασίας. 26 Φαρισαῖε τυφλέ,	τὸ δὲ ἔσωθεν ὑμῶν γέμει ἁρπαγῆς καὶ πονηρίας. 40 ἄφρονες, οὐχ ὁ ποιήσας τὸ ἔξωθεν καὶ τὸ ἔσωθεν ἐποίησεν;
καθάρισον πρῶτον τὸ ἐντὸς τοῦ ποτηρίου καὶ τῆς παροψίδος,	41 πλὴν τὰ ἐνόντα δότε ἐλεημοσύνην,
ἵνα γένηται καὶ τὸ ἐκτὸς αὐτοῦ καθαρόν.	καὶ ἰδοὺ πάντα καθαρὰ ὑμῖν ἐστιν.

Here it can hardly be doubted that the remarkable variant between Mt. *καθάρισον πρῶτον τὸ ἐντὸς κτλ.* and Lk. *πλὴν τὰ ἐνόντα δότε ἐλεημοσύνην* is to be explained by the fact that New Heb. and Aram. זַכֵּי means both 'to *purify*' (occurring in Aram. as well as normal דַּכֵּי) and also 'to *give alms*' (cf. Wellhausen, *Einleitung*², p. 27). For the latter sense cf. the numerous occurrences in Midrash Rabba on Exodus, par. xxxiv; e.g. sect. 5 (New Heb.), 'If misfortune has befallen thy companion, consider how to give him alms (לזכות בו) and provide for him'; sect. 11 (Aram.), 'The Rabbis Yoḥanan and Resh Lakish were going down to bathe in the hot baths of Tiberias. A poor man met them. He said to them, "Give me alms" (זכון בי). They said to him, "When we come out we will give thee alms" (זכיין בך). When they came out, they found him dead.' The inference is that our Lord used some such expression as דִּבְגַוָּא זַכּוֹן 'That which is within purify'; this has been rightly rendered in Mt. and made more explicit by the addition of *τοῦ ποτηρίου κτλ.*, while in Lk. it has been wrongly rendered, 'That which is within give as alms'. *Ἡρμήνευσε δ' αὐτά, ὡς ἦν δυνατός, ἕκαστος.*

In the opening of the long indictment of the Scribes and Pharisees contained in Mt. 23, presumably from Q, we find a passage (*vv.* 2–7) which has clearly formed a source for Mk. in his short summary of teaching contained in 12^{38-40}. It seems not unlikely that Mk.'s opening phrase, *Καὶ ἐν τῇ διδαχῇ αὐτοῦ ἔλεγεν*, which recurs nearly *verbatim* in 4^2 (introducing the parable of the sower), may be his manner of referring to this written discourse-source to which he had access. Lk. 20^{45-47} has followed Mk. and not Mt., though his opening statement that our Lord's words were spoken both to the multitude and to the disciples seems to indicate that he rightly identified Mk's abbreviated version with the long discourse of Mt. (Q), and selected the former. The parallel passages run as follows:

is a sure indication that he was steeped with LXX influence, and very possibly unacquainted with Hebrew.*

Mt. 23[1ff.]	Mk. 12[38—40]	Lk. 20[45—47]
ότε ὁ Ἰησοῦς ἐλάλησεν ὄχλοις καὶ τοῖς μαθηταῖς οῦ λέγων· . . . . . ντα δὲ τὰ ἔργα αὐτῶν ῦσιν πρὸς τὸ θεαθῆναι ἀνθρώποις· πλατύνουσιν τὰ φυλακτήρια αὐτῶν μεγαλύνουσιν τὰ σπεδα, [6] φιλοῦσιν δὲ πρωτοκλισίαν ἐν τοῖς νοις καὶ τὰς πρωτοκδρίας ἐν ταῖς συνγαῖς [7] καὶ τοὺς ἀσπασμοὺς ταῖς ἀγοραῖς, κτλ.	[38] Καὶ ἐν τῇ διδαχῇ αὐτοῦ ἔλεγεν· βλέπετε ἀπὸ τῶν γραμματέων τῶν θελόντων ἐν στολαῖς περιπατεῖν καὶ ἀσπασμοὺς ἐν ταῖς ἀγοραῖς [39] καὶ πρωτοκαθεδρίας ἐν ταῖς συναγωγαῖς καὶ πρωτοκλισίας ἐν τοῖς δείπνοις· [40] οἱ κατεσθίοντες τὰς οἰκίας τῶν χηρῶν καὶ προφάσει μακρὰ προσευχόμενοι, οὗτοι λήμψονται περισσότερον κρίμα.	[45] Ἀκούοντος δὲ παντὸς τοῦ λαοῦ εἶπεν τοῖς μαθηταῖς· [46] προσέχετε ἀπὸ τῶν γραμματέων τῶν θελόντων περιπατεῖν ἐν στολαῖς καὶ φιλούντων ἀσπασμοὺς ἐν ταῖς ἀγοραῖς καὶ πρωτοκαθεδρίας ἐν ταῖς συναγωγαῖς καὶ πρωτοκλισίας ἐν τοῖς δείπνοις, [47] οἳ κατεσθίουσιν τὰς οἰκίας τῶν χηρῶν καὶ προφάσει μακρὰ προσεύχονται· οὗτοι λήμψονται περισσότερον κρίμα.

The statements of Mk. in *vv.* [38, 39] can be clearly recognized in Mt., except for τῶν θελόντων ἐν στολαῖς περιπατεῖν, which seems to be a paraphrase of καὶ μεγαλύνουσιν τὰ κράσπεδα, Mt. 23[5]. In *v.* [40] of Mk., however, we meet with two statements which do not seem, as they stand, to connect themselves directly with anything in Mt. Noticing, however, that the second of these speaks of *prayer*, we observe that the New Heb. and Aram. term for φυλακτήρια (Mt. 23[5]) is תְּפִלִּין *tᵉphillîn*, which properly means 'prayers'. Thus there is a suspicious resemblance between the two statements, 'make broad their phylacteries' and 'make long their prayers'. Now the verb πλατύνουσιν is rendered in Pesh. by ܡܦܬܝܢ, and Payne Smith in his *Thesaurus* quotes instances in which this Aph'el ܐܦܬܝ 'make broad', as well as the Pa'el ܦܬܝ, has the sense '*make verbose*' (e.g. Severus Alexandrinus, *Rhetorica*, 79 *v.*, ܐܢ ܨܒܐ ܕܢܦܬܐ 'If he wishes to be verbose'). It is likely, therefore, that an original דְּמַפְּתִין תְּפִלֵּיהוֹן 'who make broad their phylacteries', rightly rendered in Mt., appears in Mk. and Lk. in the mistranslation 'who make verbose their prayers'. It should be remarked that תְּפִלִּין is not the ordinary *Aramaic* word for 'prayers' (צְלוֹתְיָא); but it might be so interpreted by a translator who was aware of this meaning of the term in New Heb.

The writer believes that this suggestion as to a misunderstanding of תְּפִלִּין is not his own, but has already been made; though he cannot recall to whom acknowledgement is due. He is himself responsible for pointing out the variant meanings of the verbal form.

* That St. Luke was a Hellenistic Jew and not a Gentile would be—apart from other evidence to the contrary—the natural deduction from the fact that the LXX has coloured his Greek style in so marked a degree; since this surely implies that he was brought up upon the Greek Bible. Had he been a Gentile, and not converted to Christianity until he was a grown man, his Greek style would presumably have been already formed and would not have taken on a LXX

The following striking Hebraisms occurring in Lk. may serve to illustrate the true meaning of the term 'Hebraism', viz. a construction or word-usage found in *Biblical Hebrew* which has been copied in translation by the LXX, and has come through LXX influence into N. T. Greek:

1. ἐγένετο introducing a time-determination. The use of וַיְהִי 'And it came to pass' is in such a case very idiomatic in Hebrew, and the LXX equivalent is καὶ ἐγένετο or ἐγένετο δέ. After וַיְהִי there follows *the note of time* or *occasion*, which may take various forms, such as—

An Infinitive with preposition בְּ; e.g. בְּבֹאָם 'when they came' (lit. 'in their coming') = LXX ἐν τῷ ἐλθεῖν αὐτούς.

An Infinitive with preposition כְּ; e.g. כְּבֹאָם 'at their coming' = LXX ὡς (or ἡνίκα) ἦλθον.

כַּאֲשֶׁר (or כִּי) 'when' with a Perfect; e.g. כַּאֲשֶׁר בָּאוּ 'when they came' = LXX ὡς (or ἡνίκα) ἦλθον.

A Participle Absolute with pronominal or nominal subject; e.g. הֵמָּה בָאִים 'they (were) coming' = LXX αὐτῶν ἐρχομένων.

A specific note of time; e.g. בַּיּוֹם הַשְּׁלִישִׁי 'on the third day' = LXX (ἐν) τῇ ἡμέρᾳ τῇ τρίτῃ; מִקֵּץ שְׁלֹשֶׁת יָמִים 'after three days' = LXX μετὰ ἡμέρας τρεῖς.

After this comes *the apodosis*, which is most frequently (though by no means invariably) introduced by '*and*' (= 'then'); e.g. וַיִּרְאוּ 'and they saw' = LXX (καὶ) εἶδον (LXX often omits καί), וְהִנֵּה רָאוּ 'and, behold, they saw' = LXX καὶ ἰδοὺ εἶδον, or simply רָאוּ 'they saw' = LXX εἶδον. The subject of the apodosis may of course vary from that of the time-determination (when this latter embodies a subject); e.g. וַיְהִי כְּבֹאָם וַיֵּצֵא אִישׁ לִקְרָאתָם 'And it came to pass, as they came, that (lit. 'and') a man went out

colouring, at any rate to the extent that it has. We do, however, possess other and apparently contrary evidence in the fact that St. Paul in Col. 4^{14} appears expressly to distinguish him from 'those of the circumcision' previously mentioned ($v.^{11}$); and this is taken by most scholars, such as Dr. Lightfoot (*Colossians*, p. 239) and Dr. Plummer (*St. Luke*, p. xix), as conclusive evidence that he was of Gentile origin, the latter scholar going so far as to maintain, 'That he was originally a heathen may be taken as certain'. Such a verdict, however, surely ignores the important criterion of style; and perhaps the conclusion which best satisfies the conflicting evidence is that he may have been a proselyte from his youth and have come over to Christianity from Judaism.

to meet them', or וַיְהִי הֵמָּה בָּאִים וְהִנֵּה אִישׁ יֹצֵא לִקְרָאתָם 'And it came to pass, they (were) coming, and, behold, a man going out to meet them'.

Instances of this Hebrew construction, with time-determination ἐν τῷ (Infinitive) and apodosis introduced by καί, may be seen in Lk. $5^{1.12}$, 9^{51}, 14^{1}, 17^{11}, 19^{15}, $24^{4.(15)}$; without καί, Lk. 1^{8}, 2^{6}, $9^{18.33}$, $11^{1.27}$, 17^{14}, 18^{35}, $24^{30.51}$. With time-determination ὡς (Aorist), and without καί in apodosis, Lk. $1^{23.41}$, 2^{15}, 19^{29}. With specific note of time, and καί in apodosis, Lk. 5^{17}, $8^{1.22}$, Acts 5^{7}; without καί, Lk. 1^{59}, $2^{1.46}$, 7^{11}, $9^{28.37}$, 20^{1}.

There are besides some cases in Lk., and many more in Acts, in which the verb of the apodosis is not an Aorist but an *Infinitive.* This modification of the construction, which is *not* found in Hebrew, and only occurs once in LXX (3 Kgs. 11^{43} B), can be paralleled from the papyri. It seems therefore in Lk. and Acts to be a modification of the Hebraic construction under the influence of a known Κοινή construction (cf. Thackeray, *Grammar of the O. T. in Greek*, p. 50). So Lk. 3^{21}, $6^{1.6.12}$, Acts 4^{5}, $9^{3*.32.37}$, 14^{1}, 16^{16}, 19^{1}, $22^{6.17}$, 28^{17}. It may be noted that in some of these examples, viz. Acts 9^{32}, 14^{1}, $22^{6.17}$, the note of time or occasion has been variously modified so as to lose its clear-cut Hebraic form. In other cases, viz. Lk. 16^{22}, Acts 9^{43}, 11^{26}, 28^{8}, it is altogether absent. This is quite un-Hebraic. Hebrew might say וַיָּמָת הָאֶבְיוֹן 'And the poor man died', without note of time except as inferred from the context ('and'='and *then*'), or, inserting note of time, וַיְהִי מִקֵּץ יָמִים וַיָּמָת הָאֶבְיוֹן 'And it came to pass, after some time (lit. "from the end of days"), that (lit. "and") the poor man died'; it would not say וַיְהִי וַיָּמָת הָאֶבְיוֹן = ἐγένετο δὲ ἀποθανεῖν τὸν πτωχόν (Lk. 16^{22}). The reason why St. Luke modified his Gospel-style in this respect in Acts demands investigation. It would seem to imply a not inconsiderable interval between the two works, during which his wider intercourse with Gentile heathen in the course of his missionary labours exercised an influence on his style.

Outside Lk. and Acts ἐγένετο introducing a time-determination is only found in the five-times repeated phrase καὶ ἐγένετο ὅτε ἐτέλεσεν Ἰησοῦς in Mt. 7^{28}, 11^{1}, 13^{53}, 19^{1}, 26^{1}, and also in Mt. 9^{10}, Mk. 1^{9}, 2^{23}, 4^{4} (cf. 2^{15}). In Semitic it is specifically a construction belonging to

* With time-determination *before* ἐγένετο.

Biblical Hebrew, and not found in Aramaic except where this language copies the Hebrew construction in translation, as in the Targums.*

These facts prove that in the construction under discussion we have a true Hebraism, which can only have entered into N. T. Greek through the influence of the LXX. Incidentally, its absence from Jn. tells against the use of the LXX by the writer of this Gospel.

2. Enforcement of verb by cognate substantive in Dative. When Hebrew desires to emphasize a verbal idea, it prefixes the Infinitive Absolute to the Finite verb. In LXX the place of the Infinitive is commonly taken by *the cognate substantive in the Dative*; e.g. Gen. 2[17] מוֹת תָּמוּת 'Thou shalt surely *die*' (lit. 'dying thou shalt die') = LXX *θανάτῳ ἀποθανεῖσθε*, Judg. 15[13] לֹא כִּי־אָסֹר נֶאֱסָרְךָ וּנְתַנּוּךָ בְיָדָם וְהָמֵת לֹא נְמִיתֶךָ 'Nay, but we will *bind* thee (lit. 'binding we will bind thee') and deliver thee into their hand; but we will not *slay* thee' (lit. 'slaying we will not slay thee') = LXX *Οὐχί, ὅτι ἀλλ' ἢ δεσμῷ δήσομέν σε καὶ παραδώσομέν σε ἐν χειρὶ αὐτῶν, καὶ θανάτῳ οὐ θανατώσομέν σε.* An alternative method employed by LXX is the rendering of the Infinitive by *a Participle*; e.g. Judg. 1[28] וְהוֹרֵישׁ לֹא הוֹרִישׁוֹ 'and did not expel them at all' (lit. 'and expelling did not expel them') = LXX *καὶ ἐξαίρων οὐκ ἐξῆρεν αὐτόν.*

No examples of the second form of the idiom are found in N. T. except in the LXX quotations Mt. 13[14], Mk. 4[12], Acts 7[34], but the first occurs three times in the Lucan literature; viz. Lk. 22[15] *ἐπιθυμίᾳ ἐπεθύμησα*, Acts 5[28] *παραγγελίᾳ παρηγγείλαμεν*, Acts 23[14] *ἀναθέματι ἀνεθεματίσαμεν* (cf. also Acts 2[30] *ὅρκῳ ὤμοσεν*).† Elsewhere in N. T. we find it only in Mt. 13[14], 15[4] = Mk. 7[10] (both O. T. quotations), Jn. 3[29] *χαρᾷ χαίρει*, Jas. 5[17] *προσευχῇ προσηύξατο.*

This enforcement of the verbal idea by the Infinitive, while found occasionally in other Semitic languages (cf. Babylonian *edišu lidiš* 'let it be ever new'; Syriac ܟܕ ܡܙܟܐ ܢܙܟܘܢ 'when they are completely victorious'), is peculiarly characteristic of Biblical Hebrew.‡

* Cf. Dalman, *WJ.* p. 32.

† Acts 2[17] *ἐνυπνίοις ἐνυπνιασθήσονται*, which occurs in an O.T. quotation from Joel 2[28] (3[1] in Heb.) is different, the substantive representing the cognate Accusative in Heb. חֲלֹמוֹת יַחֲלֹמוּן, LXX *ἐνύπνια ἐνυπνιασθήσονται.*

‡ According to Dalman (*WJ.* p. 34) it is quite unknown in the Palestinian Aramaic of the Jews, apart from the Hebraizing rendering of the Targums.

3. Use of προστίθημι in place of πάλιν or a similar adverb in imitation of Hebrew הוֹסִיף 'he added' to do something, i.e. he did it *again*. There are two constructions in Hebrew: (1) the auxiliary verb הוֹסִיף may be followed by an Infinitive with preposition לְ, e.g. וַיֹּסִפוּ . . . לַעֲשׂוֹת הָרַע 'and they added to do that which was evil' (i.e. 'they *again* did it') = LXX καὶ προσέθεντο . . . ποιῆσαι τὸ πονηρόν, Judg. 3[12], 4[1], 10[6]; or (2) it may be followed by 'and' with a Finite verb, e.g. וַיֹּסֶף אַבְרָהָם וַיִּקַּח אִשָּׁה 'And Abraham added and took a wife' ('*again* took', or 'took a *second*') = LXX προσθέμενος δὲ Ἀβραὰμ ἔλαβεν γυναῖκα, Gen. 25[1]; וַיֹּסֶף אֱלִיהוּא וַיֹּאמַר 'And Elihu added and said' = LXX Προσθεὶς δὲ Ἐλιοῦς ἔτι λέγει, Job 36[1]. Both of these constructions occur in the Lucan literature: (1) καὶ προσέθετο ἕτερον πέμψαι δοῦλον . . . καὶ προσέθετο τρίτον πέμψαι, Lk. 20[11.12]; προσέθετο συλλαβεῖν καὶ Πέτρον, Acts 12[3]; (2) προσθεὶς εἶπεν παραβολήν, Lk. 19[11]. The usage is not found elsewhere in N. T.*

4. The phrase πορεύου εἰς εἰρήνην, Lk. 7[50], 8[48], ὕπαγε εἰς εἰρήνην, Mk. 5[34] (nowhere else in N. T.) is derived from the LXX rendering of the Hebrew לֵךְ לְשָׁלוֹם; cf. 1 Sam. 1[17], 20[13.42], 1 Kgs. 20 (LXX 21)[18], 2 Kgs. 5[19], 1 Chr. 12[17], Tob. 10[13], Judith 8[35]. The Hebrew preposition לְ is here incorrectly given the sense εἰς which it commonly possesses. It is really an idiomatic usage known as לְ *of norm*, לְשָׁלוֹם thus meaning lit. 'peace-wise' or 'health-wise', i.e. 'in peace *or* health'. The phrase belongs distinctively to Biblical Hebrew. The Targum Hebraizes in copying it in translation, but in the Peshîttā the regular rendering is ܐܙܠ ܒܫܠܡܐ, i.e. πορεύου ἐν εἰρήνῃ.

5. The expression ἐνώπιον is peculiarly characteristic of Lk. (23 times), Acts (13 times), and Apoc. which is marked by an Hebraic style (34 times). It is derived from LXX where it is extremely common (some hundreds of occurrences), and ordinarily represents Hebrew לִפְנֵי 'before' (lit. 'to the face of'), or לְעֵינֵי 'in the sight of' (lit. 'to the eyes of'). ἐνώπιον is only found once in Jn. (20[30]), and is unused in Mt. and Mk. In these Gospels we find ἔμπροσθεν, which also occurs in Lk.

ἔναντι (Lk. 1[8], Acts 7[10], 8[21]), ἐναντίον (Lk. 1[6], 20[26], 24[19], Acts 7[10], 8[32]), exclusively Lucan in N. T., are both very common in LXX, where they ordinarily render בְּעֵינֵי 'in the sight of' (lit. 'in the eyes of'),

* Cf. however the text of D in Mk. 14[25], οὐ μὴ προσθῶ πιεῖν.

i.e. 'in the *opinion* of'. Hebrew always observes a distinction between לְעֵינֵי 'in the (physical) sight of', and בְּעֵינֵי 'in the (mental) sight of'. The same distinction may be noticed for the most part in the N.T. use of *ἐνώπιον* and *ἐναντίον*.

In place of the distinctively Hebraic expressions לִפְנֵי, לְעֵינֵי, בְּעֵינֵי, Aramaic uses קֳדָם, 'before', 'in front of'.

6. The phrase *πρὸ προσώπου*, which is a common LXX rendering of לִפְנֵי, occurs in the O.T. quotation Mk. 1^{2} = Mt. 11^{10} = Lk. 7^{27}, and only besides in Lk. 1^{76}, 9^{52}, 10^{1}, Acts 13^{24}. *ἀπὸ προσώπου* = מִפְּנֵי in LXX is found in Acts 3^{19}, 5^{41}, 7^{45}, 2 Thess. 1^{9}, Apoc. 6^{16}, 20^{11} (*ἀπὸ τοῦ π.*). *ἐπὶ πρόσωπον* Lk. 21^{35}, *ἐπὶ προσώπου* Acts 17^{26}, are LXX renderings of עַל־פְּנֵי.

7. The phrase *τὸ πρόσωπον ἐστήρισεν*, Lk. 9^{51} (nowhere else in N.T.) is derived from LXX, where it renders Hebrew שִׂים פָּנִים 'set the face' (Jer. 21^{10}, Ezek. 6^{2}, 13^{17}, 14^{8}, 15^{7}, &c.).

8. *λαμβάνειν πρόσωπον*, Lk. 20^{21}, Gal. 2^{6} occurs 9 times in LXX as the rendering of Hebrew נָשָׂא פָּנִים 'take *or* lift up the face' of any one, i.e. show him partiality in judgement. More commonly this phrase is rendered in LXX by *θαυμάζειν πρόσωπον*. The Semitic phrase occurs in Aramaic as well as in Hebrew. The N.T. substantives *προσωπολήμπτης* 'a respecter of persons' (Acts 10^{34}), *προσωπολημψία* (Rom. 2^{11}, Eph. 6^{9}, Col. 3^{25}, Jas. 2^{1}) 'partiality', are derived from the LXX Hebraism.

9. The use of the verb *δίδωμι* in a wider range of senses, which may be rendered 'put', 'set', 'appoint', 'allow', &c., appears in N.T. to be exclusively Lucan; cf. Lk. 7^{43}, $12^{51.58}$, 15^{22}, 19^{23}, Acts 2^{19} (quotation from Joel 3^{3}), 2^{27}, 13^{35} (both quotations from Ps 16^{10}), 10^{40}, 19^{31}. This usage comes from LXX where *δίδωμι* is the regular rendering of Hebrew נָתַן which, meaning primarily 'give', is regularly used also in such wider senses. Cf. the LXX rendering in Gen. 17^{20} *δώσω αὐτὸν εἰς ἔθνος μέγα*, Gen. 31^{7} *οὐκ ἔδωκεν αὐτῷ ὁ θεὸς κακοποιῆσαί με*, Deut. 1^{13} *δότε ἑαυτοῖς ἄνδρας σοφούς*, Deut. 2^{25} *ἐνάρχου δοῦναι τὸν τρόμον σου*. Such instances might be indefinitely multiplied.

These examples should serve clearly to illustrate the character of N.T. Hebraisms derived from the Greek of the LXX. We observe that they are characteristically Lucan, and in some cases exclusively so. Other N.T. Hebraisms may be found in the Greek of the Apocalypse (cf. Dr. Charles's Commentary, Index II), and these owe their origin to a different cause, viz. first-hand imitation of Biblical Hebrew style—a cause which was perhaps also operative in the Birth-narrative of Lk. The Marcan Aramaisms collected by Canon Allen in the article mentioned by Prof. Schmiedel are wholly different in character; and the statement that they only prove that this evangelist 'wrote a kind of Jewish Greek that he had derived from a reading of the LXX' is most misleading. For example, one of Canon Allen's most striking Aramaisms is the very frequent use of the Historic Present in Mk., which he rightly ascribes to the influence of the Aramaic usage of the Participle in narrative (cf. pp. 87 ff. of the present volume). How could this usage have been derived from reading the LXX, when, as Sir John Hawkins has shown (*HS.*[2], p. 213), it is there comparatively rare? The total occurrences in the whole LXX are 337, and of these 232 occur in the four Books of Kingdoms, leaving only 105 for the whole of the rest of the LXX. 'Out of the 232 instances in the four books of Kingdoms, the First Book (= 1 Samuel) contains very nearly two-thirds, viz. 151, which happens to be exactly the same number as Mark contains. But then 1 Kingdoms exceeds Mark in length by about one-third, as may be seen by comparing the two books in the pages of any English Bible—e.g. in the R.V. minion 8vo 1885, in which 1 Sam. occupies 26 pages, and Mark (without the Appendix) about 15 pages and a half. Consequently it appears that the historic presents are scattered considerably more thickly over the pages of the latter than of the former, the average to a page being in 1 Sam. about 6 and in Mark between 9 and 10' (*HS.*[2] *loc. cit.*) Moreover, the same scholar has proved, in the most conclusive manner, in dealing with the Synoptists and the LXX, that Mark is considerably the least familiar with this version, Matthew occupies an intermediate place, while Luke shows most familiarity with it (*HS.*[2] pp 198 ff.).

The marking of the distinction between Aramaisms and Hebraisms may thus be seen to be a matter of fundamental importance to our inquiry. If Aramaic and Hebrew were so similar in structure and phraseology that close translations made from the two languages, or original Greek compositions influenced by their style, were practically indistinguishable, then it might not matter whether the stylistic peculiarities of such documents were classed as Aramaisms or Hebraisms; though even so—since such phenomena would properly rank as the common property of two (if not more) languages of the Semitic group—it would scientifically be more correct to describe them as *Semitisms*. It is true that Aramaic and Hebrew, having sprung from a common ancestor, do in fact exhibit a considerable number of such common characteristics, the occurrence of which in isolated Greek passages of brief length might leave us in doubt whether the influencing factor was the one language or the other. In dealing, however, with Greek works such as the Gospels, we are concerned not with brief sentences but with lengthy documents; and if so be that in any of these we have actual or virtual translation from a Semitic original, the distinction between Aramaic style and Hebrew style is bound to assert itself.*

If, then, we find a New Testament document such as St. Mark's Gospel, which lacks the clearly-marked Hebraisms of the Lucan literature—unmistakably derived from the LXX, and at the same time contains different marks of Semitic style which can only be referred to Aramaic, the conclusion should surely be obvious. Here we have the work, not of a Hellenist who studied the LXX, but of a Palestinian Jew who either actually wrote in Aramaic, or whose mind was so moulded by Aramaic idiom that his Greek perforce reflected it. Such a work is naturally found to contain, together with the specific Aramaisms, a number of Semitisms which may be paralleled both from Aramaic and Hebrew, and which may or may not be reflected in the Greek of the LXX. But it is the specific Aramaisms which must determine the character of the work (Palestinian and not Hellenistic). The other Semitisms serve but to add weight after the conclusion has been drawn.†

* In speaking of 'Hebrew style' it may be well to reiterate the fact that we are referring to Biblical or Classical Hebrew. The 'New' Hebrew employed in the Mishna and Midrashim, which was the language of the Rabbinic Schools at or about the Christian era and subsequently, is structurally nearer akin to Aramaic than to Hebrew. This artificial product, however, fulfilled much the same function as did the dog-Latin employed by scholars in the Middle Ages, and there is no reason for supposing that it ever came into popular use.

† Cf. Allen, 'The Aramaic Element in St. Mark', *Expository Times*, xiii (1902), pp. 328 ff., an article which effectively disposes of the criticisms of Schmiedel.

Whether the Marcan Aramaisms prove actual translation from an original Aramaic document, as distinct from the virtual translation of a writer who, though using Greek as his medium of expression, is casting his words in the Aramaic mould which is more familiar to him, is a question which still remains open. The present writer, comparing the evidence for an Aramaic Marcan document with that which he himself adduces in this volume for an Aramaic Fourth Gospel, feels that the case for the former is not of equal cogency with that for the latter. To a large extent, as is natural, the evidence for the two works runs upon identical lines; and here the argument for Jn. is materially strengthened by the parallel usages of Mk. There is, however, a still larger mass of evidence which can be cited for Jn. to which no adequate analogue exists in Mk. Examination of the usages discussed in the present volume will be found to yield the following results:

Usages common to Jn. and Mk.

Parataxis (p. 56).
Frequency of Historic Present (p. 87).
Frequency of Imperfect ἔλεγεν, ἔλεγον (p. 92).
Sparse use of δέ, and preference for καί (p. 69).
ἵνα = conjunctive 'that' (p. 70).
πρός = 'with' (p. 28).

Usages of Jn. found more rarely in Mk.

Asyndeton * (p. 49).
Casus pendens † (p. 63).
καί linking contrasted statements = 'and yet' ‡ (p. 66).
ἵνα mistranslation of ־ְדּ relative. One case in Mk. (p. 76).
ὅτι mistranslation of ־ְדּ relative. Two cases in Mk. (p. 77).
Relative completed by a Pronoun. Two cases in Mk. (p. 84).
οὐ μή . . . εἰς τὸν αἰῶνα = 'never'. Two parallels in Mk. (p. 99).
πιστεύειν εἰς. One case in Mk. (p. 34).

* Allen quotes Asyndeton as characteristic of Mk. (*St. Mark*, pp. 18 f.), but his instances bear no comparison with the frequency of the usage in Jn.

† The present writer has noted only Mk. 6^{16}, 7^{20}, 12^{10}, 13^{11}.

‡ The only cases collected from Mk. are 4^{32}, $5^{26.31}$, 14^{49}.

To these may be added an Aramaism of which one case occurs in each, viz.:

Anticipation of Genitive by Possessive Pronoun (p. 85).

Usages characteristic of Jn. not found in Mk.

Frequency of Personal Pronouns (p. 79).

Frequency of Emphatic Demonstratives οὗτος, ἐκεῖνος (p. 82).

ἵνα mistranslation of דְּ = 'when' (p. 77).

ὅτι mistranslation of דְּ = 'when' (p. 78).

ἔρχομαι Present as *Futurum instans* (p. 94).

οὐ . . . ἄνθρωπος = 'no one' (p. 99).

ἵνα μή employed to the exclusion of μήποτε (pp. 69, 100).

To these may be added an Aramaism of which one case only occurs in Jn., viz.:

Anticipation of direct Object of verb by Pronoun (p. 86).

Two cases of a construction which is Hebraic rather than Aramaic, viz.:

Change of construction after Participle (p. 96).

The Marcan usages noted above which find parallels in Jn. do not exhaust the Aramaisms of Mk. Others are cited by Allen (cf. *St. Mark*, pp. 48 ff.) and by Wellhausen (*Einleitung*[2], pp. 7 ff.), of which the most noteworthy are the frequent use of the adverbial πολλά = שַׂגִּיא, and of the auxiliary ἤρξατο, -αντο = שָׁרִי; but they are not equally impressive because—though they fit in with the theory of translation from an Aramaic original—they are the kind of Aramaisms which might naturally be introduced by a writer of Greek whose native tongue was Aramaic. We may also note the fact that the Κοινή construction ἵνα = conjunctive 'that' which characterizes Mk. (though to a less extent than Jn.) is a usage which an Aramaic-speaking writer of Greek would naturally tend to exaggerate. On the other hand, the use of ἵνα in place of a relative, which can scarcely be understood except on the theory of mistranslation, while frequent in Jn. (cf. pp. 75 f.), occurs but once in Mk. What is needed to substantiate the theory of an Aramaic original for Mk. is some cogent evidence of mistranslation; and this has not as yet been advanced. In contrast, the writer believes that the evidence which he has collected in

Chap. VII in proof of mistranslation in Jn. must be recognized, on the whole, as exceedingly weighty.

Granted, however, the possibility of an Aramaic original for the Fourth Gospel, the question naturally arises—What evidence do we possess sufficient to enable us to prove this theory, and in a measure to reconstruct the original text?

The evidence is naturally drawn from our knowledge of Palestinian Aramaic at or about the period at which the Gospel is presumably to be dated.* The following are the main sources of our knowledge:

1. The Aramaic sections of the O.T., viz. Jer. 10^{11}, Ezr. 4^{8}—6^{18}, 7^{12-26}, Dan. 2^{4b}—7^{28}. The Ezra-sections, if they are what they profess to be, date from the middle of the fifth century B.C.† The Book of Daniel is dated with approximate certainty under the persecution of Antiochus Epiphanes, 168–167 B.C. The dialect of 2^{4b}—7^{28} is W. Aramaic, and is practically identical with that of the Ezra-sections, exhibiting affinities to the dialects of the Palmyrene and Nabataean inscriptions which date from the third century B.C. to the second century A.D.‡ This source is therefore of great value as closely approximating to what must have been the type of Aramaic spoken in Palestine in the first century of the Christian era.

2. The Targums or Aramaic paraphrases of the O.T. The synagogue-practice of expounding the Hebrew text of the O.T. by an Aramaic paraphrase is undoubtedly very ancient. Both the Babylonian and Jerusalem Talmuds understand the term מְפֹרָשׁ in Neh. 8^{8}—R.V. 'And they read in the book, in the law of God *distinctly* (marg. *with an interpretation*); and they gave the sense, so that they understood the reading'—as referring to the use of

* On this subject the standard work is Dr. G. Dalman's *Grammatik des jüdisch-palästinischen Aramäisch*. Cf. especially pp. 5–40. This may usefully be supplemented by the discussion in the same writer's *The Words of Jesus*, pp. 79–88.

† Ezr. 4^{6-23}, though inserted into a section which relates the efforts of the Samaritans to thwart Zerubbabel's rebuilding of the Temple in the latter part of the sixth century B.C., really relates to the interruptions caused by the Samaritans and other enemies of the Jews to the project of the rebuilding of the *city-walls*, probably shortly before the twentieth year of Artaxerxes (444 B.C.) when Nehemiah intervened and secured the support of the Persian king. Cf. Driver, *Introd. to Lit. of O.T.*[9] p. 547.

‡ Cf. Driver, *Introd. to Lit. of O.T.*[9] pp. 503 ff.

an Aramaic paraphrase;* and this view, though disputed, has something to be said in its favour.† If, however, the practice of

* Cf. Bab. Megilla 3*a*; Nedarim 37*b*; Jerus. Megilla 74*d*. The same explanation is given in Midrash Bereshith Rabba, par. xxxvi. 12.

† Cf. Berliner, *Targum Onkelos*, ii, p 74, who compares the use of מְפָרַשׁ in the words of the Persian king's rescript in Ezr. 4[18], נִשְׁתְּוָנָא דִּי־שְׁלַחְתּוּן עֲלֶינָא מְפָרַשׁ קְרִי קָדָמָי, i. e. most naturally, 'The letter which ye sent unto us hath been read before me *in translation*', i. e. translated from Aramaic into Persian. The principal rival explanation (offered by Dr. Bertholet) is 'divided' (sc. into sections), i. e. 'section by section'; and on this explanation the following words וְשׂוֹם שֶׂכֶל 'and giving the sense' may refer to an Aramaic paraphrase. The synagogue-custom as known to us was to read a verse of the Law in the Hebrew and follow it by the Aramaic paraphrase. In the Prophets three verses might be read together and followed by the Aramaic rendering.

Even in pre-exilic times (cf. 2 Kgs. 18[26]) Aramaic was the *lingua franca* of international communication. It must have been widely used, along with Babylonian, in the Neo-Babylonian kingdom. Cuneiform tablets of the late Assyrian, Neo-Babylonian, and Achaemenian periods bear Aramaic dockets; and scribes or secretaries were employed for the purpose of writing Aramaic upon parchment along with those whose business it was to write Babylonian in cuneiform upon clay tablets (cf. the writer's *Judges*, pp. 255, 495). Probably Aramaic was the exclusive medium of intercourse between the exiled Jews and their captors, and was used by them in commercial dealings with foreigners. Thus the Jews who returned from exile must have come back with a knowledge of Aramaic at least as thorough as was their knowledge of Hebrew, and must have found that in Palestine Aramaic had established itself and gained ground owing to the mixture of races and the decay of national feeling among the Jews who had remained in Palestine.

The fact that Hebrew of a more or less classical character remained the literary language of the Jews to within at least a century before the Christian era does not of course imply that it was widely and generally *spoken* by the Jews up to that period. That it *was* understood and spoken in the earlier post-exilic period is implied by the fact that e. g. the prophecies of Haggai, Zechariah, and Malachi, which were intended for a popular audience, are written in Hebrew; and by the allusion in Neh. 13[24], which shows, however, at the same time, how easy the condition of affairs made it for the less precise Jews to drop Hebrew and adopt another language.

All that we can say, then, with any certainty, is that after the return from exile Hebrew and Aramaic must for a time have been used concurrently by the Jews. Religious, national, and literary feeling strove for the retention of Hebrew; but external influence making itself felt in the exigences of daily life favoured the advance of Aramaic, and gradually led to its general adoption. Literary and cultivated Jews read Hebrew, and no doubt spoke it to some extent among themselves at least for some time after the return. The mass of the people who did not read books came more and more to speak Aramaic exclusively and to lose the knowledge of Hebrew.

using a Targum is not to be carried so far back as the days of Ezra, the fact that it became customary long before the Christian era is at any rate not in dispute.

The date at which written Targums first came into existence cannot certainly be determined.* It is related that in the fourth century A.D. Samuel ben Isaac once entered a synagogue, and seeing a scribe reading the Targum from a book, admonished him thus: 'This is forbidden thee; for that which is received orally must only be delivered orally, and only that which is received in writing may be read from the book' (Jerus. Megilla iv. 1). There is, however, considerably older evidence for the existence of written Targums—for private reading and not for public worship. The Mishna† states that portions of the text of the Bible were 'written as a Targum' (Yadaim iv. 5); and there exists a Tannaitic ‡ tradition that a Targum of the Book of Job existed in the days of Gamaliel the Elder (the grandson of Hillel and instructor of St. Paul; cf. Acts $5^{34 ff.}$, 22^{3}), and after being withdrawn from use by his orders, reappeared in the days of his grandson Gamaliel II.§ The Targum of Onkelos on the Pentateuch, which became the official Targum of the Babylonian schools, must have been committed to writing and finally redacted at least as early as the third century A.D., since its Masora dates from the first half of that century. Two Palestinian Amoraim of the third century advised their congregation to read the Hebrew text of the Parasha (section of the Pentateuch read as lesson) twice in private and the Targum once, according to the practice of public worship. Joshua ben Levi commended this practice to his sons (Berakhoth 8 *b*), while Ammi, a pupil of Johanan, made it a rule

* See on this subject Berliner, *Targum Onkelos*, ii, pp. 88 ff., and the admirable article 'Targum' by Dr. W. Bacher in the *Jewish Encyclopaedia*.

† The Mishna (i.e. 'Repetition' of the Law, or in a wider sense its *Exposition*) was compiled towards the end of the second century A.D.

‡ The Tannaim ('Teachers') were the Rabbinic authorities of the first two centuries of the Christian era whose work is embodied in the Mishna. They were succeeded by the Amoraim ('Speakers' or 'Interpreters'), third to fifth centuries A.D., who chiefly concerned themselves with the exposition of the Mishna. The outcome of this work was the Gemara, 'Supplement' or 'Complement' of the Mishna, which, together with the latter, forms the Talmud.

§ Cf. the passage from Tosefta Shabbath, ch. xiv, quoted by Berliner, *op. cit.* p. 89.

generally binding (*ib.* 8 *a*). 'These two dicta were especially instrumental in authorizing the custom of reciting the Targum.'* Thus we may gather how the practice of interpreting the Hebrew Scriptures in Aramaic, at one time presumably dependent upon the extempore skill of the individual Mᵉthurgᵉman, gradually assumed a fixed form; first, no doubt, orally, then in written shape.

The principal Targums which concern us are as follows:

The so-called Targum of Onkelos † on the Pentateuch. This is sometimes called the Babylonian Targum, as adopted and standardized in Babylonia not later, as we have seen, than the third century A.D. While exhibiting certain Babylonian peculiarities in diction, it 'is composed in a dialect fundamentally Palestinian'.‡ Its contents prove that it must have been drawn up in Palestine in the second century, since both its Halakhic and Haggadic elements § exhibit the influence of the school of Akiba (who perished in the rebellion of Bar Cokhba, A.D. 135) and other prominent Tannaïm.‖

The Palestinian Targum of the Pentateuch is, as it has come down to us, much later in date. The Targum of Pseudo-Jonathan is wrongly assigned to Jonathan (the reputed author of the Targum of the Prophets), possibly through mistaken interpretation of the abbreviation ת"י = *Targum Yerushalmi*, Jerusalem Targum, as *Targum Yehonathan*. As finally redacted it is not earlier than the seventh century A.D., but it is thought to contain many elements which are older than the Targum of Onkelos.¶ Comparison of these two Targums yields evidence that they were originally identical, their agreement being often *verbatim*.

* Cf. Bacher, *op. cit.* p. 58.

† The name אונקלס Onkelos appears to have arisen through confusion made in Bab. Megilla iii. 1 of a reference in Jerus. Megilla i. 11 to the Greek translation of Aquila עקילס Akylas. Cf. Berliner, *op. cit.* pp. 92 ff.

‡ Nöldeke, *Mandäische Grammatik*, p. xxvii, quoted by Bacher, *op. cit.* p. 59 *a*.

§ *Hălākhā* ('walking' or 'way'; so 'custom') is the exposition and application of the legal elements of Scripture; *Haggādā* ('narration') the elaboration of its historical and didactic portions.

‖ Cf. Berliner, *op. cit.* p. 107.

¶ Dalman, *Gramm.* pp. 21 ff., and *WJ.* pp. 84 f., disputes this inference, holding the most primitive elements to be 'exactly the parts taken from the Onkelos Targum'.

In addition to the complete Targum of Pseudo-Jonathan there survive fragments of a Jerusalem Targum, apparently not all contemporaneous. In the view of Dr. Bacher, 'Both the Pseudo-Jonathan and the fragments contain much that has survived from a very early period; indeed the nucleus of the Palestinian Targum is older than the Babylonian which was redacted from it' (*op. cit.* p. 61 *a*).

The Targum of Jonathan on the Prophets* is assigned by tradition to Jonathan ben Uzziel, who was Hillel's most famous pupil. The history of its transmission appears to follow the same lines as that of the Targum of Onkelos. Palestinian in origin (as is expressly stated in the Bab. Talmud), it gained official recognition in Babylonia in the third century A.D. It is frequently quoted by Joseph, the head of the Academy of Pumbeditha in Babylonia in the early part of the fourth century A.D., who, in referring to Isa. 8[6] and Zech. 12[11], remarks that 'if there were no Targum to it, we should not know the meaning of these verses' (Sanhedrin 94 *b*; Moed Ḳaṭon 28 *b*; Megilla 3 *a*). Such reference implies the recognition of the Prophetic Targum as an ancient authority.

These Targums—and especially the Targums of Onkelos and of Jonathan on the Prophets—are of great value to us as illustrating the Palestinian Aramaic of the early centuries of the Christian era. Though, in the form in which we know them, they are later than the first century, they embody material which—whether in written or oral form—must have come down from that period; and from the linguistic point of view it is clear that they are faithful witnesses. Their dialect is closely allied to the dialect of the Book of Daniel, such slight differences as exist being mainly orthographical.† The only drawback to their use is that, being translations of Hebrew, they tend at times to Hebraize their Aramaic; but instances of this tendency are not difficult to detect, and are unlikely, therefore, to lead us astray.‡

* The term 'Prophets' is of course used in the Jewish sense, including the four historical books known as 'the Former Prophets', viz. Josh., Judg., Sam., and Kgs.

† Cf. Driver, *Introd. to Lit. of O.T.*[9] p. 503; Nöldeke in *Encycl. Bibl.* 283.

‡ Cf. e.g. the passages cited on pp. 61 ff. On Hebraisms in the Targums cf. Dalman, *WJ.* p. 83.

3. The Palestinian (so-called Jerusalem) Talmud and the Midrashim contain short sections—stories and the like—in Aramaic interspersed amid the New Hebrew in which they are for the most part written. These Aramaic sections are the latest portions of these works, dating from the fourth to the sixth centuries A.D. They are clearly in the dialect of the people, and such linguistic peculiarities as this dialect exhibits connects it with Galilee rather than with Judaea.*

4. The Palestinian Syriac Lectionary, of unknown date, exhibits an Aramaic dialect akin to that of the Palestinian Talmud and Midrashim. As offering us the text of a great part of the Gospels translated into Palestinian Aramaic this Lectionary is of considerable interest. Like the Targums, however, in relation to the Hebrew text, it shows a certain tendency to adapt its language to its Greek original.

In addition to these Palestinian Aramaic sources, we may gain not inconsiderable aid through comparison of the ancient Syriac versions of the O. and N.T., making, of course, such allowances as are necessary for the dialectical differences between Eastern and Western Aramaic. The Peshîṭtā translation of the O.T. is undoubtedly very ancient. Made directly from the Hebrew, it exhibits the traditions of Jewish exegesis, as appears from the points of connexion which it offers with Targumic renderings.† It may well have been the work of Jewish scholars, and can hardly be later than the early second century A.D., if so late. As compared with the Targums, it exhibits less of a tendency to accommodate its language to the Hebrew constructions of the original.

No Syriac version of the N.T. is as old as that of the O.T. We know that Tatian made his Diatessaron, or Harmony of the Four Gospels (*τὸ διὰ τεσσάρων εὐαγγέλιον*), in Greek, and that this was translated into Syriac during his lifetime, *c.* A.D. 170.‡ It

* Cf. Dalman, *Gramm.* pp. 12 ff., 31 ff.

† Cf. the illustrations of this tendency collected by Dr. Driver in his *Notes on the Heb. Text of the Books of Samuel*², pp. lxxi f., and by the present writer in his *Notes on the Heb. Text of the Books of Kings*, pp. xxxiv f., and *Book of Judges*, p. cxxviii.

‡ For authorities cf. Dr. Nestle's article 'Syriac Versions' in Hastings's *Dictionary of the Bible*, iv, p. 646*a*. The view that the Diatessaron was first composed in

continued in use at Edessa till the fifth century, when Rabbula, bishop of Edessa (A.D. 411–35), prepared a revision of the text of the separate Gospels (called *Evangelion da-M^e pharr^e shê*, 'Gospel of the Separate'), and ordered its substitution for the Diatessaron (*Evangelion da-M^e ḥall^e ṭê*, 'Gospel of the Mixed'), and the collection and confiscation of the copies of the latter. This was carried out with such thoroughness that no copy of the Syriac Diatessaron has survived, and we only know the work through an Armenian translation of St. Ephrem's Commentary upon it, and a late Arabic translation in which the text has been accommodated to that of the Peshîṭṭā.

Dr. Burkitt has shown that Syrian writers prior to Rabbula used the *Evangelion da-M^e pharr^e shê*,* which has survived to us in the fragmentary remains of a recension of the Four Gospels discovered and edited by Dr. Cureton in 1858, and in the (nearly complete) palimpsest of the Gospels discovered by Mrs. Lewis at the convent on Mount Sinai in 1892; and further, that Rabbula, when he forbad the use of the Diatessaron, made a revision of this separate version of the Gospels in conformity with the Greek text current at Antioch at the beginning of the fifth century. This appears to have been the origin of the N.T. Peshîṭṭā. He has also shown that the *Evangelion da-M^e pharr^e shê* used the O.T. Peshîṭṭā, and must therefore be later than it.† His conclusion is that the Diatessaron was the earliest form of the N.T. possessed by the Syrian Church, the *Evangelion da-M^e pharr^e shê* being dated by him *c.* A.D. 200. According to this view the early Christian Church at Edessa had no N.T. prior to the Diatessaron in A.D. 170. 'For the first generation of Syriac-speaking Christians the Law and the Prophets sufficed.'‡ This is a conclusion which is open to question, and it may be that the old version represented by the Sinaitic and Curetonian should be placed at an earlier date.

The Old Syriac and Peshîṭṭā versions of the N.T., as well as

Greek and then translated into Syriac appears to be more probable than that it was originally composed in Syriac. Cf. Burkitt, *Evangelion da-Mepharreshe*, ii, p. 206. For the latter view cf. J. F. Stenning in Hastings's *DB.*, v, p. 452.

* Burkitt, *Evangelion da-Mepharreshe*, ii, pp. 101 ff.

† *op. cit.* pp. 201 ff.

‡ *op. cit.* p. 212.

the Palestinian Syriac Lectionary, are of great value to our inquiry as illustrating Aramaic constructions in relation to the Greek of the Gospels. When, for example, we get a varying Greek construction, one form of which we suspect of being an Aramaism, and the Syriac versions render both alike in accordance with our suspected Aramaism, our primary inference receives strong confirmation. There are many instances of this in the Fourth Gospel (cf. e.g. pp. 72 ff.).

The *Acta Thomae*, an original Syriac work * of fairly early date (early third century A.D.†) is sometimes used in the following pages for purposes of illustration.

The evidence which is brought forward in this volume in proof that the Greek text of the Fourth Gospel is a translation from Aramaic is concerned with the broad general characteristics of the Aramaic language, and does not depend upon dialectal details. Though dialects of the language may be distinguished, belonging to different places and different periods, their distinctive characteristics (if we except the earliest monuments of the language, of the 9th–8th centuries B.C.) are but slight in comparison with the common features which unite all branches of the language. Thus the exact dialectal form of the original which we presuppose is a matter of minor importance. We may have doubts as to the precise word or verbal termination or suffix which we should select; we can have no reasonable doubt as to constructions which properly characterize the language as a whole.

* The fact that this work was originally written in Syriac has been conclusively proved by Dr. Burkitt in *Journal of Theol. Studies*, i, pp. 280 ff.; ii, p. 429; iii, p. 94.

† Cf. R. Duval, *La Littérature syriaque*, pp. 98 ff.

CHAPTER I

PRELIMINARY TESTING OF THE THEORY BY EXAMINATION OF THE PROLOGUE

As a preliminary to the classified discussion of particular usages, it is instructive to take the Prologue of the Gospel and examine it verse by verse. Thus we may gain at the outset a clearer conception of the texture of the writer's language as a whole; and, when we come to classify, may realize that we are not dealing merely with isolated phenomena, but with illustrations of a continuous characteristic which admits of but one explanation—the theory of an Aramaic original.

vv. $^{1.2}$. The phrase πρὸς τὸν θεόν in the sense '*with* God' is remarkable, as Westcott observes. He cites the parallel usage in Mt. 13^{56}, Mk. 6^{3}, 9^{19}, 14^{49}, Lk. 9^{41}, 1 Jn. 1^{2}. The last of these passages is an echo of the Gospel-prologue, presumably by the same author—ἥτις ἦν πρὸς τὸν πατέρα. With regard to the Synoptic instances we notice (1) that they are all from the Marcan source, and (2) that Mt. 17^{17}, Lk. 22^{53} alter Mark's πρὸς ὑμᾶς to the more natural μεθ' ὑμῶν, while Mt. 26^{55} omits the phrase altogether. The parallel passages are as follows:

Mk. 6^{3} καὶ οὐκ εἰσὶν αἱ ἀδελφαὶ αὐτοῦ ὧδε πρὸς ἡμᾶς;
Mt. 13^{56} καὶ αἱ ἀδελφαὶ αὐτοῦ οὐχὶ πᾶσαι πρὸς ἡμᾶς εἰσίν;

Mk. 9^{19} ἕως πότε πρὸς ὑμᾶς ἔσομαι;
Mt. 17^{17} ἕως πότε μεθ' ὑμῶν ἔσομαι;
Lk. 9^{41} ἕως πότε ἔσομαι πρὸς ὑμᾶς;

Mk. 14^{49} καθ' ἡμέραν ἤμην πρὸς ὑμᾶς ἐν τῷ ἱερῷ διδάσκων.
Mt. 26^{55} καθ' ἡμέραν ἐν τῷ ἱερῷ ἐκαθεζόμην διδάσκων.
Lk. 22^{53} καθ' ἡμέραν ὄντος μου μεθ' ὑμῶν ἐν τῷ ἱερῷ.

Clearly, then, we are dealing with a phrase confined in the Gospels to the Marcan source and to Jn. which was so far strange to the other Synoptists that they were moved on occasions to alter or expunge it. The view that it may represent an Aramaic phrase is at once suggested by the fact that it occurs three times in Mk., for which on other grounds an Aramaic original, or at any rate Aramaic influence, has been postulated. In Aramaic the common preposition לְוָת (possibly akin to the verb לְוִי 'join') denotes (1) connexion with, *apud*, παρά, (2) motion towards, *ad*, πρός. It may be suggested that feeling for the second meaning so commonly borne by לְוָת has moved the translator of an Aramaic original to represent the preposition by πρός even when used in the former sense.*

The usage of πρός = 'with' is frequent in St. Paul; cf. 1 Thess. 3^{4}, 2 Thess. 2^{5}, 3^{10}, 1 Cor. $16^{6.7}$, 2 Cor. 5^{8}, 11^{9}, Gal. 1^{18}, 2^{5}, $4^{18.20}$, Phil. 1^{26}, Philem. [13]. There are, however, many other indications that this Apostle's language is tinged with Aramaic influence.

v. [4]. ὃ γέγονεν ἐν αὐτῷ ζωὴ ἦν. This reading has the consensus of early attestation, the punctuation which connects ὃ γέγονεν with the preceding sentence seeming 'to be little if at all earlier than Cent. IV' (WH.). Yet, as is well known, considerable difficulty has arisen in connexion with the interpretation, 'That which hath been made in Him was life'. The Aramaic equivalent would be דַּהֲוָא בֵּיהּ חַיִּין (הֽוּא). Here the opening דְּ, answering to 'that which', might equally well bear the meaning 'inasmuch as, since, because'; cf. the use of דִּי in Dan. 2^{41} וְדִי־חֲזַיְתָה 'And *inasmuch as* thou sawest'; 2^{20} דִּי חָכְמְתָא וּגְבוּרְתָא דִּי־לֵהּ הִיא '*because* wisdom and might belongeth unto Him'. The Heb. relative אשר often bears the same sense. Adopting this interpretation, we obtain the meaning, 'Because in Him was life'; and this admirably suits the connexion—He was the source of all creation because He Himself was Life.

v. [5]. καὶ τὸ φῶς ἐν τῇ σκοτίᾳ φαίνει, καὶ ἡ σκοτία αὐτὸ οὐ κατέλαβεν. The difficulty of κατέλαβεν is familiar. Dr. Ball, in his article

* It was only after finishing this chapter that the writer noticed that the facts that πρός here = Aram. לְוָת, and that the other Gospel-occurrences emanate from the Marcan source with its Aram. background, had been anticipated by Dr. Rendel Harris in the first of a series of articles on 'The origin of the Prologue to St. John's Gospel' in the *Expositor*, xii (1916), pp. 156 f. The coincidence in conclusion serves to prove that it is unmistakable for an Aramaic scholar.

mentioned in the Introduction, has made the brilliant suggestion that confusion may have arisen in Aramaic between the Aph'el form אַקְבֵּיל *'aḳbēl* 'darken' and the Pa'el form קַבֵּיל *ḳabbēl* from an outwardly identical root, meaning 'receive, take'. It may be further noted that in Syriac the latter root actually occurs in the Aph'el in the sense 'receive'—cf. Lk. 15^{27} in Sin. and Pesh. ܕܟܕ ܚܠܝܡ ܐܩܒܠܗ 'because he hath received him whole' (cf. other instances cited by Payne Smith, 3470). The difference between לא אקבליה 'obscured it not' and לא קבליה *αὐτὸ οὐ κατέλαβεν* is slight; and if the construction was the common one of the participle with the substantive verb, לָא מַקְבֵּיל הֲוָא יָתֵיהּ 'was not obscuring it', there would, in an unvocalized text, be no distinction between מַקְבֵּיל 'obscuring' and מְקַבֵּיל 'receiving'. The sense 'darken' is equally suitable to Jn. 12^{35} *ἵνα μὴ σκοτία ὑμᾶς καταλάβῃ*, דְּלָא יְקַבְּלִינְכוֹן קַבְלָא 'that darkness shroud you not'.

v. ^{6}. *ἐγένετο ἄνθρωπος . . . ὄνομα αὐτῷ Ἰωάννης*, i.e. . . . הֲוָא גַּבְרָא שְׁמֵיהּ יוֹחָנָן. 'Whose name was' is only elsewhere so expressed in N.T. in *ch.* 3^{1} *ἄνθρωπος ἐκ τῶν Φαρισαίων Νικόδημος ὄνομα αὐτῷ*, Apoc. 6^{8} *ἵππος χλωρός· καὶ ὁ καθήμενος ἐπάνω αὐτοῦ, ὄνομα αὐτῷ ὁ θάνατος*, Apoc. 9^{11} *τὸν ἄγγελον τῆς ἀβύσσου· ὄνομα αὐτῷ Ἑβραϊστὶ Ἀβαδδών*.

Elsewhere in N.T. the ordinary expression is *ὀνόματι* (classical); cf. Matt. 27^{32}, Mk. 5^{22}, Lk. 1^{5}, 5^{27}, 10^{38}, 16^{20}, 23^{50}, 24^{18}, Acts 5$^{1.34}$, 8^{9}, 9$^{10.11.12.33.36}$, 10^{1}, 11^{28}, 12^{13}, 16$^{1.14}$, 17^{34}, 18$^{2.7.24}$, 19^{24}, 20^{9}, 21^{10}, 27^{1}, 28^{7} (30 occurrences). Other expressions are: *ὀνόματι καλούμενος*, Lk. 19^{2}; *καὶ τὸ ὄνομα αὐτῆς*, Lk. 1^{5}; *ᾧ (ᾗ) ὄνομα*, Lk. 1$^{26.27}$, 2^{25}, 8^{41}, 24^{13}, Acts 13^{6}; *οὗ τὸ ὄνομα*, Mk. 14^{32}.

Pal. Syr. renders the Gospel-occurrences of *ὀνόματι* by ܫܡܗ 'his name', ܕܫܡܗ 'who his name' (i.e. 'whose name'), ܘܫܡܗ 'and his name'. Pesh. renders *ὀνόματι* by ܕܫܡܗ (ܕܫܡܗ̇) 'who his (her) name', ܕܫܡܗ ܗܘܐ 'who his name was', and once (Acts 16^{14}) ܫܡܗ̇ ܗܘܐ 'her name was'. *ὀνόματι καλούμενος*, Lk. 19^{2} = Pal. Syr. ܕܫܡܗ ܡܬܩܪܐ 'who his name was called', Pesh. ܕܫܡܗ ܗܘܐ 'who his name was'. *καὶ τὸ ὄνομα αὐτῆς*, Lk. 1^{5} = Pal. Syr. ܘܫܡܗ̇ 'and her name', Pesh. ܫܡܗ̇ ܗܘܐ 'her name was'. *ᾧ ὄνομα*, Lk. 1^{27} = Pal. Syr. caret, Pesh. ܕܫܡܗ 'who his name'; Lk. 2^{25} = Pal. Syr. ܫܡܗ ܕܗܘܐ 'who was his name' (i.e. 'whose name was'), Pesh. ܫܡܗ ܗܘܐ 'his name was'; Lk. 8^{41} =

Pal. Syr. ܕܫܡܗ, Pesh. ܕܫܡܗ 'who his name'; Acts 13[6] = Pesh. ܕܫܡܗ ܗܘܐ 'who his name was'. ᾗ ὄνομα, Lk. 1[26], 24[13] = Pal. Syr. (1[26] caret) ܕܫܡܗ̇, Pesh. ܕܫܡܗ̇ 'which its name'. οὗ τὸ ὄνομα, Mk. 14[32] = Pal. Syr. caret, Pesh. ܐܝܢܐ ܕܡܬܩܪܐ 'that which was called'. ὄνομα αὐτῷ, Jn. 1[6] = Pal. Syr. ܕܫܡܗ 'who his name', Pesh. ܫܡܗ 'his name'; Jn. 3[1] = Pal. Syr. ܫܡܗ 'his name', Pesh. ܫܡܗ ܗܘܐ 'his name was'; Rev. 6[8] = Pesh. ܫܡܐ ܠܗ 'name to it'; Rev. 9[11] = ܕܫܡܐ ܠܗ 'which, name to it'.

In the Aramaic parts of the O.T. we find, Ezr. 5[14] ויהיבו לששבצר שמה 'and they were given to Sheshbazzar his name' (i.e. 'to one whose name was S.'); Dan. 2[26], 4[5.16] די שמה בלטשאצר 'who his name Belteshazzar'.

The Hebrew modes of expressing 'whose name was N.' are two, viz. (1) 'and his name N.', Gen. 24[29], 38[1.2], Judg. 13[2], 17[1], Ru. 2[1], 1 Sam. 1[1], 9[1.2], 17[12], 21[8], 22[20], 2 Sam. 4[4], 9[2.12], 13[3], 16[5], 17[25], 20[1], 1 Chr. 2[34], Est. 2[5], Jer. 37[13] (22 occurrences), or (2) 'N. his name', 1 Sam. 17[4.23], 2 Sam. 20[21], 1 Kgs. 13[2], 2 Chr. 28[9], Job 1[1], Zech. 6[12] (7 occurrences). Besides these two phrases, we once find (Dan. 10[1]) דניאל אשר נקרא שמו בלטאשצר 'Daniel, who his name was called Belteshazzar'. In all these cases the rendering of Targg. exactly corresponds with the Hebrew, except that in Targ. of Est. 2[5] we find ושמיה מרדכי אתקרי 'and his name *was called* Mordecai' for 'and his name Mordecai' of Heb. The rendering of Pesh. exactly corresponds with Heb. except in Ru. 2[1], 1 Sam. 9[2], 2 Sam. 9[2], where we find 'who his name' for 'and his name'; in 1 Sam. 13[3], where the phrase is omitted; and in Zech. 6[12], where, in place of 'Branch his name', we have 'and his name Sunrise'. In LXX Heb. ושמו 'and his name' is rendered καὶ ὄνομα αὐτῷ, except in Gen. 24[29], 38[1.2], where we have ᾧ (ᾗ) ὄνομα. Heb. שמו 'his name' is represented by ὄνομα αὐτῷ except in Job 1[1], where we have ᾧ ὄνομα.

Outside O.T. we find that 'whose name was' is rendered in Syriac, 'his name', 'his name was', 'who his name', 'who his name was'. Cf. in Wright's *Apocryphal Acts*, ܚܕ ܡܢ ܪ̈ܫܐ ܕܐܢܛܝܘܟܝ. ܫܡܗ ܐܠܟܣܢܕܪܘܣ 'one of the chief men of Antioch, his name Alexander' (p. ܪܡܓ); ܚܕ ܕܝܢ ܓܒܪܐ ܐܘܢܣܝܦܘܪܘܣ ܫܡܗ ܗܘܐ 'Now a certain man, Onesiphorus his name was' (p. ܪܡܓ); ܓܒܪܐ ܒܠܢܝܐ ܕܫܡܗ ܣܣܢܝܘܣ 'a bath-keeper, who his name

Secundus' (p. ܝܒ); ܒܪ ܗܘܦܪܟܐ ܕܫܡܗ ܗܘܐ ܡܢܠܐܘܣ 'a procurator's son, who his name was Menelaus' (p. ܛܐ).

Thus it appears that *ὄνομα αὐτῷ Ἰωάννης, Νικόδημος ὄνομα αὐτῷ* exactly represent a Semitic construction common to Aramaic and Hebrew, and that the Greek represents the regular rendering of the Hebrew phrase. It is also noteworthy that the only other occurrences of *ὄνομα αὐτῷ* are found in Apoc., which is strongly Semitic in colouring.

v. [7]. *ἵνα πάντες πιστεύσωσιν δι' αὐτοῦ* probably = דִּיהֵימְנוּן בֵּיהּ כֹּלָּא, which is most naturally taken to mean, 'that all might believe in *it*' (the light) rather than 'through him' (John). Cf., for the sense postulated, 12[36] *ὡς τὸ φῶς ἔχετε, πιστεύετε εἰς τὸ φῶς, ἵνα υἱοὶ φωτὸς γένησθε*, and 12[46] *ἐγὼ φῶς εἰς τὸν κόσμον ἐλήλυθα, ἵνα πᾶς ὁ πιστεύων εἰς ἐμὲ ἐν τῇ σκοτίᾳ μὴ μείνῃ.*

v. [8]. *οὐκ ἦν ἐκεῖνος τὸ φῶς.* The emphatic pronoun *ἐκεῖνος*—so characteristic of the Fourth Gospel—has its counterpart in the Aram. הָהוּא, Syriac ܗܘ 'that one', or in the Personal Pronoun הוּא. See below (p. 82).

ἀλλ' ἵνα μαρτυρήσῃ περὶ τοῦ φωτός. The difficulty of the supposed ellipse (usually supplied by the words, 'he came') is familiar. The whole verse would run in Aramaic, לָא הֲוָא הוּא נְהוֹרָא אִילָּהֵן דְּיִסְהֵיד עַל נְהוֹרָא (cf. Pal. Syr. ܠܐ ܗܘܐ ܗܘ ܢܘܗܪܐ ܐܠܐ ܕܢܣܗܕ ܥܠ ܢܘܗܪܐ). It is probable that ד is here wrongly rendered *ἵνα*, and should have its relative force—'(*one*) *who*'. The sense then is, 'That one was not the light, but *one who* was to bear witness of the light'. Cf., for such a use of ד or די without expressed antecedent ('one who', 'he who'), Ezr. 7[25], וְדִי לָא יָדַע תְּהוֹדְעוּן 'and *him who* knoweth not ye shall teach'; Dan. 2[23] וּכְעַן הוֹדַעְתַּנִי דִּי־בְעֵינָא מִנָּךְ 'and now Thou hast made known to me *that which* we asked of Thee'. Cf. the similar use of אשר in Hebrew in Gen. 44[9.10] אֲשֶׁר יִמָּצֵא אִתּוֹ מֵעֲבָדֶיךָ וָמֵת . . . אֲשֶׁר יִמָּצֵא אִתּוֹ יִהְיֶה־לִּי עָבֶד '*He* with *whom* it is found of thy servants shall die . . . *He* with *whom* it is found shall be my slave', where the rendering of Targ. Onk. is דְּיִשְׁתְּכַח עִימֵּיהּ. Other instances of ד relative mistranslated by *ἵνα* are given below (pp. 75 f.).*

* In favour of the ordinary view that the construction implies an ellipse stand two other passages cited by Westcott—9[3] *Οὔτε οὗτος ἥμαρτεν οὔτε οἱ γονεῖς αὐτοῦ, ἀλλ' ἵνα φανερωθῇ τὰ ἔργα τοῦ Θεοῦ ἐν αὐτῷ*, where before *ἵνα* we have to supply

v. [9]. *πάντα ἄνθρωπον ἐρχόμενον εἰς τὸν κόσμον* is rightly recognized by J. Lightfoot (*Horae Hebraicae, ad loc.*) and by Schlatter (*Sprache*, pp. 18 f.) as the common Rabbinic phrase כָּל בָּאֵי עוֹלָם 'all comers into the world', i.e. all that are in it.* The Aram. equivalent would be כָּל אֱנָשׁ אָתֵי בְעָלְמָא. Thus Westcott's proposal to regard *τὸ φῶς* as the subject of *ἦν ἐρχόμενον* ('The true light . . . was coming, &c.': so R.V. *margin*) is excluded, and *ἦν τὸ φῶς τὸ ἀληθινόν* can only mean, 'It was the true light', referring to the preceding verse. For this sense we seem to need a demonstrative pronoun; and this probably stood in Aramaic as הוּא, which was misread הֲוָא and rendered *ἦν*.

v. [10]. *καὶ ὁ κόσμος αὐτὸν οὐκ ἔγνω.* Notice the adversative force of *καί* = 'and *yet*', here and in *v.* [11] *καὶ οἱ ἴδιοι κτλ.* This is very frequent in Semitic (cf. p. 66).

v. [11]. *εἰς τὰ ἴδια ἦλθε, καὶ οἱ ἴδιοι αὐτὸν οὐ παρέλαβον*, i.e. לְוָת דִּילֵיהּ אֲתָא וְדִילֵיהּ לָא קַבְּלוּנֵיהּ (cf. Pal. Syr. and Pesh.). The use of *τὰ ἴδια, οἱ ἴδιοι* cannot, of course, be claimed as unusual; but the expressions are striking, and at once suggest to an Aramaic scholar the phrase דִּילֵיהּ 'which to him', i.e. 'that which pertains (*or* those who pertain) to him'—'his belongings'. *ἴδιος* is a favourite term in Jn.; occurring 15 times (1[11 bis. 42], 4[44], 5[18.43], 7[18], 8[44], 10[3.4.12], 13[1], 15[19], 16[32], 19[27]), as against 5 in Mt., 1 in Mk., 4 in Lk.

v. [12]. *ὅσοι δὲ ἔλαβον αὐτόν, ἔδωκεν αὐτοῖς κτλ.* The construction

in thought some such words as 'he was born blind'; and 15[25] where before *ἀλλ' ἵνα πληρωθῇ ὁ λόγος κτλ.* there is an implied ellipse of 'This cometh to pass'. Cf. also Mk. 14[49]. Similarly, Schlatter (*Sprache*, p. 18) cites parallels from Mechilta on Ex. 20[19] אלו אפשר להעביר מלאך המות הייתי מעבירו אלא שכבר נגזרה גזירה 'If it were possible to remove the angel of death I should have removed him, but because the decree has already been decreed' (sc. 'I cannot do so'), and from Siphrê on Num. 25[1] אין אנו נזקקים לו בכך אלא שתגלה עצמך לו 'We are not under such obligation to him, but (sc. it is necessary) that thou, &c.' In spite of these parallels for an ellipse, it is clear that ד = *ἵνα* in the Aramaic rendering of our passage most naturally stands for the relative 'one who'; and this conclusion is supported by the other instances collected on pp. 75 f., where *ἵνα* is a mistranslation of a relative.

* Schlatter quotes a remarkable parallel to our passage from the Midrash Rabba on Leviticus, par. xxxi. 6—אתה מאיר לעליונים ולתחתונים ולכל באי עולם 'Thou (God) givest light to those that are above and to those that are below, and to all comers into the world'.

with *Casus pendens* is very frequent in Semitic—Pal. Syr. ܗܘܠܝܢ ܕܝ ܕܩܒܠܘ ܝܬܗ ܝܗܒ ܠܗܘܢ, Pesh. ܐܝܠܝܢ ܕܝܢ ܕܩܒܠܘܗܝ ܝܗܒ ܠܗܘܢ. For the occurrences of the construction in Jn. see p. 64.

τοῖς πιστεύουσιν εἰς τὸ ὄνομα αὐτοῦ, i.e. לִמְהֵימְנִין בִּשְׁמֵיהּ. The striking phrase *πιστεύειν εἰς* is strongly reminiscent of the Hebrew and Aramaic construction (Heb. הֶאֱמִין בְּ, Aram. הֵימִין בְּ). This is admitted by Moulton (*NTG.*^{3} p. 68), whose words are—'It would seem therefore that the substitution of *εἰς* or *ἐπί* for the simple dative may have obtained currency mainly in Christian circles, where the importance of the difference between simple belief (הֶאֱמִין לְ) and personal trust (ה׳ בְּ) was keenly realized. The prepositional construction was suggested no doubt by its being a more literal translation of the Hebrew phrase with בְּ.' The occurrences of *πιστεύειν εἰς* are as follows: (*εἰς τὸν Ἰησοῦν, εἰς τὸν υἱὸν τοῦ Θεοῦ, εἰς αὐτόν*, &c.) Jn. 2^{11}, $3^{16.18.36}$, 4^{39}, $6^{29.35.40}$, $7^{5.31.38.39.48}$, 8^{30}, $9^{35.36}$, 10^{42}, $11^{25.26.45.48}$, $12^{11.37.42.44.46}$, $14^{1.12}$, 16^{9}, 17^{20}, 1 Jn. 5^{10}; elsewhere, Matt. 18^{6} = Mk. 9^{42}, Acts 10^{43}, 14^{23}, 19^{4}, Rom. 10^{4}, Gal. 2^{16}, Phil. 1^{29}, 1 Pet. 1^{8}; (*εἰς τὸ φῶς*) Jn. 12^{36}; (*εἰς τὸ ὄνομα αὐτοῦ*) Jn. 1^{12}, 2^{23}, 3^{18}, 1 Jn. 5^{13}; (*εἰς τὴν μαρτυρίαν*) 1 Jn. 5^{10} (37 Johannine cases in all; 9 other cases).

v. ^{13}. *οἳ οὐκ ἐξ αἱμάτων . . . ἐγεννήθησαν*, i.e. דְּלָא מִן דְּמָא וְלָא מִן צְבוּת בִּסְרָא וְלָא מִן צְבוּת גַּבְרָא אִילָהֵן מִן אֱלָהָא אִתְיְלִידוּ. A point of great interest is the fact that the Latin variant ὃς . . . *ἐγεννήθη* becomes considerably more plausible upon the assumption of an Aramaic original. Since the particle דְּ is invariable, it might form the relative either to 'as many as received Him', or to 'He gave'. The question of reading in Aramaic depends, then, upon the difference between the plural אִתְיְלִידוּ 'they were born', and the singular אִתְיְלִיד 'He was born'—a difference which involves solely the insertion or omission of the letter ו. Moreover, since the following *v.* ^{14} begins with *καί* = ו, it is quite possible that the plural form איתילידו may have arisen through dittography of this ו. Very probably דְּ may not have had the relative sense at all, but (as in *v.* ^{4}) may have been intended to express the sense 'inasmuch as', thus giving the reason why the fact previously mentioned became possible—'inasmuch as He was born, not of blood, nor of the will of the flesh, nor of the will of man, but of God'; i.e. He, being born not after the manner of flesh, but of God, was thus able to give to those who received Him power to become sons of God.

This interpretation is of a piece with that which is given above for *vv.* 3.4—just as the Logos was the Source of all physical life '*because* in Him was life', so (*vv.* 12.13) He is the Source of spiritual life (the new birth) *because* He was born into the world, not by the ordinary process of human generation, but 'of God'. Cf. Lk. 1[35]

> Πνεῦμα ἅγιον ἐπελεύσεται ἐπὶ σέ,
> καὶ δύναμις Ὑψίστου ἐπισκιάσει σοι·
> διὸ καὶ τὸ γεννώμενον ἅγιον
> κληθήσεται υἱὸς Θεοῦ.

We note a connexion between υἱὸς Θεοῦ and τέκνα Θεοῦ of Jn. 1[12] which may not be accidental (cf. also ἐπεὶ ἄνδρα οὐ γινώσκω, Lk. 1[34], with οὐδὲ ἐκ θελήματος ἀνδρός, Jn. 1[13]). If this explanation of Jn. 1[12.13] be correct, the writer is drawing out the mystical import of the Virgin-Birth for believers on precisely the lines on which he elsewhere (5[21–29], 11[25.26], 14[19]) draws out the mystical import for them of the Resurrection.

On the other hand, the generally accepted reading οἳ . . . ἐγεννήθησαν surely involves a very strange sequence. The spiritual birth of believers is clearly the *result* of the grace described by ἔδωκεν αὐτοῖς ἐξουσίαν τέκνα Θεοῦ γενέσθαι, but *v.* 13 as phrased seems to imply that it was an antecedent condition. The author would surely have written 'and so they were born', or 'so that they should be born', had this result been the fact which he was intending to convey.

v. 14. καὶ ἐσκήνωσεν ἐν ἡμῖν. The verb ἐσκήνωσεν very clearly suggests the Jewish doctrine of the שְׁכִינָה *Sh'kīnā* (Heb.), שְׁכִינְתָּא *Sh'kīntā* (Aram.), or visible *dwelling* of Yahweh among His people, typified by the pillar of cloud standing above the Tent of Meeting, as subsequently in Solomon's Temple (Ex. 33[7–11] from the old document E; 1 Kgs. 8[10.11]. Cf. also, for the use of the verb שָׁכַן *šākan* of Yahweh's *dwelling* in the midst of Israel, Lev. 26[11.12] (H), Ex. 25[8], 29[45], Num. 5[3], 35[34] (P), 1 Kgs. 6[13], Ezek. 43[9]; of His *causing* His Name *to dwell* there, Deut. 12[11], 14[23], 16[2.6.11], 26[2], &c.). In Hebrew passages in which Yahweh is said to dwell, or to cause

His Name to dwell, in the midst of Israel, the Targumic phrase is, *He caused His Shᵉkīntā to dwell* there. Examples are—

Heb.	*Targ.*
Lev. 26^{12} 'And I will walk among you'.	'And I will cause My *Shᵉkīntā* to dwell among you'.
Ex. 25^{8} 'That I may dwell in your midst'.	'That I may cause My *Shᵉkīntā* to dwell among you'.
Ex. 29^{45} 'And I will dwell in the midst of the children of Israel'.	'And I will cause My *Shᵉkīntā* to dwell in the midst of the children of Israel'.

So, of the withdrawal of Yahweh's Presence,

Isa. 57^{17} 'I hid Myself'.	'I caused My *Shᵉkīntā* to depart (ascend) from them'.
Ps. 44^{9} 'And Thou goest not forth with our hosts'.	'And Thou dost not cause Thy *Shᵉkīntā* to dwell with our hosts'.
Ps. 88^{5} 'And they are cut off from Thy hand'.	'And they are separated from the face of Thy *Shᵉkīntā*.

Thus we may assume with some confidence that *καὶ ἐσκήνωσεν ἐν ἡμῖν* represents the Aramaic וְאַשְׁרִי שְׁכִינְתֵיהּ בֵּינָנָא 'and caused His *Shᵉkīntā* to dwell among us'. The choice of the verb *σκηνοῦν* was doubtless largely dictated by its close resemblance to the Semitic root *š-k-n*. The same usage is to be seen in Apoc. 7^{15} *καὶ ὁ καθήμενος ἐπὶ τοῦ θρόνου σκηνώσει ἐπ᾽ αὐτούς*, 21^{3} Ἰδού, *ἡ σκηνὴ τοῦ Θεοῦ μετὰ τῶν ἀνθρώπων, καὶ σκηνώσει μετ᾽ αὐτῶν.*

καὶ ἐθεασάμεθα τὴν δόξαν αὐτοῦ. Here we have a clear reference to a second term used in the Targums to describe God's Self-manifestation to mankind, יְקָרָא דַיָי 'the *Glory* of the Lord'. The conception of the יְקָרָא *Yᵉḳārā* goes back, like that of the *Shᵉkīntā*, to O.T. passages. In these the Heb. term is כָּבוֹד *Kābhōdh*. Thus, Ex. 16^{10}, 'Behold, the Glory of the Lord appeared in the cloud'; 24^{16}, 'And the Glory of the Lord abode upon mount Sinai, and the cloud covered it six days'; &c. The Targums employ *Yᵉḳārā*, like *Shᵉkīntā*, in paraphrasing passages which might, as they stand in the Heb., be taken to describe the actual appearance of God in bodily form. Thus—

Heb.	*Targ.*
Ex. 3^{1} 'And he came to the mountain of God, unto Horeb'.	'And he came to the mountain on which the *Yᵉḳārā* of the Lord was revealed, even to Horeb'.
Ex. 3^{6} 'For he was afraid to look upon God'.	'For he was afraid to look upon the manifeṣtation of the *Yᵉḳārā* of the Lord'.
Ex. 24^{10} 'And they saw the God of Israel'.	'And they saw the *Yᵉḳārā* of the God of Israel'.

We sometimes find *Shᵉkīntā* and *Yᵉḳārā* coupled; שְׁכִינַת יְקָרָא 'the Dwelling of the Glory'—

Isa. 40^{22} 'He that sitteth upon the circle of the earth'.	'That causeth the *Shᵉkīntā* of His *Yᵉḳārā* to dwell in lofty strength'.
Ps. 44^{24} 'Wherefore hidest Thou Thy face?'	'Wherefore causest Thou the *Shᵉkīntā* of Thy *Yᵉḳārā* to depart?'

Or, with inversion of order—

Isa. 6^{5} 'For mine eyes have seen the King, the Lord of hosts'.	'For mine eye hath seen the *Yᵉḳārā* of the *Shᵉkīntā* of the King of the ages'.

This last passage, from Isaiah's vision, leads us to a point which proves beyond the shadow of a doubt that when Jn. describes our Lord's Self-manifestation as δόξα he has in mind the *Yᵉḳārā* of the Targums.* In Jn. $12^{40.41}$ the writer, after quoting Isa. 6^{10}, adds the statement, ταῦτα εἶπεν Ἠσαΐας ὅτι εἶδεν τὴν δόξαν αὐτοῦ. The opening of the vision (Isa. 6^{1}) runs in Heb., 'I saw the Lord sitting upon a throne', and this is rendered in Targ., 'I saw the *Yᵉḳārā* of the Lord resting on His throne'. Other instances in Jn. of δόξα in this sense are, 2^{11} ἐφανέρωσεν τὴν δόξαν αὐτοῦ, 11^{40} ἐὰν πιστεύσῃς ὄψῃ τὴν δόξαν τοῦ Θεοῦ, 17^{24} ἵνα θεωρῶσιν τὴν δόξαν τὴν ἐμήν.

We are now in a position to maintain that the λόγος-conception

* Not of course necessarily the *written* Targums. but at any rate the conceptions which entered into the oral exposition of Scripture called Targum.

of the Prologue must undoubtedly be derived from the third and most frequent Targumic conception representing God in manifestation; that of the מֵימְרָא דַיְיָ 'the *Word* of the Lord'. We should no doubt trace the origin of the conception of the מֵימְרָא *Mēmrā* to O. T. passages in which Heb. דָּבָר *dābhār* 'Word' is employed in a connexion which almost suggests hypostatization, e.g. Ps. 107^{20}, 'He sent forth His Word and healed them'; Ps. 33^{6}, 'By the Word of the Lord were the heavens made'. This latter passage, with its reference to the Word's action in Creation, recalls the repeated וַיֹּאמֶר אֱלֹהִים 'And God *said*' in Gen. 1, where the Heb. verb אָמַר *'āmar* is identical with the Aram. root from which *Mēmrā* is derived. *Mēmrā* occurs repeatedly in the Targg. in passages where the Heb. represents God as speaking, acting, or manifesting Himself in a manner which seemed too anthropomorphic to Jewish thought of later times. This may be illustrated from the occurrences of the term in the first few chapters of Genesis.

Heb.	*Targ.*
Gen. 3^{8} 'And they heard the voice of the Lord God walking, &c.'	'And they heard the voice of the *Mēmrā* of the Lord God walking, &c.'
3^{10} 'I heard Thy voice'.	'I heard the voice of Thy *Mēmrā*'.
6^{6} 'And it repented the Lord that He had made man'.	'And the Lord repented in His *Mēmrā* because He had made man'.
6^{7} 'For it repenteth Me'.	'Because I have repented in My *Mēmrā*'.
8^{1} 'And the Lord said in His heart, I will not again curse, &c.'	'And the Lord said in (*or* by) His *Mēmrā*, I will no more curse, &c.'
9^{12} 'This is the token of the covenant which I make between Me and you'.	'This is the token of the covenant which I am making between My *Mēmrā* and you'.

So in *vv.* $^{13.15.16.17}$.

We cannot fail to notice that in Jn. 1^{14} the writer—no doubt with intention—brings together all three of these Targumic conceptions.* In *καὶ ὁ λόγος σὰρξ ἐγένετο* we have the *Mēmrā*; in *καὶ ἐσκήνωσεν ἐν ἡμῖν* the *Sh^ekīntā*; in *καὶ ἐθεασάμεθα τὴν δόξαν αὐτοῦ* the *Y^eḳārā*. This is evidence that, so far from his owing his λόγος-doctrine to an Alexandrine source, he is soaked through and through with the Palestinian Jewish thought which is represented by the Targums. Nor would the teaching of the Prologue need time for its development. Any disciple of our Lord who had heard the Targumic rendering of the O.T. in the synagogue, and who was capable of recognizing a superhuman power shining through the Master's Personality in His mighty acts, of detecting the Divine voice in His teaching, and at length of apprehending that in His Presence on earth God had come to dwell among men, could hardly fail to draw the inference that here was the grand fulfilment of O.T. conceptions so familiar to him through the Aramaic paraphrase.

πλήρης χάριτος καὶ ἀληθείας. The reference of this statement back to the main subject of the sentence, ὁ λόγος—which makes *καὶ ἐθεασάμεθα κτλ.* a parenthesis—is certainly awkward. It would be possible to assume that πλήρης is a misreading for πλήρη,† referring to τὴν δόξαν αὐτοῦ. If, however, *v.* [15], which speaks of the witness of John, and somewhat harshly breaks the connexion of thought, may be supposed to be misplaced, and properly to follow *after* the Prologue before *v.* [19] ('John bear witness . . . And this is the witness of John, &c.'), then another theory lies open. In *v.* [16] *ὅτι ἐκ τοῦ πληρώματος αὐτοῦ ἡμεῖς πάντες ἐλάβομεν*, i.e. דְּמִן מַלְיֵיהּ כּוּלָּנָא נְסַבְנָא, דְּ may mean, not 'because', but '*He who*' (the assumed mistranslation is a converse one to that noted in *vv.* [4,13]). Thus we get the statement, 'Full of grace and truth was He of whose fullness we have all received'. Aramaic, literally rendered, would express this by, 'Full of grace and truth (was) *He who* of His fullness we have all received'.

v. [18]. *μονογενὴς Θεός*. This reading has stronger attestation than the variant *μονογενὴς υἱός*, which looks like a correction. It must

* This has been noted by Dalman, *WJ.* p. 231.

† This is the reading of Cod. D. Deissmann (*LAE.* pp. 125 ff.) defends πλήρης as an indeclinable adjective, on the score of popular usage; and is followed by Moulton (*NTG.*[3] p. 50). The same view was earlier put forward by Blass, *Grammar* (Eng. tr. 1898), § 31, 6, and by C. H. Turner in *Journal of Theol. Studies* i (1900), pp. 120 ff.

be admitted, however, that the expression (though fully in accord with the teaching of the Prologue) is hardly to be expected after the preceding, 'No man hath seen God at any time'. It may be suggested that the Aramaic יְחִיד אֱלָהָא, 'the only-begotten of God', has been misunderstood as יְחִיד אֱלָהָא (Absolute for Construct State), and so rendered, 'the only-begotten God'.

It thus appears that nearly every verse of the Prologue yields evidence pointing to an Aramaic original. Besides, however, the special points which have been discussed, we notice generally (1) the simplicity of construction, with its fondness for co-ordination of sentences linked by *καί* (cf. especially *vv.* [1.3.5.10.11.14]), and (2) the many cases of parallelism in thought and expression—a marked trait of Hebrew poetic composition. Close study of this latter characteristic brings to light a most interesting fact. The Prologue seems to take the form of a hymn, written in eleven parallel couplets, with comments introduced here and there by the writer. This may be clearly seen in the Aramaic translation which follows, together with an English rendering of it. In making the translation the Judaean dialect has been used as far as possible. On the distinction between the Judaean and Galilaean dialects of Aramaic, see Dalman, *Gramm.* pp. 33 ff.*

בְּקַדְמָא הֲוָא מֵימְרָא
וּמֵימְרָא הֲוָא לְוָת אֱלָהָא.
וֵאלָהָא הֲוָא מֵימְרָא
הוּא הֲוָא בְקַדְמָא לְוָת אֱלָהָא.
כֹּלָּא בֵיהּ אִתְעֲבֵיד
וּבַר מִנֵּיהּ לָא אִתְעֲבֵיד כְּלוּם.
דַּהֲוָא בֵיהּ חַיִּין
וְחַיִּין נְהוֹרָא דִבְנֵי אֱנָשָׁא.
וּנְהוֹרָא בְקַבְלָא מַנְהַר
וְקַבְלָא לָא אַקְבְּלְנֵיהּ.

* The differences are slight. We have chosen חֲזָא 'see' rather than חֲמָא, יְדַע 'know' rather than חֲכַם, אִילָהֵן 'but' in preference to אֶלָּא; and the nominal 1st plural suffix ־ַנָא rather than ־ָן, verbal 1st plural suffix ־נָא rather than ־נָן. Possibly the Relative should be דִּי as in Biblical Aramaic; but דְּ is the Targumic form. Choice of the Judaean dialect is bound up with the view of authorship put forward on pp. 133 ff.

הֲוָא גַבְרָא מְשַׁדַּר מִן אֱלָהָא שְׁמֵיהּ יוֹחָנָן. הָדֵין אֲתָא לְסַהֲדוּ דְּיַסְהֵיד עַל נְהוֹרָא דִיהֵימְנוּן בֵּיהּ כֻּלֵּי. לָא הֲוָא הוּא נְהוֹרָא אִילָהֵן דְּיַסְהֵיד עַל נְהוֹרָא. הוּא נְהוֹרָא דְקוּשְׁטָא דְּמַנְהַר לְכָל אֱנָשׁ אָתֵי בְעָלְמָא. בְּעָלְמָא הֲוָא

וְעָלְמָא בֵּיהּ אִתְעֲבֵיד
וְעָלְמָא לָא יַדְעֵיהּ.

לְוָת דִּילֵיהּ אֲתָא
וְדִילֵיהּ לָא קַבְּלוּנֵיהּ.

כּוּלְּהוֹן דְּקַבְּלוּנֵיהּ יְהַב לְהוֹן רְשׁוּתָא לְמֶהֱוֵי (or דִיהוֹן) בְּנֵי אֱלָהָא לִמְהֵימְנִין בִּשְׁמֵיהּ. דְּלָא מִן דְּמָא (or דְּמִין?) וְלָא מִן צְבוּת בִּסְרָא וְלָא מִן צְבוּת גַּבְרָא אִילָהֵן מִן אֱלָהָא אִתְיְלִיד.

וּמֵימְרָא בִסְרָא אִתְעֲבֵיד
וְאַשְׁרִי שְׁכִנְתֵּיהּ בֵּינָנָא.

וַחֲזֵינָא יַת יְקָרֵיהּ
יְקָרָא כִיחִידָא מִן אַבָּא.

מְלֵי חִנָּא וְקוּשְׁטָא
דְּמִן מַלְיֵיהּ כּוּלָּנָא נְסַבְנָא.

וְחִנָּא חֲלַף חִנָּא.

דְּאוֹרַיְתָא מִן מֹשֶׁה אִתְיְהִיב
חִנָּא וְקוּשְׁטָא מִן מְשִׁיחָא.

אֱלָהָא לָא חֲזָא אֱנָשׁ מִן יוֹמוֹהִי. יְחִיד אֱלָהָא דְּאִית בְּעוּבָא דְאַבָּא הוּא מַלֵּי.

1. 'In the beginning was the Word,
And the Word was with God.

2. And God was the Word;
He was in the beginning with God.

3. All things by Him were made;
And without Him there was made naught;

4. Because in Him was life,
And the life was the light of mankind.

5. And the light in darkness was shining,
And the darkness obscured it not.

There was a man sent from God, his name, John. That one came for a witness, that he might bear witness of the light, that all might believe in it. That one was not the light, but one who should bear witness of the light. It was the true light that lighteth every man coming into the world. He was in the world,

> 6. And the world by Him was made,
> And the world knew Him not.
>
> 7. Unto His own He came,
> And His own received Him not.

As many as received Him, to them gave He power to become the sons of God—to those that believe in His name; because He was born, not of blood, nor of the will of the flesh, nor of the will of a man, but of God.

> 8. And the Word was made flesh,
> And set His *Sh^ekīntā* among us.
>
> 9. And we beheld His Glory,
> Glory as of the only-begotten of the Father.
>
> 10. He was full of grace and truth,
> Of Whose fullness we all have received,

And grace for grace.

> 11. For the law was given through Moses,
> Grace and truth through the Messiah.

No man hath ever seen God; the only-begotten of God, Who is in the bosom of the Father—He hath revealed.'

A striking feature of the hymn is that it contains several examples of the somewhat rare but well-marked form of parallelism which is known as *Climactic*. In this form stichos *b* of a couplet does not offer a more or less complete echo of stichos *a*, but adds something more which completes the sense of the distich, thus forming, as it were, its climax. Dr. Driver (*Literature of the O. T.*^{9} p. 363) remarks that 'this kind of rhythm is all but peculiar to the most elevated poetry'; and quotes as instances Ps. 29^{5}, 92^{2}, 93^{3}, 94^{3}, 96^{13}, 113^{1}. 'There is something analogous to it, though much less forcible and distinct, in some of the "Songs of Ascents" (Pss. 121–34), where a somewhat emphatic word is repeated from one verse (or line) in the next, as Ps. $121^{1b.2}$ (help); *v.* $^{3b.4}$; *v.* $^{4b.5a}$; *v.* $^{7.8a}$; $122^{2b.3a}$, &c.' Climactic parallelism is very characteristic of the Song of Deborah; see note in the writer's Commentary on Judges, pp. 169 f. The following examples may be noted in the poem of the Prologue:—

4. Because in Him was life
And the life | was the light of mankind.

5. And the light in darkness was shining,
And the darkness | obscured it not.

7. Unto His own He came,
And His own | received Him not.

9. And we beheld His glory,
Glory | as of the only-begotten of the Father.

10. He was full of grace and truth,
Of Whose fullness | we all have received.

Of the remaining couplets, 1, 2, and 8 may be reckoned as synonymous, while 3, 6, and 11 are antithetical.

It should be noted that the couplets, besides being parallel, appear also to be rhythmical, each line containing three stresses. In *v.* [17], in place of διὰ Ἰησοῦ Χριστοῦ the translation offers 'through the Messiah' simply, *metri gratiâ*. Ἰησοῦ may very naturally have come in as a later addition.

Additional Note on the interpretation of Jn. 1[13] *as referring to the Virgin-Birth* (*cf. p.* 34).

There is an essential unity in the teaching of St. Luke, St. Paul, and St. John as to the mode and meaning of the Incarnation which ought not to be overlooked. All go back in thought to the appearance of Jesus Christ on earth as a new Creation, to be compared and contrasted with the first Creation of the world and of mankind; and all therefore draw upon Gen. 1, 2 in working out their theme. Just as God's first creative act was the formation of *light*, breaking in upon the physical darkness which had previously covered primeval chaos, so was the birth of Christ the dawn of Light in the midst of the spiritual darkness of the world. That this idea was in St. Paul's mind is definitely stated by him in 2 Cor. 4[5,6], οὐ γὰρ ἑαυτοὺς κηρύσσομεν ἀλλὰ Χριστὸν Ἰησοῦν *κύριον, . . . ὅτι ὁ Θεὸς ὁ εἰπών Ἐκ σκότους φῶς λάμψει, ὃς ἔλαμψεν ἐν ταῖς καρδίαις ἡμῶν πρὸς φωτισμὸν τῆς γνώσεως τῆς δόξης τοῦ Θεοῦ ἐν προσώπῳ Χριστοῦ.* Cf. also 1 Cor. 4^{6}, 2 Cor. 6^{14}, Eph. 5^{8}, Col. 1^{13}. Allusion to Gen. 1, which is clearly seen in the opening words of Jn. 1, 'In the beginning', seems also to be behind *vv.*$^{4.5}$, where it is stated that the Logos, as the Agent in Creation, represented the introduction of Light into the world, and, by an almost imperceptible transition, the writer's thought passes from the introduction of life and light at Creation to its spiritual introduction at the Incarnation. Moreover, just as the introduction of light into the world at Creation did not immediately abolish physical darkness, but led to the setting by God of a *division* (וַיַּבְדֵּל, Gen. 1^{4}) between light and darkness, so (Jn. 1^{5}) in the Incarnation the Light was shining in darkness and the darkness did not obscure it; its introduction into the world producing a *κρίσις* whereby Light and darkness were sharply distinguished and men had to range themselves under the one or the other (Jn. 3$^{19-21}$; cf. 9^{39}, 12$^{35.36.46}$).* Turning to the Birth-narrative of St. Luke, it is surely not fanciful to find in the words of the angel in 1^{35}, *Πνεῦμα ἅγιον ἐπελεύσεται ἐπὶ σέ, καὶ δύναμις Ὑψίστου ἐπισκιάσει σοι*, an implied reference to Gen. 1^{2}, where the Spirit of God is pictured as *brooding* or *hovering* (מְרַחֶפֶת) over the face of the waters in the initial process of Creation which issues in the production of light.† So for St. Luke the Divine Birth means the dawning of *ἀνατολὴ ἐξ ὕψους, ἐπιφᾶναι τοῖς ἐν σκότει καὶ σκιᾷ θανάτου καθημένοις* (1$^{78.79}$), and *φῶς εἰς ἀποκάλυψιν ἐθνῶν* (2^{32}).

Again, the connexion in thought between the Old Creation and

* A similar mystical interpretation of the Genesis passage is given in Midrash Bereshith Rabba, par. iii. 10; 'Rabbi Yannai said, When He began to create the world, the Holy One (blessed be He) observed the works of the righteous and the works of the wicked. "And the earth was a waste", i.e. the works of the wicked. "And God said, Let there be light", i.e. the works of the righteous. "And God divided between the light and between the darkness"—between the works of the righteous and the works of the wicked. "And God called the light, day", i.e. the works of the righteous. "And the darkness he called, night", i.e. the works of the wicked. "And there was morning", i.e. the works of the righteous. "And there was evening", i.e. the works of the wicked. "One day", inasmuch as the Holy One (blessed be He) gave them one day. And what is this? The Day of Atonement.'

† This Genesis passage is applied in Midrash Bereshith Rabba to the endowment of the Messiah with the Divine Spirit; 'This is the Spirit of the King-Messiah, as it is said, "And the Spirit of the Lord shall rest upon Him".'

the New is explicit in St. Paul's teaching as to the first Adam and the second Adam in 1 Cor. 15^{45}; οὕτως καὶ γέγραπται Ἐγένετο ὁ πρῶτος ἄνθρωπος Ἀδὰμ εἰς ψυχὴν ζῶσαν· ὁ ἔσχατος Ἀδὰμ εἰς πνεῦμα ζωοποιοῦν. This is worked out in the frequent antithesis between σάρξ and πνεῦμα, and in the representation of baptism as a burial with Christ in which ὁ παλαιὸς ἡμῶν ἄνθρωπος is put off, and the baptized rises with Christ to newness of life (Rom. $6^{3\,ff.}$). We find the same antithesis between σάρξ and πνεῦμα in Jn. 3^{6}, 6^{63}, the whole of the discussion with Nicodemus in *ch.* 3 turning on the new birth which is ἐκ τοῦ πνεύματος. In 6^{63} it is stated, in contrast to σάρξ, that τὸ πνεῦμά ἐστιν τὸ ζωοποιοῦν, a thought of which the connexion with St. Paul's ἐγένετο . . . ὁ ἔσχατος Ἀδὰμ εἰς πνεῦμα ζωοποιοῦν can hardly be accidental. This connexion would, it may be presumed, be generally explained by the theory of the influence of Pauline Theology upon the writer of the Fourth Gospel; and this may be so. A fact, however, which is surely beyond question is that St. Paul's οὕτως καὶ γέγραπται refers not simply to the quotation from Gen. 2^{7}, 'He breathed into his nostrils the breath of life, and man became a living soul', *but to the whole passage relating to the first Adam and the second Adam*, from ἐγένετο down to ζωοποιοῦν. ὁ ἔσχατος Ἀδὰμ εἰς πνεῦμα ζωοποιοῦν depends upon ἐγένετο introducing the quotation equally with what goes before, from which it should be divided by a comma merely, and not by a colon (WH.) or full stop (R.V.). Had it been St. Paul's own addition, could he possibly have phrased the sentence thus, and not have written at least ὁ δὲ ἔσχατος Ἀδὰμ ἐγένετο εἰς πνεῦμα ζωοποιοῦν?

If, however, the whole passage is a quotation, whence was it derived? There can be no doubt that the form in which St. Paul's argument is cast is influenced by Rabbinic speculation, and that the Rabbinism of Palestine.* Though born at Tarsus, he claims

* The expression אָדָם הָרִאשׁוֹן 'the first Adam' is well known in early Midrashic literature. אָדָם הָאַחֲרוֹן 'the second Adam', i.e. the Messiah, is not known to us in Midrash before the *Nᵉwê shālôm*, the work of a Spanish Jew in the 15th century A.D (cf. Thackeray, *The Relation of St. Paul to Contemporary Jewish Thought*, pp. 40 ff.); but the Midrash Bereshith Rabba (ascribed by tradition to R. Hoshaiah, 3rd century A.D.) brings the Messiah into contrast with 'the first Adam' when, in commenting on Gen. 2^{4}, 'These are the generations of the heaven and the earth', it quotes earlier Rabbinical speculation as to the reason why the word for 'generations' is written *plene* with ו only in this passage and in Ruth 4^{18},

to be Ἑβραῖος ἐξ Ἑβραίων (Phil. 3[5]), i. e. not a Ἑλληνιστής (cf. Acts 6[1]), and he obtained his education at Jerusalem under Gamaliel, who was one of the most prominent Rabbinic teachers of the time (Acts 22[3]). But prior to St. Paul's conversion the earliest circle of Christian believers at Jerusalem was drawn not merely from the peasant-class, but embraced (according to Acts 6[7]) 'a great company of the priests', who would scarcely have been unversed in Rabbinic teaching, but may be supposed to have applied such learning as they had acquired to the service of the new Faith.

It is by no means improbable, therefore, that the passage as a whole may have been drawn from a collection of O. T. *Testimonia*, composed with the object of meeting Rabbinic Judaism upon its own ground.* If it be objected to this suggestion that elsewhere throughout the N. T. γέγραπται introduces a definite citation from the O. T., and that this is also the case with allusions to ἡ γραφή

'These are the generations of Perez' (תולדות, but elsewhere always תולדת), and cites the inference that ו, which numerically = 6, implies that the six things which Adam lost through the Fall shall be restored at the coming of 'the son of Perez', i.e. the Davidic Messiah. The Messiah appears as a life-giver (cf. πνεῦμα ζωοποιοῦν) in the Midrash hag-gadol to Genesis (compiled by a Yemenite Jew of the 14th century) which, commenting on Gen. 16[11], states that there are six persons whose names were given to them before their birth, viz. Ishmael, Isaac, Moses, Solomon, Josiah, and the King-Messiah. On the last it says, 'The King-Messiah, because it is written, "Before the sun his name shall be *Yinnôn*". And why is his name called *Yinnôn*? because he is destined to *quicken* those who sleep in the dust.' Here the Scriptural passage quoted is Ps. 72[17] לִפְנֵי שֶׁמֶשׁ יִנּוֹן שְׁמוֹ 'Before the sun shall his name *propagate*' (or '*produce life*'), and the verbal form, only here in O. T., is treated as a Messianic title—'He who quickens'. This Midrash is quoted by Raymund Martin in his *Pugio Fidei*, chap. ii, 11, who refers it to Moses had-Darshan, born at Narbonne about the middle of the 11th century A. D. Late as this is, we have the evidence of the Talmud (*Sanhedrin*, 98 *b*) that *Yinnôn* was early regarded as a Messianic title, for in the passage in question the pupils of R. Yannai (an Amora of the first generation—2nd to 3rd century A. D.) maintain, as a compliment to their teacher, that the Messiah's name is to be *Yinnôn*. The Psalm-passage is quoted in Midrash Bereshith Rabba, par. i. 5, as evidence that the name of the Messiah existed prior to the creation of the world, though it is not there stated that *Yinnôn* is to be taken as his name.

Though no part of this Midrashic speculation can be traced back to the 1st century A. D., it serves to illustrate the kind of Rabbinic teaching which may well have formed part of St. Paul's early training.

* Cf. Sanday, *The Gospels in the Second Century*, p. 272; 'We know that types and prophecies were eagerly sought out by the early Christians, and were soon collected in a kind of common stock from which every one drew at his pleasure.'

(with the possible exception of 1 Tim. 5[18], where our Lord's words Ἄξιος ὁ ἐργάτης τοῦ μισθοῦ αὐτοῦ seem to be included under the term), it may be replied that St. Paul's quotation *does* consist of such a citation from the O. T. *plus* a deduction therefrom, and would *ex hypothesi* be derived from a collection of proofs based on the O. T. and therefore drawn ἐκ τῶν γραφῶν. We may further draw attention to the use of this formula of citation in the Epistle of Barnabas 4[14], where our Lord's words in Mt. 22[14] are quoted: προσέχωμεν μήποτε, ὡς γέγραπται, πολλοὶ κλητοί, ὀλίγοι δὲ ἐκλεκτοὶ εὑρεθῶμεν. Similarly, the formula λέγει γὰρ ἡ γραφή is used in Barnabas 16[5] to introduce a quotation from Enoch 89[56.66].

If, then, this interpretation of 1 Cor. 15[45] as wholly a quotation be correct, the implication is that some time before St. Paul wrote his Epistle in A.D. 55–6, the antithesis between the first Adam and Christ as the second Adam had been worked out in Christian Rabbinic circles and was used in argument. This conclusion surely modifies the question of the dependence of the Fourth Gospel upon St. Paul in regard to the teaching here involved, suggesting as it does the alternative theory that both may have been dependent upon a common earlier method of theological expression of the truths of the Incarnation.

St. Luke supplies us with further food for thought in this connexion. His Birth-narrative is certainly from a Jewish-Christian source, and is generally acknowledged to be early. If any portions of it are earlier than the rest, these are the poems which it contains; and the angel's words at the Annunciation are no less a poem cast in rhythmical parallelism than are the *Magnificat*, *Benedictus*, and *Nunc dimittis*. We have had occasion to cite passages from all these, except the *Magnificat*, in arguing the unity of their thought with that of St. Paul and St. John. We may now note the fact that St. Luke carries back our Lord's genealogy to Adam, 'who was the son of God' (3[38]). What is the reason for this? Doubtless one reason is to be found in the fact that his Gospel is pre-eminently a universal Gospel—not for the Jews only but for the whole Gentile world also. May not, however, another (and perhaps the prime) reason be that the fact that the first Adam was born not by natural generation but by an act of God, in itself suggests the reasonableness that the second Adam should likewise so be born? If this is so, it is of course likely that St. Luke may have owed his conception to St. Paul's doctrine of Christ as the second Adam; but, if our argument has been sound, St. Paul himself owed it to an earlier source, embodied in a collection of *Testimonia* for general use. If, then, St. Luke's τοῦ Ἀδάμ, τοῦ Θεοῦ links itself on to υἱὸς Θεοῦ in the words of the Annunciation, and if his thought shows connexion with St. Paul's doctrine of the two Adams, is it likely that St. Paul, in enunciating this doctrine, was ignorant of the tradition of the Virgin-Birth? *

* This point has already been brought out by Dr. Box, *The Virgin Birth of Jesus*, pp. 38 f., 150.

CHAPTER II

THE SENTENCE

Asyndeton.

It is highly characteristic of Aramaic to open its sentences abruptly without the use of a connective particle. In this respect its contrast with Hebrew is very marked, the latter language regularly employing 'And' in prose to connect a sentence with what goes before, the force of this 'And' varying as determined by the context (And, So, Then, But, Yet, &c.). This difference in usage may well be illustrated from the Book of Daniel, in which *chs.* 1^{1}—2^{4a}, 8—12 are written in Hebrew, while *chs.* 2^{4b}—7 are in Aramaic.

Dan. 1^{1}—2^{4a} (Hebrew) consists of 23 sentences. Of these, 22 (i.e. all but the opening verse of *ch.* 1) begin with 'And' (sometimes variously rendered in R.V. 'Then', 'But', 'So').

Dan. 2^{5-49} (Aramaic) contains 44 sentences. Of these, 22 begin with a connective particle, and 22 without such particle. The openings are as follows:

With connective particle.	*Without connective particle.*
v.^{6} והן 'And if'.	*v.*^{5} ענה מלכא 'Answered the king'.
v.^{9} די הן 'For if'.	*v.*^{7} ענו 'They answered'.
v.^{11} ומלתא 'And the word'.	*v.*^{8} ענה מלכא 'Answered the king'.
v.^{13} ודתא 'And the decree'.	*v.*^{10} ענו כשדיא 'Answered the Chaldaeans'.
v.^{14} באדין דניאל 'Then Daniel'.	*v.*^{12} כל קבל דנה 'Because of this'.
v.^{15b} אדין מלתא 'Then the word'.	*v.*^{15a} ענה ואמר 'He answered and said'.
v.^{16} ודניאל על 'And Daniel went in'.	*v.*^{20} ענה דניאל 'Answered Daniel'.
v.^{17} אדין דניאל 'Then Daniel'.	
v.^{19a} אדין לדניאל 'Then to Daniel'.	

v.[19b] אדין דניאל 'Then Daniel'.
v.[25] אדין אריוך 'Then Arioch'.
v.[30] ואנה 'And I'.
v.[35] באדין דקו 'Then were broken'.
v.[39] ובתרך 'And after thee'.
v.[40] ומלכו רביעיא 'And the fourth kingdom'.
v.[41] ודי חזיתה 'And whereas thou sawest'.
v.[42] ואצבעת רגליא 'And the toes'.
v.[43] ודי חזיתה 'And whereas thou sawest'.
v.[44] וביומיהון 'And in their days'.
v.[46] באדין מלכא 'Then the king'.
v.[48] אדין מלכא 'Then the king'.
v.[49] ודניאל 'And Daniel'.

v.[22] הוא גלא 'He revealeth'.
v.[23] לך אלה אבהתי 'To thee the God of my fathers'.
v.[24] כל קבל דנה 'Because of this'.
v.[26] ענה מלכא 'Answered the king'.
v.[27] ענה דניאל 'Answered Daniel'.
v.[28b] חלמך 'Thy dream'.
v.[29] אנתה מלכא 'Thou, O king'.
v.[31a] *id.*
v.[31b] צלמא דכן 'This image'.
v.[32] הוא צלמא 'That image'.
v.[34] חזה הוית 'Thou sawest'.
v.[36] דנה חלמא 'This is the dream'.
v.[37] אנתה מלכא 'Thou, O king'.
v.[45] כל קבל די חזיתה 'Whereas thou sawest'.
v.[47] ענה מלכא 'Answered the king'.

This great frequency of unconnected sentences is equally characteristic of the rest of the Aramaic portion of the Book of Daniel. In *ch.* 8 the Hebrew begins again, and here we have 27 sentences (corresponding with the verse-division). Of these, 24 begin with 'And' (sometimes rendered, 'Then', 'Now', 'So', 'Yea'), and 3 only (*vv.*[1.4.20]) without any connective particle. It will thus be seen how clear is the distinction in style between Aramaic and Hebrew even of so late a date (*c.* 167 B.C.). When we come down to the Hebrew of the Mishna, we *do* find a paucity of connective particles, entirely owing to the influence of Aramaic.

Now great frequency of sentences opening without a connective particle is a marked characteristic of the Fourth Gospel. If we take *ch.* 1—neglecting openings in *speeches* (*vv.*[20—23], &c.), where asyndeton is *natural* in Greek as in English—we find 34 asyndeton openings, as against 28 with connective particle. In the 28 sentences which have connective particles, these are *καί* 19 times, *δέ* 4 times, *ὅτι* twice, *οὖν* 3 times. 'And', which is thus more than doubly as frequent as all the others taken together, is the ordinary Semitic connective particle, which bears various forces according to the context (cf. p. 49). The openings are as follows:

With connective particle.	*Without connective particle.*
	v.[1] ἐν ἀρχῇ ἦν.
	v.[2] οὗτος ἦν.
	v.[3] πάντα δι' αὐτοῦ ἐγένετο.
	v.[4] ἐν αὐτῷ ζωὴ ἦν.
v.[5] καὶ τὸ φῶς.	v.[6] ἐγένετο ἄνθρωπος.
	v.[7] οὗτος ἦλθεν.
	v.[8] οὐκ ἦν ἐκεῖνος τὸ φῶς.
	v.[9] ἦν τὸ φῶς τὸ ἀληθινόν.
	v.[10] ἐν τῷ κόσμῳ ἦν.
	v.[11] εἰς τὰ ἴδια ἦλθε.
v.[12] ὅσοι δέ.	
v.[14a] καὶ ὁ λόγος.	
v.[14b] καὶ ἐθεασάμεθα.	v.[15] Ἰωάννης μαρτυρεῖ.
v.[16] ὅτι ἐκ τοῦ πληρώματος.	
v.[17a] ὅτι ὁ νόμος.	v.[17b] ἡ χάρις καὶ ἡ ἀλήθεια.
	v.[18a] Θεὸν οὐδεὶς ἑώρακε.
	v.[18b] μονογενὴς Θεός.
v.[19] καὶ αὕτη ἐστίν.	
v.[20] καὶ ὡμολόγησεν.	
v.[21a] καὶ ἠρώτησαν.	
v.[21b] καὶ λέγει.	
v.[21c] καὶ ἀπεκρίθη.	
v.[22] εἶπαν οὖν.	v.[23] ἔφη.
v.[24] καὶ ἀπεσταλμένοι.	
v.[25a] καὶ ἠρώτησαν.	
v.[25b] Τί οὖν βαπτίζεις;	v.[26a] ἀπεκρίθη αὐτοῖς.
	v.[26b] μέσος ὑμῶν στήκει.
	v.[28] ταῦτα ἐν Βηθανίᾳ ἐγένετο.
	v.[29] τῇ ἐπαύριον βλέπει.
v.[31] κἀγὼ οὐκ ᾔδειν αὐτόν.	
v.[32] καὶ ἐμαρτύρησεν.	

*v.*33 κἀγὼ οὐκ ᾔδειν αὐτόν.	
*v.*34 κἀγὼ ἑώρακα.	*v.*35 τῇ ἐπαύριον πάλιν ἱστήκει.
*v.*36 καὶ ἐμβλέψας.	
*v.*37 καὶ ἤκουσαν.	
*v.*38*a* στραφεὶς δέ.	
*v.*38*b* οἱ δὲ εἶπαν.	*v.*39*a* λέγει αὐτοῖς.
*v.*39*b* ἦλθαν οὖν.	*v.*39*c* ὥρα ἦν ὡς δεκάτη.
	*v.*40 ἦν Ἀνδρέας.
	*v.*41 εὑρίσκει οὗτος.
	*v.*42*a* ἤγαγεν αὐτόν.
	*v.*42*b* ἐμβλέψας αὐτῷ.
	*v.*43*a* τῇ ἐπαύριον ἠθέλησεν.
*v.*43*b* καὶ εὑρίσκει Φίλιππον.	
*v.*44 ἦν δὲ ὁ Φίλιππος.	*v.*45 εὑρίσκει Φίλιππος.
*v.*46*a* καὶ εἶπεν αὐτῷ.	*v.*46*b* λέγει αὐτῷ ὁ Φίλιππος.
	*v.*47 εἶδεν Ἰησοῦς.
	*v.*48*a* λέγει αὐτῷ Ναθαναήλ.
	*v.*48*b* ἀπεκρίθη Ἰησοῦς.
	*v.*49 ἀπεκρίθη αὐτῷ Ναθαναήλ.
	*v.*50 ἀπεκρίθη Ἰησοῦς.
*v.*51 καὶ λέγει αὐτῷ.	

In order to prove that this characteristic is found throughout the Fourth Gospel, we may take two other chapters—from the middle and end—consisting mainly of narrative. *Ch.* 11 contains 59 sentences, of which 17 have no connective particle (*vv.* 8.9 *bis*.11.23.24.25.26.27.34.35.39 *bis*.40.44 *bis*.48); *ch.* 18 contains 52 sentences, and 20 of these are without connective particle (*vv.* 1.5*b*.8.8.11.20.21.23.25.26.30.31.34.35 *bis*.36.37 *ter*.38). This is a smaller proportion than in *ch.* 1; yet, as compared with the Synoptists, it is a very high one. To take three chapters at random from the latter—Mt. 3 contains 13 sentences, *none* without connective particle; Mk. 1 contains 38 sentences, 2 only without connective particle (*vv.* 1.8); Lk. 8 contains 60 sentences, 2 only without connective particle (*vv.* 8*b*.49).

Asyndeton ἀπεκρίθη, ἀπεκρίθησαν = *asyndeton* עֲנֵה, עֲנוֹ.

In the openings of unconnected sentences given above from the Aramaic of Dan. 2, it will be noticed that 9 out of the 22 take the form, 'Answered (so and so)'. This is very characteristic,

28 examples occurring in the six Aramaic chapters, while there are only 2 cases of 'Then answered' (5^{17}, 6^{14}), and *none at all* of 'And answered'. In contrast, the whole Hebrew O.T. offers only 2 such unconnected openings, 'Answered' (Song 2^{10}, rendered 'spake' in R.V.; Ps. 118^{5b}), while there are 145 cases of 'And answered (so-and-so)', ויען, ויענו, &c.

Theodotion's version of Dan. does not always represent this Aramaic 'Answered'; but where it does, it regularly renders ἀπεκρίθη, ἀπεκρίθησαν (11 times; *once* ἀποκριθείς), preserving the asyndeton in 4 cases ($2^{5.7.10}$, 4^{27}), but elsewhere prefixing καί. These 12 passages, in all of which the Aramaic phrase is regularly followed by 'and said', before statement of the words spoken, are as follows:

2^{5}	ענה . . . ואמר	ἀπεκρίθη.
2^{7}	ענו . . . ואמרין	ἀπεκρίθησαν . . . καὶ εἶπαν.
2^{8}	ענה . . . ואמר	καὶ ἀπεκρίθη . . . καὶ εἶπεν.
2^{10}	ענו . . . ואמרין	ἀπεκρίθησαν . . . καὶ λέγουσιν.
2^{26}	ענה . . . ואמר	καὶ ἀπεκρίθη . . . καὶ εἶπεν.
2^{27}	ענה . . . ואמר	καὶ ἀπεκρίθη . . . καὶ λέγει.
2^{47}	ענה . . . ואמר	καὶ ἀποκριθεὶς . . . εἶπεν.
3^{14}	ענה . . . ואמר	καὶ ἀπεκρίθη . . . καὶ εἶπεν.
3^{16}	ענו . . . ואמרין	καὶ ἀπεκρίθησαν . . . λέγοντες.
$3^{28(95)}$	ענה . . . ואמר	καὶ ἀπεκρίθη . . . καὶ εἶπεν.
4^{16}	ענה . . . ואמר	καὶ ἀπεκρίθη . . . καὶ εἶπεν.
4^{27}	ענה . . . ואמר	ἀπεκρίθη . . . καὶ εἶπεν.

In the Fourth Gospel ἀπεκρίθη or ἀπεκρίθησαν occurs as asyndeton openings 65 times (see below), ἀποκρίνεται *once*, 13^{38}. On the other hand, we have ἀπεκρίθη οὖν, 7^{16}, 9^{25}, 12^{34}; ἀπεκρίθησαν οὖν, 2^{18}, 7^{47}, 9^{20}; ὃς δὲ ἀπεκρίθη, 5^{11}; ἀπεκρίνατο οὖν, 5^{19}; ὁ δὲ ἀπεκρίνατο, 5^{17}; ἀποκρίνεται οὖν, 13^{26}; ὁ δὲ Ἰησοῦς ἀποκρίνεται, 12^{23}; i.e. 11 cases of this verb as an opening with connective particle, as against 66 cases without. Elsewhere in the whole N.T. ἀπεκρίθη as an asyndeton opening occurs only in Mk. 12^{29}. In the Synoptists the common phrase is ὁ δὲ ἀποκριθεὶς (ἀποκριθεὶς δὲ) εἶπεν, which rather resembles the common Hebrew phrase ויען ויאמר 'And he answered and said', of which it is frequently the rendering in LXX.

Of the 65 cases of asyndeton opening ἀπεκρίθη, ἀπεκρίθησαν in

Jn., 38 introduce the words spoken without further verb, viz. 1^{49}, 3^{5}, $5^{7.11}$, $6^{7.68.70}$, $7^{20.46}$, $8^{19.33.34.49.54}$, $9^{3.11.27}$, $10^{25.32.33.34}$, 11^{9}, $13^{8.36}$, 16^{31}, $18^{5.8.20.23.34.35.36.37}$, $19^{7.11.15.22}$, 21^{5}; we *once* have ἀπεκρίθη . . . λέγων, 1^{26}; while in the 26 other cases the opening is ἀπεκρίθη (ἀπεκρίθησαν) . . . καὶ εἶπεν (εἶπαν), viz. $1^{48.50}$, 2^{19}, $3^{3.9.10.27}$, $4^{10.13.17}$, $6^{26.29.43}$, $7^{21.52}$, $8^{14.39.48}$, $9^{30.31.36}$, 12^{30}, 13^{7}, 14^{23}, 18^{30}, 20^{28}. It is difficult to resist the conclusion that ἀπεκρίθη καὶ εἶπεν is a literal rendering of the Aram. עֲנָה וְאָמַר, and ἀπεκρίθησαν καὶ εἶπαν of עֲנוֹ וְאָמְרִין, for which, as we have seen, they stand in Theodotion's Daniel.

Asyndeton λέγει, λέγουσιν = *asyndeton* אָמַר (*participle*), אָמְרִין.

Similarly, we constantly find that Jn. uses λέγει as an opening without connective particle. The cases are $1^{39.46.48}$, $2^{5.7}$, 3^{4}, $4^{7.11.15.16.17.19.21.25.26.34.49.50}$, 5^{8}, 6^{8}, 7^{50}, 8^{29}, 9^{12}, $11^{23.24.27.39\,bis.40.44}$, $13^{6.8.9.10.36.37}$, $14^{5.6.8.9.22}$, $18^{5.17.26.38}$, $19^{6.15}$, $20^{13.15.16.17.29}$, $21^{3.10.12.15\,bis.16\,ter.17\,bis.22}$; a total of 63. λέγουσιν without connective particle occurs in $11^{8.34}$, 16^{29}, 21^{3}; ἐκείνη . . . λέγει, 20^{15}; ἄλλοι ἔλεγον in 10^{21}, 12^{29}. On the other hand, we have the opening καὶ λέγει in $2^{4.8}$, 19^{14}; καὶ λέγουσιν in 20^{13}; καὶ ἔλεγεν in 6^{65}, 8^{23}; καὶ ἔλεγον in 6^{42}; λέγει οὖν in 4^{9}, 7^{6}, 13^{27}, 18^{17}, 19^{10}, $21^{5.7}$; λέγουσιν οὖν in 9^{17}; ἔλεγεν οὖν in 8^{31}; ἔλεγον οὖν in 4^{33}, 5^{10}, $8^{19.25}$, $9^{10.16}$, 11^{36}, 16^{18}, 19^{21}, 20^{25}; λέγει δέ in 12^{4}; ἔλεγεν δέ in 6^{71}; ἔλεγον δέ in 10^{20}; εἶτα λέγει in 19^{27}, 20^{27}; i.e. a total of 31 openings with connective particle, as against 70 without such particle.

In Mt. λέγει as an asyndeton opening occurs 16 times, viz. 16^{15}, 17^{25}, 18^{22}, $19^{8.18.20}$, $20^{7.21.23}$, $21^{31.42}$, 22^{43}, $26^{25.35.64}$, 27^{22}; λέγουσιν 10 times, viz. 9^{28}, $19^{7.10}$, $20^{7.22.23}$, $21^{31.41}$, 22^{42}, 27^{22}. In Mk. λέγει thus *never*; λέγουσιν in 8^{19}.* In Lk. λέγει in 16^{7}, 19^{22}; λέγουσιν *never*. In Acts there are *no occurrences* of λέγει, λέγουσιν as asyndeton openings.

That the historical present in Jn., of which λέγει is the most frequent example, represents the similar usage of the participle in Aramaic, is argued later on (p. 88). There are no instances of the asyndeton opening אָמַר (participle) in Dan., because the

* The absence of this asyndeton usage in Mk. is a point against the view that this Gospel is a *literal translation* of an Aramaic document. There are very many cases where Mk. uses καὶ λέγει, ὁ δὲ λέγει as openings, where Jn. would certainly have used asyndeton λέγει. Cf. e.g., for the difference in style, the dialogue of Mk. 12^{14-17}.

writer of this book prefers the formula 'Answered and said' which we have already noticed. This latter phrase, however, so much favoured in Dan., seems to have been practically confined to *Western* Aramaic, being unused in Syriac, except in *translation*, as in the Peshiṭṭā of the O.T.* Ordinarily in Aramaic, especially in its Eastern branch, the asyndeton opening אָמַר, ܐܡܪ (participle) is one of the most characteristic features of the language in description of a dialogue; and this naturally lends itself in Greek to a rendering by the asyndeton historical present λέγει. For example, the Syriac *Acta Thomae* in the first four pages (ed. Wright) offers twelve examples of the usage. The following is a literal rendering of a dialogue-passage from this work (p. ܩܟܒ):

'And when they had embarked and sat down, Habban the merchant says to Judas, "What is the craft that thou art able to practise?" Judas says to him, 'Carpentry and architecture—the work of a carpenter". Habban the merchant says to him, "What art thou skilled to make in wood, and what in hewn stone?" Judas says to him, "In wood I have learned to make ploughs and yokes and ox-goads, and oars for ferry-boats and masts for ships; and in stone, tombstones and shrines and temples and palaces for kings". Habban the merchant says to him, "I was seeking just such a workman".'

With this we may compare the structure of the dialogue in Jn. 21^{15-17}:

'So when they had broken their fast, Jesus says to Simon Peter, "Simon, son of John, lovest thou Me more than these?" He says to Him, "Yea, Lord; Thou knowest that I love Thee". He says to him, "Feed My lambs". He says to him again a second time, "Simon, son of John, lovest thou Me?" He says to Him, "Yea, Lord, Thou knowest that I love Thee". He says to him, "Tend My sheep". He says to him the third time, "Simon, son of John, lovest thou Me?" Peter was grieved because He said to him the third time, "Lovest thou Me?" And he said to Him, "Lord, Thou knowest all things; Thou knowest that I love Thee". Jesus says to him, "Feed My sheep".'

* According to Dalman (*WJ.* p. 25) the formula is unknown in later Jewish Aramaic.

This very striking resemblance in structure between the two passages—both as regards pictorial ܐܡܪ = λέγει *and* asyndeton usage—is no mere chance and isolated phenomenon. Dialogues so framed are frequent in the Fourth Gospel (cf. especially the references to λέγει in *chs.* 4, 11, 13, 14, 18, 20), and innumerable parallels from Aramaic might be collected.*

Parataxis.

Peculiarly Semitic is the simplicity of construction employed throughout the Fourth Gospel. Sentences are regularly co-ordinated, and linked by καί. Subordinate sentences are few and far between. In 6[22–24], where the writer embarks exceptionally upon a somewhat complex sentence, he speedily becomes involved in difficulty. 13[1–4] is more successful as Greek; but this passage, in point of style, practically stands alone.† Such simplicity of construction can of course to some extent be paralleled from the Synoptic sources, particularly from Mk. But not even in Mk. does it attain anything like the vogue which it has in Jn.

Comparative rarity of Aorist Participle describing action anterior to finite verb.

In speaking above of Jn.'s phrase ἀπεκρίθη καὶ εἶπεν, we noticed that the Synoptic equivalent subordinates the prior action by use of the Aorist Participle, e.g. ὁ δὲ ἀποκριθεὶς εἶπεν, i.e. the natural Greek construction. Though we occasionally find this latter construction in Jn.—e.g. 1[36] καὶ ἐμβλέψας . . . λέγει—it is far less common than in the Synoptists. An approximate count yields the following figures, the proportions of which are worked out according to the pages of WH.

* The asyndeton construction is also frequent in Rabbinic Hebrew (under the influence of Aramaic), though here in description of past events the Perfect is normally used. Several examples are cited by Schlatter (*Sprache*, pp. 25 f.). Cf. e.g. Midrash Rabba on Exodus, par. v. 18 (Moses and Aaron before Pharaoh), 'He said to them, Who are ye? They said to him, We are the messengers of the Holy One, blessed be He. What are ye seeking? They said to him, Thus saith the Lord, &c.'

† We may note that *v.*[2] contains two out of the only seventeen occurrences of the Genitive absolute which are found in Jn.

	pp. in WH.	*Occurrences.*	*Proportion per page.*
Mt.	68	338	5
Mk.	41	224	5½
Lk.	72	324	4½
Jn.	53	58	1

Prof. Moulton (*NTG.*[3] i, p. 12), in speaking of "co-ordination of clauses with the simple *καί*, in place of the use of participles or subordinate clauses', remarks that 'in itself the phenomenon proves nothing more than would a string of "ands" in an English rustic's story—elementary culture, and not the hampering presence of a foreign idiom that is being perpetually translated into its most literal equivalent'. This may be so 'in itself'; here, however, we have to ask why, if avoidance of the participial construction in favour of co-ordination is natural to Κοινή Greek, we find this striking disproportion between Jn. and the Synoptists which the figures reveal. The answer has been supplied elsewhere by Dr. Moulton himself. 'The over-use of locutions which can be defended as good Κοινή Greek' is a test of 'Greek which is virtually or actually translated'.*

Comparative rarity of Genitive absolute.

As compared with the Synoptists, the use of the Genitive absolute in Jn. is infrequent. The approximate figures are, Mt. 48, Mk. 36, Lk. 59, Jn. 17; i.e. the Synoptists exhibit but slight variation in their use of the construction, and use it about 2½ times as often as Jn. While the Synoptists use the construction, almost without exception, in temporal clauses, Jn. 'employs it with more elasticity of meaning than is found in the Triple Tradition. A causal meaning ("*as*" or "*because*") is implied, probably or certainly, in 2[3], 5[13], 6[18]. "*Though*" is certainly implied in 12[37], 21[11], and perhaps in 20[19]' (Abbott, *JG.* 2028–31).

The rarity of the Genitive absolute in Jn. is due partly to the use of parataxis: e.g. 1[21] *καὶ ἠρώτησαν αὐτόν Τί οὖν; σὺ Ἠλείας εἶ; καὶ λέγει Οὐκ εἰμί.* 1[46] *καὶ εἶπεν αὐτῷ Ναθαναήλ, . . λέγει αὐτῷ ὁ Φίλιππος.*

* *Cambridge Biblical Essays*, p. 474. The quotation has already been given in full on p. 7.

1[18] λέγει αὐτῷ Ναθαναήλ . . . ἀπεκρίθη Ἰησοῦς καὶ εἶπεν αὐτῷ (contrast Mt. 17[26] εἰπόντος δέ Ἀπὸ τῶν ἀλλοτρίων, ἔφη αὐτῷ ὁ Ἰησοῦς. Lk. 21[5] καί τινων λεγόντων . . . εἶπεν). 4[46] ἦλθεν οὖν . . . καὶ ἦν τις βασιλικός. 7[45] Ἦλθον οὖν οἱ ὑπηρέται πρὸς τοὺς ἀρχιερεῖς καὶ Φαρισαίους, καὶ εἶπον αὐτοῖς ἐκεῖνοι (contrast Mt. 8[28] καὶ ἐλθόντος αὐτοῦ . . . ὑπήντησαν αὐτῷ. Mt. 17[14.24], 21[23]). 6[17] καὶ σκοτία ἤδη ἐγεγόνει, καὶ οὔπω ἐληλύθει πρὸς αὐτοὺς ὁ Ἰησοῦς (contrast Mt. 8[16] ὀψίας δὲ γενομένης προσήνεγκαν αὐτῷ). 10[22.24] καὶ περιεπάτει ὁ Ἰησοῦς ἐν τῷ ἱερῷ . . . ἐκύκλωσαν οὖν αὐτὸν οἱ Ἰουδαῖοι (contrast Lk. 11[29] Τῶν δὲ ὄχλων ἐπαθροιζομένων ἤρξατο λέγειν).

The place of the Genitive absolute is also taken in Jn. by a temporal clause introduced by ὅτε, a construction for which, as compared with the Synoptists, this writer shows a relative fondness. Neglecting cases in which ὅτε has an antecedent (e.g. Jn. 4[21] ἔρχεται ὥρα ὅτε. So 4[23], 5[25], 9[4], 16[25]), there are 16 cases of ὅτε introducing a temporal clause in Jn., as against 13 in Mt., 10 in Mk., 10 in Lk. If Jn. were as long as Mt., there would be proportionately 21 cases; if as long as Lk., 22 cases; if as short as Mk. 13 cases. The occurrences of ὡς = 'when' introducing a temporal clause in Jn. are 16; Lk. 16; Mt. and Mk. *none*.

In cases where the subject of the ὅτε or ὡς clause is the same as that of the principal clause, the temporal clause so introduced of course takes the place of an Aorist Participle in the nominative. These in Jn. are—ὅτε, 6[24], 13[12], 17[12], 19[6.8.23.30], 21[18]; ὡς, 2[9], 4[1.40], 11[6.20.29.32.33], 19[33], 21[9]. There remain 8 cases in which, the subject of the ὅτε clause being different from that of the principal clause, the Genitive absolute might have been used; and 5 similar cases of the ὡς clause. These are—ὅτε, 1[19], 2[22], 4[45], 12[16.17], 13[31], 20[24], 21[15]; ὡς, 2[23], 6[12.16], 7[10], 18[6]. Similar cases in Lk. are—ὅτε 6, ὡς 8; Mt. ὅτε 7; Mk. ὅτε 9. Thus cases in which a ὅτε or ὡς clause takes the place of a Genitive absolute are in Jn. 13, as against Lk. 14, Mt. 7, Mk. 9. Though the figures in Jn. and Lk. are thus similar, it should be borne in mind that Lk. is considerably longer (72 pp. WH. as against 53 pp.), and also contains much more *narrative*, to which, in distinction from speeches, by far the greater number of such temporal clauses belong. Thus we are justified in finding in Jn., as compared with the Synoptists, a preponderance of temporal clauses introduced by ὅτε or ὡς, which serve to explain along with parataxis) the comparative rarity of the Genitive absolute in this Gospel.

Now the use of כַּדִּי, כַּד, Syr. ܟܕ = 'when' to introduce a temporal clause is very common in Aramaic. This is the ordinary construction employed in the Syriac versions to render a temporal clause which Greek expresses by the Genitive absolute. The first few cases of the Genitive absolute in Lk. will serve to illustrate this (the rendering 'when' followed by the finite verb gives the literal representation of the Syriac construction).

Lk. 2[2] *ἡγεμονεύοντος τῆς Συρίας Κυρηνίου.*

Pal. Syr. ܟܕ ܗܘܐ ܩܘܪܝܢܝܘܣ ܒܣܘܪܝܐ 'when Quirinius was in Syria'.

Pesh. ܒܗܓܡܘܢܘܬܐ ܕܩܘܪܝܢܝܘܣ ܒܣܘܪܝܐ 'in the hegemony of Q. in S.'

Sin. ܒܫܢܝ ܩܘܪܝܢܝܘܣ ܗܓܡܘܢܐ ܕܣܘܪܝܐ 'in the years of Q., governor of S.'

Lk. 2[42.43] *καὶ ὅτε ἐγένετο ἐτῶν δώδεκα, ἀναβαινόντων αὐτῶν κατὰ τὸ ἔθος τῆς ἑορτῆς, καὶ τελειωσάντων τὰς ἡμέρας, κτλ.*

Pal. Syr. ܘܟܕ ܗܘܐ ܒܪ ܬܪܬܥܣܪܝ ܫܢܝܢ ܣܠܩܘܢ ܠܐܘܪܫܠܡ ܟܡܢܗܓܗ ܕܚܓܐ: ܘܟܕ ܫܠܡܘܢ ܝܘܡܝܐ 'And when He was twelve years old, they went up to Jerusalem according to the custom of the feast; and when they had fulfilled the days, &c.' Construction of Sin. and Pesh. identical.

Lk. 3[1] *ἡγεμονεύοντος Ποντίου Πιλάτου τῆς Ἰουδαίας, κτλ.*

Pal. Syr. ܟܕ ܗܘܐ ܦܢܛܝܘܣ ܦܝܠܛܘܣ ܗܓܡܘܢ ܒܝܗܘܕ 'when Pontius Pilate was governor in Judaea'.

Sin. ܒܗܓܡܘܢܘܬܐ ܕܦܢܛܝܘܣ ܦܝܠܛܘܣ ܒܝܗܘܕ 'in the hegemony of Pontius Pilate in Judah'. So Pesh.

Lk. 3[15] *προσδοκῶντος δὲ τοῦ λαοῦ, καὶ διαλογιζομένων πάντων ἐν ταῖς καρδίαις αὐτῶν.*

Pal. Syr. ܟܕ ܕܝܢ ܗܘܐ ܡܣܟܐ ܥܡܐ ܘܡܬܚܫܒܝܢ ܟܘܠܗܘܢ ܒܠܒܝܗܘܢ 'Now when the multitude was expectant, and all of them were debating in their hearts'.

Sin., Cur. ܘܐܢܫܐ ܕܫܡܥܝܢ ܗܘܘ ܠܗ ܡܬܪܥܝܢ ܗܘܘ ܒܪܥܝܢܝܗܘܢ 'And the men that were hearing him were reflecting in their minds'.

Pesh. ܟܕ ܕܝܢ ܡܣܟܐ ܗܘܐ ܥܡܐ ܥܠ ܝܘܚܢܢ: ܘܟܠܗܘܢ ܡܬܚܫܒܝܢ

ܗܘܘ ܒܠܒܗܘܢ 'Now when the people were speculating concerning John, and all of them were debating in their heart'.

Lk. 3[21] Ἐγένετο δὲ ἐν τῷ βαπτισθῆναι ἅπαντα τὸν λαὸν καὶ Ἰησοῦ βαπτισθέντος καὶ προσευχομένου ἀνεῳχθῆναι τὸν οὐρανόν.

Pal. Syr. ܐܬܥܒܕ ܕܝ ܟܕ ܐܬܥܡܕ ܟܠܗ ܟܢܫܐ ܘܐܦ ܡܪܢ ܝܫܘܥ ܕܝ ܐܬܥܡܕ ܘܨܠܝ: ܐܬܦܬܚܘ ܫܡܝܐ 'Now it came to pass, when all the multitude had been baptized, and also the Lord Jesus had been baptized and had prayed, that the heavens were opened'.

Sin. ܘܟܕ ܥܡܕ ܗܘܐ ܟܠܗ ܥܡܐ ܐܦ ܝܫܘܥ ܥܡܕ ܘܟܕ ܡܨܠܐ ܗܘܐ ܐܬܦܬܚܘ ܫܡܝܐ 'And when all the people had been baptized, Jesus also was baptized. And when He was praying, the heavens were opened'.

Pesh. ܗܘܐ ܕܝܢ ܟܕ ܥܡܕ ܟܠܗ ܥܡܐ: ܘܐܦ ܝܫܘܥ ܥܡܕ: ܘܟܕ ܡܨܠܐ ܐܬܦܬܚܘ ܫܡܝܐ 'Now it came to pass, when all the people were baptized, Jesus also was baptized. And when He was praying, the heavens were opened'.

Lk. 4[2] καὶ συντελεσθεισῶν αὐτῶν ἐπείνασεν.

Pal. Syr. caret.

Sin. ܘܡܢ ܒܬܪ ܐܪܒܥܝܢ ܝܘܡܝܢ ܕܨܡ ܗܘܐ ܟܦܢ 'and after forty days on which He fasted, He was hungry'.

Pesh. ܘܟܕ ܫܠܡ ܐܢܘܢ ܠܚܪܬܐ ܟܦܢ 'and when He had completed them, afterwards He was hungry'.

Two cases occur in which Mk.'s ὅτε with finite verb (suiting the theory of an Aramaic background) is altered into the Genitive absolute in the other Synoptists.

Mk. 1[32] ὅτε ἔδυ ὁ ἥλιος.
Lk. 4[40] δύνοντος δὲ τοῦ ἡλίου.
Mt. 8[16] ὀψίας δὲ γενομένης.*

Mk. 4[6] καὶ ὅτε ἀνέτειλεν ὁ ἥλιος.
Mt. 13[6] ἡλίου δὲ ἀνατείλαντος.
Lk. 8[6] omits.

* Mk. also has ὀψίας δὲ γενομένης before ὅτε ἔδυ ὁ ἥλιος. If this is part of the original Mk. and not a conflation, and if Mk. wrote in Aramaic, the text must have run וּבְרַמְשָׁא כַּד עֲרַב שִׁמְשָׁא 'And in the evening, when the sun was set'. It would be more natural to write וְכַד הֲוָא בְרַמְשָׁא וַעֲרַב שִׁמְשָׁא 'And when it was evening, and the sun was set'; but would this have been translated as we have it?

It is interesting to note that this construction of 'when' with a finite verb *and* the absence of an alternative construction resembling the Genitive absolute in Greek, is not common to Semitic, but is *specifically Aramaic*. Hebrew uses כַּאֲשֶׁר 'when' with a finite verb somewhat rarely, but far more frequently employs the Infinitive construct with pronominal suffix, and prefixed ב 'in' or כ 'as'; e.g. בִּרְאוֹתוֹ 'when he saw', lit. 'in his seeing'. Further, it has a usage of the *Participle absolute* (cf. Driver, *Tenses*,[3] § 165) closely resembling the Greek Genitive absolute, and regularly rendered by it in LXX. In the passages where this construction occurs in O.T. it will be found that Targ. Hebraizes its Aramaic to a large extent, while exhibiting a tendency to use the true Aramaic construction. Pesh., on the other hand, regularly breaks away from the Hebrew construction, and renders by ܟܕ 'when' with a finite verb. The English renderings aim at exactly reproducing the Semitic constructions.

Gen. 42[35] ויהי הם מריקים שקיהם והנה איש צרור כספו בשקו 'And it came to pass, they emptying their sacks, and behold, each man's bundle of money in his sack'.

LXX ἐγένετο δὲ ἐν τῷ κατακενοῦν αὐτοὺς τοὺς σάκκους αὐτῶν, καὶ ἦν ἑκάστου ὁ δεσμὸς τοῦ ἀργυρίου ἐν τῷ σάκκῳ αὐτῶν.

Targ. והוה אינון מריקין שקיהון והא גבר צרר כספה בשקיה, exactly follows Hebrew.

Pesh. ܘܗܘܐ ܕܟܕ ܗܢܘܢ ܡܣܪܩܝܢ ܣܩܝܗܘܢ܆ ܗܐ ܨܪܪܐ ܕܟܣܦܗ ܕܓܒܪܐ ܒܦܘܡ ܥܕܠܗ 'And it came to pass that when they were emptying their sacks, behold, each man's bundle of money in the mouth of his bale'.

1 Kgs. 13[20] ויהי הם ישבים על השלחן ויהי דבר יהוה 'And it came to pass, they sitting at the table, and there came the word of Yahweh'.

LXX καὶ ἐγένετο αὐτῶν καθημένων [ἐπὶ τῆς τραπέζης], καὶ ἐγένετο λόγος Κυρίου.

Targ. והוה עד דאינון מסתחרין על פתורא והוה פתגם נבואה מן קדם יהוה 'And it came to pass, whilst they were sitting round the table, and (= then) there came a word of prophecy from before Y.'

Pesh. ܘܟܕ ܗܢܘܢ ܝܬܒܝܢ ܥܠ ܦܬܘܪܐ ܗܘܐ ܦܬܓܡܗ ܕܡܪܝܐ 'And when they were sitting at the table, there came the word of the Lord'.

2 Kgs. 2^{11} ויהי המה הלכים הלוך ודבר והנה רכב אש וג׳ 'And it came to pass, they going on—going and talking (= and talking as they went), and, behold, a chariot of fire, &c.'

LXX *καὶ ἐγένετο αὐτῶν πορευομένων, ἐπορεύοντο καὶ ἐλάλουν· καὶ ἰδοὺ ἅρμα πυρὸς κτλ.*

Targ. והוה עד דאינון אזלין מיזל וממללין והא רתיכין דאישתא 'And it came to pass, whilst they were going on—going and talking, and (= then) behold, chariots of fire'.

Pesh. ܘܗܘܐ ܕܟܕ ܗܢܘܢ ܡܡܠܠܝܢ ܘܡܗܠܟܝܢ ܗܘܘ ܡܪܟܒܬܐ ܕܢܘܪܐ 'And it came to pass that when they were talking and going on, and (= then) behold, a chariot of fire'.

2 Kgs. 8^{5} ויהי הוא מספר למלך את אשר החיה את המת והנה האשה אשר החיה את בנה צעקת אל המלך 'And it came to pass, he telling the king how he (Elisha) had raised the dead, and, behold, the woman whose son he had raised crying unto the king'.

LXX *καὶ ἐγένετο αὐτοῦ ἐξηγουμένου τῷ βασιλεῖ ὡς ἐζωπύρησεν υἱὸν τεθνηκότα, καὶ ἰδοὺ ἡ γυνὴ ἧς ἐζωπύρησεν τὸν υἱὸν αὐτῆς βοῶσα πρὸς τὸν βασιλέα.*

Targ. והוה הוא משתעי למלכא דאחי ית מיתא והא איתתא דאחי ית ברה קבלא קדם מלכא, as in Hebrew.

Pesh. ܘܟܕ ܡܫܬܥܐ ܗܘܐ ܠܡܠܟܐ ܕܐܚܝ ܡܝܬܐ ܚܙܐ ܐܢܬܬܐ ܕܐܚܝ ܒܪܗ ܡܬܟܫܦܐ ܩܕܡ ܡܠܟܐ 'And when he was relating to the king that he had raised the dead, he saw the woman whose son he had raised making supplication before the king'.

2 Kgs. 8^{21} ויהי הוא קם לילה ויכה את אדום הסביב עליו . . . וינס העם לאהליו 'And it came to pass, he arising (*or* arose) by night and smote Edom who surrounded him . . . and the people fled to their home'.

LXX *καὶ ἐγένετο αὐτοῦ ἀναστάντος, καὶ ἐπάταξεν τὸν Ἐδὼμ τὸν κυκλώσαντα ἐπ' αὐτὸν . . . καὶ ἔφυγεν ὁ λαὸς κτλ.*

Targ. והוה הוא קם בלילוא ומחא ית איניש אדום דמקפין ליה . . . ואפך עמא לקירווהי, construction as in Hebrew.

Pesh. ܘܟܕ ܩܡ ܒܠܠܝܐ ܕܢܚܪܘܒ ܠܐܕܘܡܝܐ ܕܡܚܕܪܝܢ ܠܗ . . . ܘܥܪܩܘ ܥܡܐ ܠܡܫܟܢܝܗܘܢ 'And when he arose by night that he might destroy the Edomites who were surrounding him . . . and (= then) the people fled to their homes'.

2 Kgs. 13^{21} ויהי הם קברים איש והנה ראו את הגדוד 'And it came to pass, they burying a man, and, behold, they saw the robber-hand'.

LXX *καὶ ἐγένετο αὐτῶν θαπτόντων τὸν ἄνδρα, καὶ ἰδοὺ ἴδον τὸν μονόζωνον.*

Targ. והוה עד דאינון קברין גברא והא חזו ית משרית 'And it came to pass, whilst they were burying a man, and (= then) they saw, &c.'

Pesh. ܘܟܕ ܗܘܘ ܩܒܪܝܢ ܓܒܪܐ܆ ܚܙܘ ܓܝܣܐ 'And when they were burying a man, they saw, &c.'

2 Kgs. 19^{37} ויהי הוא משתחוה בית נסרך אלהיו ואדרמלך ושראצר בניו הכהו 'And it came to pass, he worshipping in the house of Nisroch his god, and Adrammelech and Sharezer his sons smote him'.

LXX *καὶ ἐγένετο αὐτοῦ προσκυνοῦντος ἐν οἴκῳ Ἐσδρὰχ θεοῦ αὐτοῦ, καὶ Α. καὶ Σ. οἱ υἱοὶ αὐτοῦ ἐπάταξαν αὐτόν.*

Targ. והוה הוא סגיד בית נסרך טעותיה ואדרמלך ושראצר בנוהי קטלוהי, as in Hebrew.

Pesh. ܘܟܕ ܣܓܕ ܗܘܐ ܒܒܝܬ ܢܣܪܘܟ ܐܠܗܗ܆ ܐܕܪܡܠܟ ܘܫܪܐܨܪ ܒܢܘܗܝ ܩܛܠܘܗܝ 'And when he was worshipping in the house of N. his god, A. and S. his sons killed him'.

Casus pendens.

It is characteristic of Hebrew and Aramaic to simplify the construction of a sentence, and at the same time to gain emphasis, by reinforcing the subject by a Personal Pronoun. Such reinforcement is specially favoured if the subject happens to be further defined by a relative clause, since otherwise the sentence would—to the Semitic ear—appear involved and overweighted. The same principle is also adopted with the object, when this, for the sake of emphasis, is brought to the beginning of the sentence; and other oblique cases may be similarly treated. Examples in Hebrew are—Gen. 3^{12}, 'The woman whom Thou gavest to be with me, she gave me (הִוא נָתְנָה־לִּי) of the tree and I did eat'; Gen. 15^{4}, 'But one that shall come out of thine own bowels, he shall be thine heir' (הוּא יִירָשֶׁךָ); Gen. 24^{7}, 'Yahweh, the God of heaven, who took me from my father's house, &c., He shall send (הוּא יִשְׁלַח) His angel before thee'; Deut. 13^{1}, 'All the word that I command you, it shall ye observe to do' (אֹתוֹ תִשְׁמְרוּ לַעֲשׂוֹת); Ezek. 18^{24}, 'In his trespass that he hath trespassed, and in his sin that he hath sinned, in them shall he die' (בָּם יָמוּת). See further, Driver, *Tenses*, § 123 γ *Obs.*

Similarly in Aramaic—Dan. $2^{37, 38}$, 'Thou, O king, the king of kings, to whom the God of heaven gave, &c., thou art that head of gold' (אַנְתְּה הוּא רֵאשָׁה דִּי דַהֲבָא); Dan. 3^{22}, 'Those men that took up Shadrach, Meshach, and Abed-nego, the flame of the fire slew them' (קַטִּיל הִמּוֹ שְׁבִיבָא דִּי נוּרָא); Dan. 4^{17-19}, 'The tree that thou sawest, &c., it is thou, O king' (אַנְתְּה הוּא מַלְכָּא); Ezr. 5^{14}, 'And moreover, the vessels of the house of God, &c., them did Cyrus the king take out (הַנְפֵּק הִמּוֹ כּוֹרֶשׁ) of the temple of Babylon'; Ezr. 7^{24}, 'All priests and Levites, &c., it shall not be lawful to impose tribute, &c., upon them' (לְמִרְמֵא עֲלֵיהֹם); Ezr. 7^{26}, 'Every one that will not perform the law of thy God and the law of the king, let judgement diligently be executed upon him' (לֶהֱוֵא מִתְעֲבֵד מִנֵּהּ).

This reinforcement of a *Casus pendens* by the Pronoun is a marked characteristic of the Fourth Gospel. We may note the following illustrations:

1^{12} *ὅσοι δὲ ἔλαβον αὐτόν, ἔδωκεν αὐτοῖς ἐξουσίαν τέκνα Θεοῦ γενέσθαι.*

1^{18} *μονογενὴς Θεὸς ὁ ὢν εἰς τὸν κόλπον τοῦ πατρὸς ἐκεῖνος ἐξηγήσατο.*

1^{33} *ὁ πέμψας με βαπτίζειν ἐν ὕδατι ἐκεῖνός μοι εἶπεν.*

3^{26} *ὃς ἦν μετὰ σοῦ . . . ἴδε οὗτος βαπτίζει.**

3^{32} *ὃ ἑώρακεν καὶ ἤκουσεν τοῦτο μαρτυρεῖ.*

5^{11} *Ὁ ποιήσας με ὑγιῆ ἐκεῖνός μοι εἶπεν.*

5^{19} *ἃ γὰρ ἂν ἐκεῖνος ποιῇ, ταῦτα καὶ ὁ υἱὸς ὁμοίως ποιεῖ.*

5^{36} *τὰ γὰρ ἔργα ἃ δέδωκέν μοι ὁ πατὴρ ἵνα τελειώσω αὐτά, αὐτὰ τὰ ἔργα ἃ ποιῶ, μαρτυρεῖ περὶ ἐμοῦ ὅτι ὁ πατήρ με ἀπέσταλκεν* (we should surely omit the comma after *ποιῶ.* and make *αὐτὰ τὰ ἔργα* the subject of *μαρτυρεῖ*, reinforcing *τὰ γὰρ ἔργα* after *ἃ δέδωκέν μοι κτλ.*)

5^{37} *καὶ ὁ πέμψας με πατὴρ ἐκεῖνος μεμαρτύρηκεν περὶ ἐμοῦ.*

5^{38} *ὃν ἀπέστειλεν ἐκεῖνος τούτῳ ὑμεῖς οὐ πιστεύετε.*

6^{39} *ἵνα πᾶν ὃ δέδωκέν μοι μὴ ἀπολέσω ἐξ αὐτοῦ.*

6^{46} *ὁ ὢν παρὰ τοῦ Θεοῦ, οὗτος ἑώρακεν τὸν πατέρα.*

7^{18} *ὁ δὲ ζητῶν τὴν δόξαν τοῦ πέμψαντος αὐτὸν οὗτος ἀληθής ἐστιν.*

8^{26} *κἀγὼ ἃ ἤκουσα παρ' αὐτοῦ ταῦτα λαλῶ εἰς τὸν κόσμον.*

10^{1} *ὁ μὴ εἰσερχόμενος διὰ τῆς θύρας . . . ἐκεῖνος κλέπτης ἐστὶν καὶ λῃστής.*

* Schlatter (*Sprache*, pp. 49 f.) quotes a number of instances from Rabbinic Hebrew in which הֲרֵי זֶה 'behold, this one, &c.' reinforces a *Nominativus pendens*. Thus e. g. Mechilta on Ex. 16^4, כל מי שיש לו מה יאכל היום ואומר מה אוכל מחר הרי זה מחוסר אמנה, 'Whosoever hath what he may eat to-day, and saith, What shall I eat to-morrow? behold, this one lacketh faith.'

10^{25} τὰ ἔργα ἃ ἐγὼ ποιῶ ἐν τῷ ὀνόματι τοῦ πατρός μου ταῦτα μαρτυρεῖ περὶ ἐμοῦ.

12^{48} ὁ λόγος ὃν ἐλάλησα ἐκεῖνος κρινεῖ αὐτὸν ἐν τῇ ἐσχάτῃ ἡμέρᾳ.

12^{49} ὁ πέμψας με πατὴρ αὐτός μοι ἐντολὴν δέδωκεν.

14^{12} ὁ πιστεύων εἰς ἐμὲ τὰ ἔργα ἃ ἐγὼ ποιῶ κἀκεῖνος ποιήσει.

14^{13} καὶ ὅτι ἂν αἰτήσητε ἐν τῷ ὀνόματί μου τοῦτο ποιήσω.

14^{21} ὁ ἔχων τὰς ἐντολάς μου καὶ τηρῶν αὐτὰς ἐκεῖνός ἐστιν ὁ ἀγαπῶν με.

14^{26} ὁ δὲ παράκλητος, τὸ πνεῦμα τὸ ἅγιον ὃ πέμψει ὁ πατὴρ ἐν τῷ ὀνόματί μου, ἐκεῖνος ὑμᾶς διδάξει πάντα.

15^{2} πᾶν κλῆμα ἐν ἐμοὶ μὴ φέρον καρπὸν αἴρει αὐτό, καὶ πᾶν τὸ καρπὸν φέρον καθαίρει αὐτό.

15^{5} ὁ μένων ἐν ἐμοὶ κἀγὼ ἐν αὐτῷ οὗτος φέρει καρπὸν πολύν.

17^{2} ἵνα πᾶν ὃ δέδωκας αὐτῷ δώσει αὐτοῖς ζωὴν αἰώνιον.

17^{24} ὃ δέδωκάς μοι, θέλω ἵνα ὅπου εἰμὶ ἐγὼ κἀκεῖνοι ὦσιν μετ' ἐμοῦ.

18^{11} τὸ ποτήριον ὃ δέδωκέν μοι ὁ πατὴρ οὐ μὴ πίω αὐτό;

Against these 27* instances in Jn. we can only set 11 in Mt. (4^{16}, $13^{20.22.23.38}$, 15^{11}, 19^{29}, 21^{42}, 24^{13}, 25^{29}, 26^{23}), 4 in Mk. (6^{16}, 7^{20}, 12^{10}, 13^{11}), and 6 in Lk. ($8^{14.15}$, 12^{48}, 20^{17}, 21^{6}, 23^{50-52}); and of these Mt. 4^{16} and Mt. 21^{42} = Mk. 12^{10} = Lk. 20^{17} are O.T. quotations.

Of course it cannot be claimed that the use of *Casus pendens* is specifically a Semitism, since—to go no farther—it is a familiar colloquialism in English. Prof. Moulton remarks that 'it is one of the easiest of anacolutha, as much at home in English as in Greek' (*NTG.*[3] i, p. 69). The fact which concerns us is the remarkable frequency of its occurrence in Jn. as compared with the Synoptists. If Lk., for example, is a fair specimen of Κοινή Greek, why should we find that a construction which occurs there but 6 times is employed in Jn. with six times the frequency? An adequate answer is forthcoming in the assumption that a common Aramaic construction has been exactly reproduced in translation.

* Abbott (*JG.* 1921) adds $10^{35.36}$, ὃν ὁ πατὴρ ἡγίασεν καὶ ἀπέστειλεν εἰς τὸν κόσμον ὑμεῖς λέγετε ὅτι Βλασφημεῖς; '"*Whom* the Father sanctified . . . do ye say [to him] Thou blasphemest?", best explained as [ἐκεῖνος] ὅν.' 7^{38}, ὁ πιστεύων εἰς ἐμέ . . . ποταμοὶ ἐκ τῆς κοιλίας αὐτοῦ (also cited by Abbott) is not included as involving—on our theory—a mistranslation. Cf. p. 109.

CHAPTER III

CONJUNCTIONS

καί, οὖν.

As compared with the Synoptists, *καί* in Jn. is infrequent in narrative. The occurrences, as given by Abbott (*JG.* 2133; cf. Bruder's *Concordance*^{2}, pp. 456 ff.) are, Mt. about 250 times, Mk. more than 400 times, Lk. about 380 times, Jn. less than 100 times. This comparative infrequency seems to be due partly to the writer's use of asyndeton (cf. p. 50), partly to his fondness for *οὖν*, which he uses some 200 times, as against Mt. 57 times, Mk. 6 times, Lk. 31 times. *καί* is frequent in Jn. in speeches, linking co-ordinate clauses, as in a Semitic language. A striking Semitic usage may be seen in its employment to link *contrasted* statements, where in English we should naturally employ 'and *yet*' or '*but*'. This is most frequent in speeches, though occasionally we find it also in the reflections of the author upon his narrative. So $1^{10.11}$, 2^{20}, $3^{10.11.19.32}$, 4^{20}, $5^{39.40.43.44}$, 6^{70}, $7^{4.19.30}$, $8^{20.52.57}$, $9^{30.34}$, 11^{8}, 12^{34}, 16^{5}, 20^{29}, 21^{11}. Cf., in Hebrew, Gen. $2^{16.17}$, 'Of every tree of the garden thou *mayest* eat; and (=*but*) of the tree of knowledge of good and evil, thou shalt not eat of it'; $3^{2.3}$, 'Of the fruit of the trees of the garden we may eat; and (=*but*) of the fruit of the tree which is in the midst of the garden God hath said, Ye shall not eat, &c.'; $17^{20.21}$, 'And as regards Ishmael I have heard thee; behold I have blessed him, &c. And (=*But*) my covenant will I establish with Isaac'; 32^{30} (Heb. 32^{31}), 'I have seen God face to face, and (=and *yet*) my life is preserved' (other instances of this common usage in *Oxford Heb. Lex.* p. 252 *b*). The same usage in Aramaic—where it is equally common—may be illustrated from Dan. $2^{5.6}$, 'If ye make not known to me the dream and its interpretation, ye shall be cut in pieces, &c.; and (=*but*) if ye shew the dream and the interpretation thereof, ye shall receive of me gifts, &c.'; $3^{5.6}$, 'At what time ye hear . . . ye shall fall down and worship the golden image, &c.; and (=*but*) whoso falleth not down, &c.'; $3^{17.18}$, 'If our God, whom we serve, be able to deliver us, He will deliver, &c.; and (=*but*) if not, be it known, &c.'; 4^{7} (Aram. 4^{4}), 'And I told the dream before them, and (=*yet*) its interpretation they did not make known to me'.

In Hebrew and Aramaic 'and' may very idiomatically introduce a contrasted idea in such a way as to suggest a *question*, this being implied by the contrast without the use of an interrogative particle. So in Hebrew, Judg. 14^{16}, 'Behold, to my father and my mother I have not told it, and shall I tell it unto *thee*?' (lit. 'and to thee I shall tell it!'); 2 Sam. 11^{11}, 'The ark, and Israel, and Judah are abiding in tents; and my lord Joab, and the servants of my lord, are encamped in the open field; and shall *I* go into my house, to eat and to drink, &c.?' (lit. 'and *I* shall go, &c.!' see further instances in *Oxf. Heb. Lex.* p. 252). The same usage may be illustrated in Aramaic from passages in *Acta Thomae* (ed. Wright).

ܟܠܗܘܢ ܒܢܝܢܐ ܒܩܝܛܐ ܗܘ ܡܬܒܢܝܢ. ܘܐܢܬ ܒܣܬܘܐ ܒܢܐ ܐܢܬ. (p. ܩܦܗ). 'All buildings are built in summer; and *thou* buildest in winter!'

ܡܛܠܬܟ ܐܫܬܐܠܬ ܡܢ ܡܪܝ ܡܠܟܐ ܡܙܕܝ ܘܡܢ ܚܫܡܝܬܐ. (p. ܪܢܚ) ܘܐܢܬ ܠܐ ܨܒܐ ܐܢܬ ܠܡܣܬܡܟܘ ܥܡܝ. 'On thy account I excused myself from my lord, king Mazdai, and from the supper; and *thou* dost not choose to sup with me!'

ܐܢܬ ܩܢܘܡܟ ܡܢ ܠܘܬܢ ܠܐ ܢܦܩܬ. ܐܠܐ ܐܢ ܚܕܐ ܫܥܐ. ܘܠܐ ܝܕܥ (p. ܪܡܓ) ܐܢܬ ܐܝܟܢܐ ܚܒܝܫܝܢ ܗܘܝܢ. 'Thou thyself hast not departed from us, except for a moment; and thou knowest not how we were shut up!'

With inverted order, (p. ܪܡܓ) ܐܢܬ ܝܬܒ ܐܢܬ ܘܫܡܥ ܐܢܬ ܩ̈ܠܐ ܣܪ̈ܝܩܬܐ ܘܡܠܟܐ ܡܙܕܝ ܒܪܘܓܙܗ ܒܥܐ ܕܢܘܒܕܟ. '*Thou* sittest and hearkenest to vain words; and king Mazdai in his wrath is seeking to destroy thee!'

In a precisely similar way *καί* introduces a paradox in several passages in Jn., and the paradox, being hypothetical, is treated as a question.

2^{20} Τεσσεράκοντα καὶ ἓξ ἔτεσιν οἰκοδομήθη ὁ ναὸς οὗτος, καὶ σὺ ἐν τρισὶν ἡμέραις ἐγερεῖς αὐτόν;

3^{10} Σὺ εἶ ὁ διδάσκαλος τοῦ Ἰσραὴλ καὶ ταῦτα οὐ γινώσκεις;

8^{57} Πεντήκοντα ἔτη οὔπω ἔχεις καὶ Ἀβραὰμ ἑώρακας;

9[34] Ἐν ἁμαρτίαις σὺ ἐγεννήθης ὅλος, καὶ σὺ διδάσκεις ἡμᾶς;

11[8] Ῥαββεί, νῦν ἐζήτουν σε λιθάσαι οἱ Ἰουδαῖοι, καὶ πάλιν ὑπάγεις ἐκεῖ;

The use of 'and' with the sense 'and *so*' is very frequent in Semitic. Some few cases of καί so used are to be found in Jn., e.g. 5[10] Σάββατόν ἐστιν, καὶ οὐκ ἔξεστίν σοι ἆραι τὸν κράββατον, 6[57] καθὼς ἀπέστειλέν με ὁ ζῶν πατὴρ κἀγὼ ζῶ διὰ τὸν πατέρα, καὶ ὁ τρώγων με κἀκεῖνος ζήσει δι' ἐμέ, 11[48] ἐὰν ἀφῶμεν αὐτὸν οὕτως, πάντες πιστεύσουσιν εἰς αὐτόν, καὶ ἐλεύσονται οἱ Ῥωμαῖοι καὶ ἀροῦσιν ἡμῶν καὶ τὸν τόπον καὶ τὸ ἔθνος. Usually, however, this consecutive connexion is expressed in Jn. by οὖν, which, as we have seen, is extraordinarily frequent (200 occurrences). It is highly probable that οὖν represents an original 'and' ('and *so*') in Aramaic in many cases *; in others it may have been inserted by the translator to introduce a sentence which stood asyndeton in the original. The cases cited by Abbott (*JG.* 2191 *a*), in which Mk. omits οὖν while Mt. or Lk. has it in parallel passages, suggests that the particle in Jn. is due to the translator. Οὖν is usually rendered in Pal. Syr. by ܘ 'and' simply; but sometimes by ܕܝܢ = δέ.

μέν, δέ, γάρ.

μέν, which is very rare in Jn., is infrequent also in the Synoptists. The occurrences are, Mt. 20, Mk. 6, Lk. 10, Jn. 8.

* The writer's conclusion as to οὖν given above stands as he had worked it out before reading the words of Prof. Burkitt in *Evangelion da-Mepharreshe*, ii, p. 89: 'In the course of working at the Syriac equivalents for S. Mark's εὐθὺς and S. John's οὖν it has occurred to me that fundamentally they mean the same thing and that they really correspond to the Hebrew "*wāw* consecutive". Not, of course, that either of these Gospels is a translation from the Hebrew; but if the authors of these Gospels were familiar with the Old Testament otherwise than through the awkward medium of the LXX, they might well have felt themselves in need of something to correspond to the Hebrew idiom. The essence of the meaning of "*wāw* consecutive" is that the event related is regarded as happening in due sequence to what has gone before. To express this καὶ is too inadequate a link, while δὲ implies a contrast which is wholly wanting in the Hebrew: the turn of thought is more or less our English "and so". But this is exactly what S. Mark means by his καὶ εὐθύς, and it is what is generally meant in the Fourth Gospel by οὖν. Simon's wife's mother was sick of a fever *and so* they tell Jesus of her (καὶ εὐθὺς Mk. 1[30]): S. Mark does not mean to emphasize the haste they were in to tell the news. Similarly in S. John there are literally scores of verses beginning with εἶπεν οὖν or εἶπον οὖν where "he said therefore" brings out too prominently the idea of causation. All that is meant is וַיֹּאמֶר "*and so* he said", or "*and so* they said", as the case may be.' That οὖν corresponds to the Hebrew *wāw* consecutive was noticed by Ewald, *Die johann. Schriften* (1861), p. 45, n. 2.

δέ is uncommon in Jn. and Mk. as compared with Mt. and Lk.*

The numbers are, Mt. 496, Mk. 156, Lk. 508, Jn. 176.†

Thus, while the average number of occurrences per page (WH.) are $7\frac{1}{3}$ in Mt. and 7 in Lk., in Mk. they are only $3\frac{2}{3}$ and in Jn. $3\frac{1}{3}$.

Now W. Aramaic, like Hebrew, has no equivalent of *δέ*, both languages employing 'and' in its place, or (Aramaic) an asyndeton opening. The comparative avoidance of *δέ* in Mk. and Jn. is therefore strongly suggestive of translation from Aramaic in which the Semitic use of 'and', or of no connective particle at all, was usually copied. In Syriac the need for such a particle as *δέ* was, under Greek influence, so much felt that the Greek particle was introduced in the form ܕܝܢ *dēn*, in Pal. Syr. ܕܝ *dī*.

γάρ is less frequent in Jn. than in the Synoptists. The occurrences are Mt. 125, Mk. 67, Lk. 101, Jn. 66. If Jn. were as long as Mt., there would be proportionately 86 occurrences; if as long as Lk., 92 occurrences; if as short as Mk., 53 occurrences. If Mk. were as long as Mt., there would be 96 occurrences; if as long as Lk., 109 occurrences; if as long as Jn., 82 occurrences.

In W. Aramaic such particles and phrases as correspond more or less to *γάρ*, אֲרֵי, בְּדִיל דְּ, Biblical Aram. כָּל־קֳבֵל דִּי, &c., are really much more weighty, bearing rather the sense *because, since.* In many cases in which Greek would use *γάρ*, Aramaic would be content with 'and' simply; and this may account for the comparative infrequency of *γάρ* in Jn. Syriac, feeling the need for a light particle like *γάρ*, introduced it in the form ܓܝܪ *gēr*.

ἵνα.

The frequency of *ἵνα* in Jn. is one of the most remarkable phenomena in this Gospel. The approximate number of occurrences is 127; whereas in Mt. we find 33, in Mk. 60, in Lk. 40. If Jn. were as long as Mt., there would be proportionately 163 occurrences; if as long as Lk., 178 occurrences; if as short as Mk., 101 occurrences. *ἵνα μή* occurs in Jn. 18 times, in Mt. 8 times, in Mk. 5 times, in Lk. 8 times. On the other hand, *μήποτε* in the sense 'that . . . not', 'lest', never occurs in Jn.,‡ whereas it is found in Mt. 8 times, in Mk. *twice*, in Lk. 6 times.

* In Apoc. *δέ* is excessively rare, occurring some 5 times only.

† The numbers for the Synoptists are those given by Sir John Hawkins, *HS.*[2] p. 151.

‡ Similarly in Apoc. we find *ἵνα μή* 11 times, *μήποτε never.*

Now there exists in Aramaic a particle—in origin a demonstrative—which is used with peculiar frequency to denote various shades of connexion. This particle appears in W. Aramaic as דִּי *dī* or דְּ *dĕ*, in Syriac as ܕ *dĕ*. As a particle of relation it denotes *who, which, that* (properly a connecting link between the relative sentence and its antecedent—*that one*, usually completed by a pronoun or pronominal suffix in the relative clause; e.g. דִּי אֲמַר לֵיהּ 'who he said to him', i.e. 'to whom he said'), and also the relative *when*. It may be used as a mark of the genitive, e.g. שַׁלִּיטָא דִּי־מַלְכָּא 'the king's captain' (lit. 'the captain, *that of* the king'). Further, it is especially frequent as a conjunction, *that*, in the sense *in that, inasmuch as, because*, and in a final sense, *in order that*. Our purpose is to show that ἵνα occurs in Jn. in all the senses of דִּי or דְּ except that which marks the genitive relation.

The frequent occurrence of ἵνα in a telic sense calls for no comment, beyond note of the fact that the use of ἵνα μή to the exclusion of μήποτε favours the theory of literal translation of the Aramaic phrase דְּלָא 'that . . . not'.* Further, the use of ἵνα = conjunctive *that*, followed by a finite verb, where in classical Greek we should expect an Infinitive, is a well-ascertained characteristic of Κοινή Greek, and has come through the Κοινή into modern Greek in the form νά. What *is* remarkable, however, in Jn.'s usage of this idiom, as compared with Mt. and Lk., is its extreme frequency. This is also—though to a less extent—true of Mk.; and it is instructive to notice how many different expedients Mt. or Lk., or both of them, frequently employ in order to get rid of Mk.'s ἵνα, whether used in a final sense or otherwise.†

Mk. 4[21] Καὶ ἔλεγεν αὐτοῖς ὅτι Μήτι ἔρχεται ὁ λύχνος ἵνα ὑπὸ τὸν μόδιον τεθῇ ἢ ὑπὸ τὴν κλίνην;

Mt. 5[15] οὐδὲ καίουσιν λύχνον καὶ τιθέασιν αὐτὸν ὑπὸ τὸν μόδιον.

Lk. 8[16] Οὐδεὶς δὲ λύχνον ἅψας καλύπτει αὐτὸν σκεύει ἢ ὑποκάτω κλίνης τίθησιν.

* Contrast the translation of Hebrew פֶּן 'lest', Isa. 6[10], by μήποτε (as in LXX) in Mt. 13[15], Mk. 4[12], with Jn. 12[40] ἵνα μὴ ἴδωσιν τοῖς ὀφθαλμοῖς κτλ. (cf. p. 100).

† The following Synoptic comparisons were kindly supplied to the writer by Sir John Hawkins.

Mk. 4^{22} οὐ γὰρ ἔστιν κρυπτόν ἐὰν μὴ ἵνα φανερωθῇ.
Mt. 10^{26} οὐδὲν γάρ ἐστιν κεκαλυμμένον ὃ οὐκ ἀποκαλυφθήσεται.
Lk. 8^{7} οὐ γάρ ἐστιν κρυπτὸν ὃ οὐ φανερὸν γενήσεται.

Mk. 5^{18} καὶ ἐμβαίνοντος αὐτοῦ εἰς τὸ πλοῖον παρεκάλει αὐτὸν ὁ δαιμονισθεὶς ἵνα μετ' αὐτοῦ ᾖ.
Mt. 8^{34} om.
Lk. $8^{37.38}$ αὐτὸς δὲ ἐμβὰς εἰς πλοῖον ὑπέστρεψεν. ἐδεῖτο δὲ αὐτοῦ ὁ ἀνὴρ ἀφ' οὗ ἐξεληλύθει τὰ δαιμόνια εἶναι σὺν αὐτῷ.

Mk. 5^{23} καὶ παρακαλεῖ αὐτὸν πολλὰ λέγων ὅτι Τὸ θυγάτριόν μου ἐσχάτως ἔχει, ἵνα ἐλθὼν ἐπιθῇς τὰς χεῖρας αὐτῇ ἵνα σωθῇ καὶ ζήσῃ.
Mt. 9^{18} ἰδοὺ ἄρχων εἷς προσελθὼν προσεκύνει αὐτῷ, λέγων ὅτι Ἡ θυγάτηρ μου ἄρτι ἐτελεύτησεν, ἀλλὰ ἐλθὼν ἐπίθες τὴν χεῖρά σου ἐπ' αὐτήν, καὶ ζήσεται.
Lk. $8^{41.42}$ καὶ πεσὼν παρὰ τοὺς πόδας Ἰησοῦ παρεκάλει αὐτὸν εἰσελθεῖν εἰς τὸν οἶκον αὐτοῦ, ὅτι θυγάτηρ μονογενὴς ἦν αὐτῷ . . . καὶ αὐτὴ ἀπέθνησκεν.

Mk. 5^{43} καὶ διεστείλατο αὐτοῖς πολλὰ ἵνα μηδεὶς γνοῖ τοῦτο.
Mt. 9^{26} om.
Lk. 8^{56} ὁ δὲ παρήγγειλεν αὐτοῖς μηδενὶ εἰπεῖν τὸ γεγονός.

Mk. 6^{25} Θέλω ἵνα ἐξαυτῆς δῷς μοι ἐπὶ πίνακι τὴν κεφαλὴν Ἰωάννου τοῦ βαπτιστοῦ.
Mt. 14^{8} Δός μοι, φησίν, ὧδε ἐπὶ πίνακι τὴν κεφαλὴν Ἰωάννου τοῦ βαπτιστοῦ.
Lk. om.

Mk. 6^{41} καὶ ἐδίδου τοῖς μαθηταῖς ἵνα παρατιθῶσιν αὐτοῖς.
Mt. 14^{19} ἔδωκεν τοῖς μαθηταῖς τοὺς ἄρτους, οἱ δὲ μαθηταὶ τοῖς ὄχλοις.
Lk. 9^{16} καὶ ἐδίδου τοῖς μαθηταῖς παραθεῖναι τῷ ὄχλῳ.

Mk. 9^{9} Καὶ καταβαινόντων αὐτῶν ἐκ τοῦ ὄρους, διεστείλατο αὐτοῖς ἵνα μηδενὶ ἃ εἶδον διηγήσωνται.
Mt. 17^{9} Καὶ καταβαινόντων αὐτῶν ἐκ τοῦ ὄρους ἐνετείλατο αὐτοῖς ὁ Ἰησοῦς λέγων Μηδενὶ εἴπητε κτλ.
Lk. om.

Cases in which Mk.'s ἵνα is retained by one or both of the other Synoptists are Mk. 6^{56} = Mt. 14^{36}; Mk. 8^{30} = Mt. 16^{20} (contrast

Lk. 9^{21}); Mk. 9^{18} = Lk. 9^{40} (contrast Mt. 17^{16}); Mk. 10^{37} = Mt. 20^{21}; Mk. 10^{48} = Mt. 20^{31} = Lk. 18^{39}; Mk. 12^{19} = Lk. 20^{28} (contrast Mt. 22^{24}).

In face of this evidence it can hardly be maintained that the deviations of Mt. and Lk. from Mk. resulting in elimination of the construction with *ἵνα* are merely accidental. Mk.'s use of *ἵνα*, which in proportion to the length of his Gospel is 3 times as frequent as that of Mt., and 2½ times as frequent as that of Lk., must have appeared to these latter Evangelists to some extent offensive to normal style. Since it is generally acknowledged that in other respects Mk. exhibits Aramaic influence, it is reasonable to suspect that this influence may account for the characteristic under discussion; and such an inference is supported by the fact, already noted, that the Aramaic דִּי or דְּ, which is the natural representative of *ἵνα* with a telic force, has a much wider range of usage, standing, for example, for the conjunctive *that* which *ἵνα* in Mk. so frequently represents.

If, however, the theory of Aramaic influence may be taken as accounting for the excessive use of *ἵνα* in Mk., the case for such influence in Jn. must be regarded as much stronger still, for *ἵνα* is there proportionately nearly twice as frequent, while it is some 5 times as frequent as in Mt., and some 4½ times as frequent as in Lk.

It is instructive to notice that there are certain phrases in which the Greek of the Gospels varies between the construction of *ἵνα* with finite verb and the Infinitive construction, and that in these the Syriac versions normally represent both constructions by ܕ *dĕ* followed by the finite verb, i.e. the construction which, on our theory, is literally rendered by the *ἵνα* construction.

One such is introduced by *οὐκ εἰμὶ ἄξιος* (or *ἱκανός*)

Jn. 1^{27} οὗ οὐκ εἰμὶ [ἐγὼ] ἄξιος ἵνα λύσω αὐτοῦ τὸν ἱμάντα τοῦ ὑποδήματος.

Pal. Syr. ܕܝ ܕܟܫܝܪ ܐܢܐ ܗܘܐ ܕܐܫܪܐ ܥܪܩܬܐ ܕܡܣܢܗ

Sin. ܗܘ ܕܠܐ ܫܘܐ ܐܢܐ ܕܐܫܪܐ ܥܪܩܐ ܕܡܣܢܘܗܝ

Pesh. ܗܘ ܕܐܢܐ ܠܐ ܫܘܐ ܐܢܐ ܕܐܫܪܐ ܥܪ̈ܩܐ ܕܡܣܢܘ̈ܗܝ

'That one who I am not worthy that I should loose the latchet of His sandal' (Pesh. 'the latchets of His sandals').

Mk. 1[7] οὗ οὐκ εἰμὶ ἱκανὸς κύψας λῦσαι τὸν ἱμάντα τῶν ὑποδημάτων αὐτοῦ.
Pal. Syr. ܕ ܕܠܝܬ ܐܢܐ ܫܘܐ ܕܐܬܟܦܦ ܐܫܪܐ ܥܪܩܬܐ ܕܡܣܢܘܗܝ
Sin. deest.
Pesh. ܗܘ ܕܠܐ ܫܘܐ ܐܢܐ ܕܐܬܓܚܢ ܐܫܪܐ ܥܪܩܐ ܕܡܣܢܘܗܝ

'That one who I am not worthy that I should stoop should loose the latchet (Pesh. latchets) of His sandals'.

Lk. 3[16] οὗ οὐκ εἰμὶ ἱκανὸς λῦσαι τὸν ἱμάντα τῶν ὑποδημάτων αὐτοῦ.
Pal. Syr. ܕ ܕܠܝܬ ܐܢܐ ܫܘܐ ܕܐܫܪܐ ܥܪܩܬܐ ܕܡܣܢܗ
Sin. ܗܘ ܕܠܐ ܫܘܐܢܐ ܕܐܫܪܐ ܥܪܩܐ ܕܡܣܢܘܗܝ
Pesh. ܗܘ ܕܠܐ ܫܘܐ ܐܢܐ ܕܐܫܪܐ ܥܪܩܐ ܕܡܣܐܢܘܗܝ

'That one who I am not worthy that I should loose the latchet (Sin., Pesh. latchets) of His sandals'.

Acts 13[25] οὗ οὐκ εἰμὶ ἄξιος τὸ ὑπόδημα τῶν ποδῶν λῦσαι.
Pesh. ܗܘ ܕܠܐ ܫܘܐ ܐܢܐ ܕܐܫܪܐ ܥܪܩܐ ܕܡܣܐܢܘܗܝ

'That one who I am not worthy that I should loose the latchets of His sandals'. The rendering of Pesh. is here verbally identical with its rendering in Jn. 1[27].

Lk. 15[19.21] οὐκέτι εἰμὶ ἄξιος κληθῆναι υἱός σου.
Pal. Syr. ܥܘܕ ܠܝܬ ܐܢܐ ܫܘܐ ܕܐܬܩܪܐ ܒܪܟ
Sin., Cur. ܘܠܐ ܫܘܐ ܡܟܝܠ ܕܒܪܟ ܐܬܩܪܐ
Pesh. ܘܠܐ ܡܟܝܠ ܫܘܐ ܐܢܐ ܕܒܪܟ ܐܬܩܪܐ

I am no longer worthy that I should be called thy son'.

In the Q passage Mt 8[8] = Lk. 7[6] where we have the ἵνα construction after οὐκ εἰμὶ ἱκανός, the Syriac versions naturally represent this by ܕ with the finite verb.

Lk. 7[7] διὸ οὐδὲ ἐμαυτὸν ἠξίωσα πρὸς σὲ ἐλθεῖν.
Pal. Syr. ܡܢ ܐܦ ܠܐ ܚܫܒܬ ܢܦܫܝ ܠܐ ܕܫܘܐ ܐܢܐ ܕܐܬܐ ܠܘܬܟ
Sin. om.
Pesh. ܡܛܠ ܗܘ ܐܢܐ ܠܐ ܫܘܝܬ ܕܠܘܬܟ ܐܬܐ

'Therefore I did not count myself worthy that I should come to Thee'.

Thus out of all these passages only Jn. 1[27] and Mt. 8[8] = Lk. 7[6] have the ἵνα construction, and this agrees with the construction with ܕ which is used in all passages by the Syriac versions.

Again, *συμφέρει* is followed both by the *ἵνα* construction and by the Infinitive, and both constructions are represented in the Syriac versions by ܕ followed by the finite verb.

Jn. 11[50] *συμφέρει ὑμῖν ἵνα εἷς ἄνθρωπος ἀποθάνῃ.*

Pal. Syr. ܛܒ ܠܟܡ ܕܚܕ ܒܪܢܫ ܝܡܘܬ

Sin. and Pesh. ܦܩܚ ܠܢ ܕܚܕ ܓܒܪܐ ܢܡܘܬ

'It is good (Sin., Pesh. profitable) to us that one man should die'.

Jn. 18[14] *συμφέρει ἕνα ἄνθρωπον ἀποθανεῖν.*

Pal. Syr. ܛܒ ܗܘ ܕܚܕ ܒܪܢܫ ܝܡܘܬ

Sin. and Pesh. ܘܠܐ (ܦܩܚ Pesh.) ܕܚܕ ܓܒܪܐ ܢܡܘܬ

'It is good (Sin. fitting, Pesh. profitable) that one man should die'.

Mt. 19[10] *οὐ συμφέρει γαμῆσαι.*

Pal. Syr. ܠܐ ܛܒ ܕܝܣܒܬܗ ܐܢܫ

'It is not good that a man should marry'.

But Sin., Cur., Pesh. ܠܐ ܦܩܚ ܠܡܣܒ ܐܢܬܬܐ

'It is not profitable to take a wife'.

συμφέρει ἵνα is also found in Jn. 16[7], Mt. 5[29.30], 18[6].

The construction *συντίθεμαι ἵνα* in Jn. 9[22], *ἤδη γὰρ συνετέθειντο οἱ Ἰουδαῖοι ἵνα ἐάν τις αὐτὸν ὁμολογήσῃ Χριστόν, ἀποσυνάγωγος γένηται*, is reproduced in the Syriac versions by ܕ with the finite verb; so Pal. Syr. ܕܟܒܪ ܗܘܬ ܕܐܬܠܡܘ ܝܗܘܕܝܐ ܒܝܢܬܗܘܢ ܕܐܢ ܗܘ ܕܡܢ ܐܢܫ ܕܝܘܕܐ ܡܫܝܚܐ ܗܘ ܢܦܩ ܠܒܪ ܡܢ ܟܢܫܬܐ. In the other two occurrences of *συντίθεμαι*, it is followed by the normal construction of the Infinitive, and this again is represented in Syriac by ܕ with the finite verb: Lk. 22[5] *συνέθεντο αὐτῷ ἀργύριον δοῦναι*, Pal. Syr. ܘܩܡܘ ܕܢܬܠܘܢ ܠܗ ܟܣܦܐ 'they agreed that they should give him money'; Acts 23[20] *οἱ Ἰουδαῖοι συνέθεντο τοῦ ἐρωτῆσαί σε*, Pesh. ܝܗܘܕܝܐ ܐܬܛܟܣܘ ܕܢܒܥܘܢ ܡܢܟ 'the Jews have planned together that they should ask of thee'.

Similarly, in the variants *ἐδίδου . . . ἵνα παρατιθῶσιν* Mk. 6[41], *ἐδίδου παραθεῖναι* Lk. 9[16], Pesh. reads ܝܗܒ . . . ܕܢܣܝܡܘܢ 'gave . . . that they might set' in both places (Pal. Syr. and Sin. desunt in Lk.); in Lk. 8[38] *ἐδεῖτο . . . εἶναι σὺν αὐτῷ* is rendered by Pal. Syr. . . . ܒܥܐ ܕܝܗܘܐ ܥܡܗ, by Sin. and Pesh. ܒܥܐ ܗܘܐ . . . ܕܠܘܬܗ ܢܗܘܐ 'was begging . . . that he might be with Him', as in *παρεκάλει . . . ἵνα μετ' αὐτοῦ ᾖ* of Mk. 5[18]; in Lk. 8[56] *ὁ δὲ παρήγγειλεν αὐτοῖς μηδενὶ εἰπεῖν* is rendered by Pal. Syr. ܘܗܘ ܦܩܕ ܠܗܘܢ ܕܠܐܢܫ ܠܐ ܢܐܡܪܘܢ, by Sin.,

Cur. ܘܗܘ ܦܩܕ ܐܢܘܢ ܕܠܐܢܫ ܠܐ ܢܐܡܪܘܢ, by Pesh. ܗܘ ܕܝܢ ܐܙܗܪ ܐܢܘܢ ܕܠܐܢܫ ܠܐ ܢܐܡܪܘܢ 'He commanded (Pesh. warned) them that they should tell no man', as in καὶ διεστείλατο αὐτοῖς πολλὰ ἵνα κτλ. of Mk. 5[43]. Such illustrations could be almost indefinitely multiplied.

ἵνα as a mistranslation of ܕ *relative, 'who', 'which'.*

So far, the most that we have accomplished is to establish a good case for the hypothesis that the excessive use of ἵνα in Mk., and still more in Jn., may be due to the fact that the writers of these Gospels were accustomed *to think in Aramaic.* The frequent use of the ἵνα construction in place of an Infinitive is not in itself sufficient to prove *translation from Aramaic*; for an Aramaic-speaking Jew, in writing Greek, would naturally tend to exaggerate the use of a Κοινή construction which resembled his own native idiom. Now, however, we have to notice a usage of ἵνα in Jn. which can hardly be explained except by the hypothesis of actual *mistranslation* of an original Aramaic document. There are several passages in which ἵνα seems clearly to represent a mistranslation of ܕ employed in a relative sense. Translate them into Aramaic in the only possible way, representing ἵνα by ܕ, and an Aramaic scholar would, without question, give to that ܕ the sense 'who' or 'which'.

1[8] οὐκ ἦν ἐκεῖνος τὸ φῶς, ἀλλ' ἵνα μαρτυρήσῃ περὶ τοῦ φωτός. This passage has already been discussed in our notes on the Prologue (p. 32). The accepted interpretation of ἵνα with a telic force involves the assumption of an ellipse—'but (he came) that he might bear witness, &c.' If ἵνα is a mistranslation of ܕ relative no such ellipse is required, the passage meaning, 'He was not the light, but *one who* was to bear witness of the light'.

5[7] ἄνθρωπον οὐκ ἔχω ἵνα . . . βάλῃ με εἰς τὴν κολυμβήθραν. Pal. Syr., quite literally, ܓܒܪ ܠܝܬ ܠܝ ܕ . . . ܝܪܡܐ ܝܬܝ ܠܟܘܠܡܒܐ. The obvious meaning of this in Aramaic is, 'I have not a man *who* . . . shall put me into the pool'.

6[30] Τί οὖν ποιεῖς σὺ σημεῖον, ἵνα ἴδωμεν; Pal. Syr., quite literally, ܡܐ ܐܬܐ ܐܢܬ ܥܒܕ ܕܢܚܡܐ. The sense intended may well be, 'What sign then doest thou *which* we may see?' though, since the final sense of ܕ would here be appropriate in Aramaic as in the Greek ἵνα, the evidence of this passage is not pressed.

6^{50} οὗτός ἐστιν ὁ ἄρτος ὁ ἐκ τοῦ οὐρανοῦ καταβαίνων ἵνα τις ἐξ αὐτοῦ φάγῃ καὶ μὴ ἀποθάνῃ. Pal. Syr., quite literally, ܗܢܘ ܗܘ ܠܚܡܐ ܕܢܚܬ ܡܢ ܫܡܝܐ ܕܢܐܟܘܠ ܐܢܫ ܡܢܗ ܘܠܐ ܢܡܘܬ. This is naturally to be rendered, 'This is the bread which came down from heaven, *which*, if a man eat thereof, he shall not die' (expressed in Aramaic, '*which* a man shall eat thereof and shall not die').

9^{36} Καὶ τίς ἐστιν, κύριε, ἵνα πιστεύσω εἰς αὐτόν; Pal. Syr., quite literally, ܘܡܢ ܗܘ ܡܪܝ: ܕܐܗܝܡܢ ܒܗ. This means, without a doubt, 'And who is he, Lord, on whom I should believe?' (the Aramaic construction is, '*who* I should believe on him'). This meaning is surely much more natural and appropriate than is the final sense given to ἵνα by A.V., R.V., 'that I may believe on him', which can hardly fail to make us discount the quality of the man's faith, suggesting, as it does, that his gratitude to our Lord made him willing to believe on any one whom He named.

14^{16} ἄλλον παράκλητον δώσει ὑμῖν ἵνα ᾖ μεθ' ὑμῶν εἰς τὸν αἰῶνα. Pal. Syr., quite literally, ܗܘ ܢܬܠ ܠܟܘܢ ܚܪܢ ܦܪܩܠܛܐ ܕܝܗܘܐ ܥܡܟܘܢ ܠܥܠܡ. The natural meaning is, 'He shall give you another Comforter, *who* shall abide with you for ever'. So 𝔏 (vt.[mq]) 'qui'.

If the fact that ἵνα in these passages is a mistranslation of דְ relative be thought to need further evidence to clinch it, this may be found in the variation between Mk. 4^{22} and the parallel passages Mt. 10^{26}, Lk. 8^{17} already noted. Here Mk.'s ἐὰν μὴ ἵνα φανερωθῇ is reproduced in Mt. by ὃ οὐκ ἀποκαλυφθήσεται, and in Lk. by ὃ οὐ φανερὸν γενήσεται. Thus ἐὰν μὴ ἵνα φανερωθῇ seems clearly to represent an original אִילָהֵן דְּאִתְגְּלִי 'except that which shall be revealed', i.e. 'which shall not be revealed', and this is the rendering of Pesh. ܕܠܐ ܢܬܓܠܐ (Pal. Syr., Sin. vacant).*

ὅτι *similarly a mistranslation of* דְ *relative.*

In Jn. 9^{17} Τί σὺ λέγεις περὶ αὐτοῦ, ὅτι ἠνέῳξέν σου τοὺς ὀφθαλμούς; the use of ὅτι is very awkward, and the 'in that' of R.V. unconvincing. The passage, however, at once becomes clear when we recognize that ὅτι is simply a mistranslation of דְ relative—'What sayest thou of him *who* hath opened thine eyes?' This

* That ἵνα is here a mistranslation of דְ relative has been noted by Wellhausen, *Einleitung*², p. 15.

sense; which is naturally to be deduced from the Aramaic, is given by the Arabic Diatessaron الذي فتح; and the best-attested reading of 𝔏 (vt. vg.) is 'qui aperuit'. Similarly, in 8^{45} ἐγὼ δὲ ὅτι τὴν ἀλήθειαν λέγω is rendered by Pal. Syr. ܐܢܐ ܕܝ ܕܐܢܐ ܐܡܪ ܩܘܫܛܐ, which would naturally bear the sense, 'I *who* speak the truth'. This meaning, which offers a superior antithesis to 'he is a liar' of the preceding verse, is offered by the Diatessaron الذي 'who', and by two MSS. of 𝔏 (vg.) 'qui'. In our notes on the Prologue a similar case of mistranslation is suggested in 1^{16} ὅτι ἐκ τοῦ πληρώματος αὐτοῦ κτλ. (cf. p. 39), and, conversely, ד = 'because, inasmuch as' seems to have been wrongly treated as the relative in $1^{4.13}$ (cf. pp. 29, 34). A case in Mk. where ὅτι seems to be a mistranslation of ד relative (ᾧ) is 4^{41}, Τίς ἄρα οὗτός ἐστιν ὅτι καὶ ὁ ἄνεμος καὶ ἡ θάλασσα ὑπακούει αὐτῷ; 'Who then is this *whom* (ᾧ . . . αὐτῷ) even the wind and the sea obey?'* Another may very possibly be seen in 8^{24}, Βλέπω τοὺς ἀνθρώπους ὅτι ὡς δένδρα ὁρῶ περιπατοῦντας, where the difficult ὅτι may represent a wrong rendering of ד (οὕς).† In Mt. 13^{16} ὑμῶν δὲ μακάριοι οἱ ὀφθαλμοὶ ὅτι βλέπουσιν, καὶ τὰ ὦτα [ὑμῶν] ὅτι ἀκούουσιν, the words ὅτι βλέπουσιν . . . ὅτι ἀκούουσιν are rendered by Sin., Cur., Pesh. ܕܚܙܝܢ . . . ܕܫܡܥܝܢ, which may mean 'because they see, &c', or '*which* see, &c.' The latter sense is given by the Diatessaron التي تبصر . . . التي تسمع, and by several MSS. of 𝔏 (vt. vg.) 'qui vident . . . quae audiunt'. Hegesippus quotes the passage in the form μακάριοι οἱ ὀφθαλμοὶ ὑμῶν οἱ βλέποντες, καὶ τὰ ὦτα ὑμῶν τὰ ἀκούοντα.‡ Since Hegesippus (according to Eusebius, *HE*. iv. 22) was a Hebrew by birth and made quotations from Syriac and Hebrew, we may infer that in this case his quotation is based upon a Syriac translation of Mt. The rendering of 𝔏 vt. here and in the passages previously noticed shows the influence of a Syriac version upon this translation, and illustrates the natural sense which a reader of Aramaic would attach to the particle ܕ in the contexts in question. Conversely, the same influence upon the so-called Western text is seen in Jn. 8^{53} D, μὴ σὺ μείζων εἶ τοῦ Ἀβραάμ· ὅτι ἀπέθανεν, where WH. rightly has ὅστις ἀπέθανεν.

* Noted by Wellhausen, *Einleitung*², p. 15. † Cf. Allen, *St. Mark, ad loc.*

‡ Cf. Grabe, *Spicilegium SS. Patrum*; edit. alt. ii, p. 213—a reference which the present writer owes to Dr. Cureton's discussion of the passage in *Remains of a very antient recension of the Four Gospels in Syriac*, p. xxv.

ἵνα as a mistranslation of דְּ *= 'when'.*

We have noticed, when speaking of the usage of דְּ, that it can bear the meaning 'when', ὅτε. Strictly speaking in such a usage it is relatival 'which', with ellipse of 'in it'—דְּבֵיהּ 'which in it' = 'in which'; cf. Jn. 5[28], where ἔρχεται ὥρα ἐν ᾗ appears in Pal. Syr. as ܐܬܬ ܫܥܬܐ ܗܕܐ ܕܒܗ. The following cases occur in Jn. of ἵνα standing for ὅτε:

12[23] ἐλήλυθεν ἡ ὥρα ἵνα δοξασθῇ ὁ υἱὸς τοῦ ἀνθρώπου.

Pal. Syr. ܐܬܬ ܫܥܬܐ ܕܝܫܬܒܚ ܒܪܗ ܕܒܪܢܫܐ.

13[1] ἦλθεν αὐτοῦ ἡ ὥρα ἵνα μεταβῇ ἐκ τοῦ κόσμου τούτου.

Pal. Syr. ܐܬܬ ܫܥܬܗ ܕܝܫܢܐ ܡܢ ܗܕܝܢ ܥܠܡܐ.

16[2] ἔρχεται ὥρα ἵνα πᾶς ὁ ἀποκτείνας ὑμᾶς δόξῃ λατρείαν προσφέρειν τῷ Θεῷ.*

Pal. Syr. ܐܬܬ ܫܥܬܐ ܕܟܠ ܡܢ ܕܩܛܠ ܠܟܘܢ ܗܘܐ ܣܒܪ ܕܩܘܪܒܢ ܗܘ ܡܩܪܒ ܠܐܠܗܐ.

16[32] ἔρχεται ὥρα . . . ἵνα σκορπισθῆτε.

Pal. Syr. ܐܬܬ ܫܥܬܐ . . . ܕܬܬܒܕܪܘܢ.

That in all these cases ἵνα simply stands by mistranslation for ὅτε, and that no mystic final sense is to be traced in the usage such as is postulated by Westcott, is proved by the use of the normal phrase ἔρχεται ὥρα ὅτε in 4[21.23], 5[25], 16[25], and ἔρχεται ὥρα ἐν ᾗ in 5[28].

ὅτι similarly a mistranslation of דְּ *= 'when'.*

In 9[8] οἱ θεωροῦντες αὐτὸν τὸ πρότερον ὅτι προσαίτης ἦν we have a very awkward ὅτι, and R.V.'s halting rendering, 'they that saw him aforetime, that he was a beggar', is the best that can be made of the sentence. Clearly the sense demanded is '*when* (ὅτε) he was a beggar', and the natural inference is that דְּ = 'when' has been wrongly interpreted as conjunctive 'that'. Another clear instance of the same mistranslation is seen in 12[41], ταῦτα εἶπεν Ἠσαίας ὅτι εἶδεν τὴν δόξαν αὐτοῦ (R.V. 'because he saw his glory'), where the sense demanded is '*when* (ὅτε) he saw His glory'.†

* Freely quoted in the letter from the church at Lyons (Eusebius, *HE.* v. 1) with the correction ἐν ᾧ . . . δόξει for ἵνα . . . δόξῃ—ἐλεύσεται καιρὸς ἐν ᾧ πᾶς ὁ ἀποκτείνας ὑμᾶς δόξει λατρείαν προσφέρειν τῷ Θεῷ.

† It is just possible that ὅτι may here be a mistranslation of דְּ relative—'These things said Isaiah *who* saw His glory and spake concerning Him', but the sense '*when*' seems to be preferable.

CHAPTER IV

PRONOUNS

ἐγώ, ἡμεῖς, σύ, ὑμεῖς.

THE great frequency of the Pronouns of the first and second persons is a marked feature in Jn. The occurrences in this Gospel and the Synoptists are as follows:

	Mt.	Mk.	Lk.	Jn.
ἐγώ	29	17	23	134
κἀγώ	9	—	4	27
ἡμεῖς	5	3	5	18
σύ	18	10	27	60
ὑμεῖς	31	11	21	68
Totals	92	41	80	307

To a large extent this phenomenon finds its explanation in the fact that the Fourth Gospel is designed to prove our Lord's Messiahship and His Divinity (20^{31}). Thus at the opening St. John the Baptist emphasizes the character of his mission—ἐγώ—in contrast to that of Christ ($1^{20.23.26.27.31a\ 33.34}$, 3^{28b}). Our Lord lays stress upon His claims—ἐγώ ($4^{14.26}$, $5^{30.36}$, $6^{35.40.41.41.48.51.54}$, $8^{12.42}$, $10^{7.9.11.14.18}$, 11^{25}, 12^{46}, 14^{6}, 15^{1}, 16^{33}, 18^{37}), or His acts ($15^{9.26}$, $17^{4.12.14.19}$, $18^{20\,bis}$), bringing Himself into antithesis with others—the disciples, the Jews, the world, &c. (4^{32}, $5^{34.45}$, $7^{8.29.34.36}$, $8^{15.21b.22.23\,bis.38.45.55}$, $10^{10.18}$, $12^{26.47}$, $13^{14.15.33}$, $14^{3.12a.19.20.27}$, $15^{5a.10.16}$, $17^{14b.25}$); or He defines His relation to God the Father (5^{17}, 6^{57}, $8^{16b.18.26}$, $10^{30.38}$, 16^{26}, 17^{23}). Emphatic ὑμεῖς is frequently antithetical to ἐγώ, and implied or expressed antithesis often accounts for the use of ἡμεῖς and σύ.

When all such cases have been taken into consideration, there remain, however, a large number in which the Pronoun appears to be used with no special emphasis. Thus ἐγώ in $1^{30.31b}$, 3^{28a}, 4^{38},

$6^{63.70}$, 7^{17}, $8^{14.16a.21a.29.49.50.54}$, $10^{17.27.28.35}$, $11^{27.42}$, 12^{50}, $13^{7.18.26}$, $14^{4.10b.12b.16.28}$, $15^{14.20.26}$, $16^{4.7bis}$, $17^{9.14a.22}$, $18^{20bis.21.37}$; ἡμεῖς in 1^{16}, $6^{42.69}$, 7^{35}, 8^{18}, $9^{24.29}$, 19^{7}; σύ in 3^{26}, 4^{10}, 10^{24}, 14^{9}, $18^{34.37b}$; ὑμεῖς in 1^{26}, 4^{35}, $5^{20.33.34.35.39.44.45}$; $8^{31.46}$, $9^{19.30}$, 11^{49}, 13^{13}, $14^{20(4)}$, $15^{3.16b}$.

Now while in Semitic the use of the Personal Pronouns with greater or less emphasis is extremely common, we also find them employed without special emphasis in order *to mark the subject of the Participle.* In Hebrew, and still more in Aramaic, the Participle is used with great freedom to describe an event as in process of continuance, whether in the past or present, or as in process of coming into being (*Futurum instans*). In such cases, the subject being unexpressed in the verbal form, it is of course necessary to mark it, when it is pronominal, by the Pronoun. This Semitic usage of the Participle being foreign to Greek, the LXX in translating the Hebrew of the O.T. naturally represents it by a Present, a Perfect, a Future, &c., and, so doing, might well have dispensed with the Personal Pronoun. As a matter of fact, however, the translation nearly always retains the Pronoun, and that, almost invariably, in the position which it occupies in the original, before or after the verbal form.

Cases of אנכי, אני, 'I', with the Participle expressed by ἐγώ in Genesis are as follows. 7^{4} אָנֹכִי מַמְטִיר *ἐγὼ ἐπάγω ὑετόν*, 9^{12} אֲנִי נֹתֵן *ἐγὼ δίδωμι*, 15^{14} דָּן אָנֹכִי *κρινῶ ἐγώ*, 30^{1} מֵתָה אָנֹכִי *τελευτήσω ἐγώ*, $24^{13.43}$ הִנֵּה אָנֹכִי נִצָּב *ἰδοὺ ἐγὼ ἕστηκα*. So also 16^{8}, 18^{17}, $24^{3.37.42}$, 25^{32}, 27^{8}, 28^{20}, 31^{5}, 32^{12}, 42^{18}, 48^{21}, 49^{29}. The only cases without ἐγώ are $37^{16.30}$.

Cases of אנחנו, 'we', with the Participle expressed by ἡμεῖς in Genesis—Kings are: Gen. 19^{13} כִּי מַשְׁחִיתִים אֲנַחְנוּ אֶת־הַמָּקוֹם הַזֶּה *ὅτι ἀπόλλυμεν ἡμεῖς τὸν τόπον τοῦτον*, 43^{18} עַל־דְּבַר הַכֶּסֶף . . . אֲנַחְנוּ מוּבָאִים *Διὰ τὸ ἀργύριον . . . ἡμεῖς εἰσαγόμεθα*, Num. 10^{29} נֹסְעִים אֲנַחְנוּ אֶל־הַמָּקוֹם *Ἐξαίρομεν ἡμεῖς εἰς τὸν τόπον*. So Deut. 1^{28}, 5^{22}, 12^{8}, Judg. 18^{5}, 19^{18}, 1 Sam. 14^{8}, 1 Kgs. 22^{3}, 2 Kgs. 6^{1}, $7^{3.9bis}$, 18^{26}. No cases with omission of ἡμεῖς.

Similarly, in Genesis—Kings there are 40 cases of אַתָּה 'thou' with the Participle expressed by σύ (e.g. Gen. 13^{15} כָּל־הָאָרֶץ אֲשֶׁר־אַתָּה רֹאֶה *πᾶσαν τὴν γῆν ἣν σὺ ὁρᾷς*), as against 14 without σύ: and 35 cases of אַתֶּם 'ye' with the Participle expressed by ὑμεῖς (e.g. Ex. 16^{8} אֶת־תְּלֻנֹּתֵיכֶם אֲשֶׁר אַתֶּם מַלִּינִם *τὸν γογγυσμὸν ὑμῶν ὃν ὑμεῖς διαγογγύζετε*) and one case with *αὐτοί* (Ex. 10^{11}), as against 6 cases without *ὑμεῖς*.

In Theodotion's version of the Aramaic portion of Daniel and the LXX of the Aramaic sections of Ezra we find the following cases of the Personal Pronoun with the Participle expressed in Greek.

אנה 'I':

Dan. 2^{8} מִן יַצִּיב יָדַע אֲנָה *Ἐπ' ἀληθείας οἶδα ἐγώ.*

3^{25} הָא־אֲנָה חָזֵה גֻּבְרִין אַרְבְּעָה *Ὅδε ἐγὼ ὁρῶ ἄνδρας τέσσαρες.*

4^{4} חֶלְמָא אָמַר אֲנָה קֳדָמֵיהוֹן *τὸ ἐνύπνιον εἶπα ἐγὼ ἐνώπιον αὐτῶν.*

אנחנא 'we':

Dan. 3^{16} לָא־חַשְׁחִין אֲנַחְנָא *Οὐ χρείαν ἔχομεν ἡμεῖς.*

3^{17} דִּי־אֲנַחְנָא פָלְחִין *ᾧ ἡμεῖς λατρεύομεν.*

Ezr. 4^{16} מְהוֹדְעִין אֲנַחְנָה לְמַלְכָּא *γνωρίζομεν ἡμεῖς τῷ βασιλεῖ.*

אנתה 'thou':

Dan. 4^{15} וְאַנְתְּה כָּהֵל *σὺ δέ, Δανιήλ, δύνασαι.*

$6^{17.21(16.20)}$ אֱלָהָךְ דִּי אַנְתְּה פָּלַח־לֵהּ בִּתְדִירָא *Ὁ θεός σου, ᾧ σὺ λατρεύεις ἐνδελεχῶς.*

אנתון 'ye':

Dan. 2^{8} עִדָּנָא אַנְתּוּן זָבְנִין *καιρὸν ὑμεῖς ἐξαγοράζετε.*

The only exception to the expression of the Pronoun is found in Dan. 2^{23} לָךְ אֱלָהּ אֲבָהָתִי מְהוֹדֵא וּמְשַׁבַּח אֲנָה *σοί, ὁ θεὸς τῶν πατέρων μου, ἐξομολογοῦμαι καὶ αἰνῶ.*

As compared with Hebrew, the Personal Pronoun is used more freely in Aramaic with (e.g.) a *Perfect* where no special stress is apparent; cf. Dan. 4^{6} דִּי אֲנָה יִדְעֵת *ὃν ἐγὼ ἔγνων*, 5^{16} וַאֲנָה שִׁמְעֵת עֲלָךְ *καὶ ἐγὼ ἤκουσα περὶ σοῦ.*

Now it is at any rate a plausible hypothesis that the unemphatic usage of the Personal Pronoun in Jn. may often represent close translation of an Aramaic original in which the Pronoun was expressed with the Participle. Thus e.g., 1^{26} *μέσος ὑμῶν στήκει ὃν ὑμεῖς οὐκ οἴδατε* exactly represents בֵּינֵיכוֹן קָאֵם מַן דְּאַנְתּוּן לָא יָדְעִין; 1^{30} *οὗτός ἐστιν ὑπὲρ οὗ ἐγὼ εἶπον*, הָדֵין הוּא דְּאָמַר אֲנָה עֲלוֹהִי. In other cases we may find the Aramaic Pronoun coupled without special emphasis with a Perfect or Imperfect; e.g. 1^{31b} *ἀλλ' ἵνα φανερωθῇ τῷ Ἰσραὴλ διὰ τοῦτο ἦλθον ἐγὼ ἐν ὕδατι βαπτίζων*, אֵילָהֵן דְּיִתְגְּלֵי לְיִשְׂרָאֵל בְּלְ־

קֳבֵל דְּנָה אֲתֵית אֲנָה מְצַבַּע בְּמַיִין. Again, in 1[16] ἡμεῖς πάντες ἐλάβομεν, the ἡμεῖς naturally reproduces the suffix of כֻּלַּן 'all of us'.

Particularly noteworthy is the throwing of σύ to the end of the sentence, whether in a question, as in 1[21b] Ὁ προφήτης εἶ σύ; 18[37] Οὐκοῦν βασιλεὺς εἶ σύ; 19[9] Πόθεν εἶ σύ; or in a statement, as in 4[19] θεωρῶ ὅτι προφήτης εἶ σύ, 8[48] Σαμαρείτης εἶ σύ. This is never found elsewhere throughout the N. T. except in Acts 13[33], Heb. 1[5] Υἱός μου εἶ σύ, a quotation of Ps. 2[7] with accurate reproduction of the Hebrew order בְּנִי אַתָּה. Hebrew and Aramaic can, in such a statement or query, place the Pronoun after the predicate or before it (as e.g. in Gen. 27[24] אַתָּה זֶה בְּנִי), and Jn.'s use of both orders (cf. σὺ εἶ in 1[42.49], 3[10], 7[52], &c.) looks much like a close reproduction of an Aramaic original.

αὐτός, οὗτος, ἐκεῖνος.

To express the 3rd person αὐτός is fairly frequent in Jn. The figures for αὐτός (-ή) as subject in the four Gospels are as follows:

Mt. 12, Mk. 17, Lk. 51, Jn. 18.

Much more often, however, Jn. prefers to use an emphatic demonstrative οὗτος 'this one', ἐκεῖνος 'that one', and he employs these Pronouns substantivally with far greater freedom than do the Synoptists. The figures for οὗτος (αὕτη) as subject are

Mt. 35, Mk. 14, Lk. 36, Jn. 44.

For ἐκεῖνος (-η, -ο) used substantivally, whether as subject or obliquely, the figures are

Mt. 4, Mk. 3, Lk. 4, Jn. 51.

ἐκεῖνος is used adjectivally

Mt. 51, Mk. 16, Lk. 29, Jn. 18.

Jn.'s extraordinary fondness for demonstratives in preference to the Personal Pronoun finds adequate explanation in the heory that his Gospel is a close reproduction of an Aramaic original.

In the Aramaic of Dan. the 3rd Personal Pronoun הוּא *hû* as subject is rendered αὐτός by Theodotion, except where it forms the subject of a predicative statement in which the copula is understood, in which case the Greek represents it by the substantive verb: e.g. 6^{5} מְהֵימַן הוּא 'faithful (was) he' = πιστὸς ἦν, 6^{11} הוּא בָּרֵךְ 'he (was) kneeling' = ἦν κάμπτων.

Aramaic is richly supplied with demonstrative Pronouns. The following, with their Greek renderings, may be noticed.

דְּנָה *d^enā* 'this', fem. דָּא *dā*, plur. c. אִלֵּין *'illēn*, Dan. and Ezr. *passim*. Targums דֵּין *dên*, fem. דָּא *dā*; strengthened by demonstrative prefix הָ *hā-*, הָדֵין *hādên*, fem. הָדָא *hādā* = Syriac ܗܢܐ *hånå* (contracted from *hådenå*), fem. ܗܕܐ *hâdē*; plur. c. הָאִלֵּין *hā'illên* = Syriac ܗܠܝܢ *hållên*. דְּנָה both as pronominal subs. and adj. is regularly rendered οὗτος in Dan. and Ezr. (in a few cases of adj. use it is represented by the definite article only).

דִּכֵּן *dikkēn* 'this, that', c., Dan. 2^{31} צַלְמָא דִּכֵּן ἡ εἰκὼν ἐκείνη (LXX and Θ.), Dan. $7^{20.21}$ קַרְנָא דִכֵּן τὸ κέρας ἐκεῖνο (LXX, Θ.). Plur. c. אִלֵּךְ *'illēkh*, Dan $3^{12.21.23}$, $6^{12.16}$ (also found in Ezr.).

To this corresponds in Ezr.:

דֵּךְ *dēkh*, fem. דָּךְ *dākh* 'this'. קִרְיְתָא דָךְ ἡ πόλις ἐκείνη, Ezr. $4^{13.15.16.19.21}$; ἡ πόλις αὕτη, 4^{16b}; שֵׁשְׁבַּצַּר דֵּךְ, Σαρβαγὰρ ἐκεῖνος, 5^{16}; עֲבִידְתָּא דָךְ τὸ ἔργον ἐκεῖνο, 5^{8}; בֵּית אֱלָהָא דֵךְ, (τὸν) οἶκον τοῦ θεοῦ ἐκεῖνον, 5^{17}, $6^{7.8}$, οἶκον θεοῦ, 6^{12}.

In addition, we find in Talmudic Aramaic הָהוּא *hāhû* = 'that' or 'that one' (i.e. 3rd personal pronoun *hû* + demonstrative particle *hā*), contracted in Syriac into ܗܘ *hau* (Pal. Syr. also ܗܠܘ), fem. הָהִיא *hāhî* (also האי), contracted in Syriac into ܗܝ *hâi* (Pal. Syr. also ܗܠܝ), plur. הָנְהוֹ *hānhô*, Syriac m. ܗܢܘܢ *hånnūn*, fem. *hånnên*. This usage is not found in the Aramaic of Dan. and Ezr., though we may notice the use of the Personal Pronoun in Dan. 2^{32} הוּא צַלְמָא '*that* image' (explained as *Nom. pendens*—'it—the image'). This is remarkably like ἐκεῖνος τὸ Πνεῦμα τῆς ἀληθείας in Jn. 16^{13}, an expression which amounts to '*that* Spirit of truth' or '*the* Spirit, &c.' (Pal. Syr. ܗܠܘ ܪܘܚܐ ܕܩܘܫܛܐ. This version at times uses ܗܠܘ to express the definite article, e.g. ܗܠܘ ܒܪܢܫܐ = ὁ ἄνθρωπος.)

There can be no question that where ἐκεῖνος is used adjectivally it would naturally be represented by ההוא. Thus 4^{53} ἐκείνῃ τῇ ὥρᾳ would appear in the Jerus. Talmud as בהאי שעתא (Cur., Pesh. ܒܗܝ ܫܥܬܐ, but Pal. Syr. ܗܠܗ ܫܥܬܐ). When used substantivally as subject—especially when reinforcing a *Nom. pendens* (cf. p. 64)—it is probable that ἐκεῖνος represents the Personal Pronoun הוּא; but there are other cases in which it looks much like a reproduction of ההוא. Pal. Syr. represents it by ܗܘ (ܗܠܘ) in 3^{30}, 5^{35}, 7^{11}, $9^{11.12}$;

Pesh. by ܗܿܘ in 3^{30}; $5^{35.43.47}$, 7^{11}, 8^{44}, $9^{28.36}$, $10^{1.35}$, $13^{25.26}$, 14^{21}. We may note especially the rendering of oblique cases by Pesh. in the following passages:

3^{30} *ἐκεῖνον δεῖ αὐξάνειν* = ܠܗܿܘ ܗܘ ܘܠܐ ܠܡܪܒܐ (Cur. ܠܗ ܗܘ)
5^{43} *ἐκεῖνον λήμψεσθε* = ܠܗܿܘ ܬܩܒܠܘܢ (so Cur.)
5^{47} *τοῖς ἐκείνου γράμμασιν* = ܠܟܬ̈ܒܘܗܝ ܕܗܿܘ (Cur. ܕܗܘ).
9^{28} *σὺ μαθητὴς εἶ ἐκείνου* = ܐܢܬ ܗܘ ܬܠܡܝܕܗ ܕܗܿܘ (Sin. om. ܕܗܿܘ).
10^{35} *εἰ ἐκείνους εἶπεν θεούς* = ܐܢ ܠܗܿܢܘܢ ܐܡܪ ܐܠܗ̈ܐ (Sin. om.).

In cases such as these the idiomatic force of the Aramaic demonstrative satisfactorily accounts for the Greek usage. Again, the phrase *ἐκεῖνός ἐστιν*, rendered ܗܿܘ ܗܘ—lit. 'that one (is) he'—in 13^{26}, 14^{21}, is one in which ההוא would naturally be employed.

We thus reach the following conclusions as to the pronouns which we have been considering:

Substantival use—

αὐτός = *hū*.
ἐκεῖνος = *hū* and *hāhū*.
οὗτος = *hādēn*.

Adjectival use—

οὗτος = *dēn*, *dᵉnā*, or *hādēn*.
ἐκεῖνος = *dikkēn*, *dēkh*, or *hāhū*.

The Relative completed by a Pronoun.

The Aramaic relative particle דִּי, דְּ—originally, as we have already remarked (p. 70), a demonstrative '*that one*'— is invariable, and, like the Hebrew relative אֲשֶׁר, properly forms a link connecting two co-ordinate sentences. For expression of the implied relation it is therefore necessary to complete the sense of the Relative particle by a Pronoun or Pronominal suffix in the clause which it introduces. Thus e.g. such a statement as, 'I saw the man *to whom* I gave the book' has to be expressed in Semitic in the form, 'I saw the man *who* I gave the book *to him*'. There are several instances in Jn. in which the Greek copies this Semitic construction.

1^{6} Ἐγένετο ἄνθρωπος . . . ὄνομα αὐτῷ Ἰωάννης. Here the relative connexion is implied and not directly expressed. So 3[1]. On the thoroughly Semitic character of this particular idiom cf. p. 30.

1[27] *οὗ ἐγὼ οὐκ εἰμὶ ἄξιος ἵνα λύσω αὐτοῦ τὸν ἱμάντα τοῦ ὑποδήματος.*

1[33] *Ἐφ' ὃν ἂν ἴδῃς τὸ Πνεῦμα καταβαῖνον καὶ μένον ἐπ' αὐτόν* = Pal. Syr. ܗܘ ܕܐܢܬ ܚܙܐ ܪܘܚܐ ܢܚܬܐ ܘܡܩܘܝܐ ܥܠܘܗܝ lit. 'He who thou seest the Spirit descending and abiding upon him'.

9[36] *Καὶ τίς ἐστιν, κύριε, ἵνα πιστεύσω εἰς αὐτόν;* Here *ἵνα* is a mistranslation of the relative דְּ; cf. p. 76.

13[26] *Ἐκεῖνός ἐστιν ᾧ ἐγὼ βάψω τὸ ψωμίον καὶ δώσω αὐτῷ.* Peculiarly Aramaic—הָהוּא הוּא דְצָבַע אֲנָה לְחַמָא וְיָהֵב לֵיהּ 'That is he *dĕ* I shall dip the sop and give it to him', i.e. 'to whom I shall give the sop when I have dipped it'.

18[9] *Οὓς δέδωκάς μοι οὐκ ἀπώλεσα ἐξ αὐτῶν οὐδένα.*

Wellhausen (*Einleitung*[2], p. 15) cites two instances of this construction from Mk., viz. 1[7] *οὗ οὐκ εἰμὶ ἱκανὸς κύψας λῦσαι τὸν ἱμάντα τῶν ὑποδημάτων αὐτοῦ*, and 7[25] *ἧς εἶχεν τὸ θυγάτριον αὐτῆς πνεῦμα ἀκάθαρτον*, besides three cases from the text of D in Mt. 10[11], 18[20], Lk. 8[12].*

Pronominal constructions peculiar to Aramaic.

It is peculiarly idiomatic in Aramaic to anticipate a genitive by use of a possessive pronominal suffix attached to the antecedent. Thus the Aramaic of Dan. writes '*His* name of God' (2[20]), 'in *their* days of those kings' (2[44]), 'ate *their* pieces of the Jews' (i.e. slandered them, 3[8]), '*his* appearance of the fourth (3[25]), &c.; Pal. Syr. in Jn. 1 writes '*their* light of mankind' (*v.* [4]), '*its* news of the light' (*vv.* [7.8]), 'in *His* bosom of the Father' (*v.* [18]), '*his* witness of John' (*v.* [19]), &c.

There appears to be but one instance of this in the Greek of Jn., but this is so striking that it should surely count for much in estimating the theory of translation from Aramaic. In 9[18] we read *τοὺς γονεῖς αὐτοῦ τοῦ ἀναβλέψαντος*, '*his* parents of him that had received sight'. This appears naturally in Pal. Syr. as ܐܒܗܘܗܝ ܕܗܘ ܕܚܙܐ. Cf. Mk. 6[22] *εἰσελθούσης τῆς θυγατρὸς αὐτοῦ* (*v.l.* *αὐτῆς*) *τῆς Ἡρωδιάδος*, which is clearly an attempt to reproduce the Aramaic

* He also cites Mt. 3[12] = Lk 3[17], *οὗ τὸ πτύον ἐν τῇ χειρὶ αὐτοῦ*, upon the assumption that *οὗ* is reinforced by *ἐν τῇ χειρὶ αὐτοῦ*, 'In whose hand is the fan' (not 'Whose fan, &c.'); but this is very doubtful.

construction בְּרַתַּהּ דְּהֵרוֹדְיָס '*her* daughter of Herodias', i. e. '*the* daughter of H.' (noted by Allen, *St. Mark, ad loc.*).

Another peculiarly Aramaic idiom is the anticipation of the direct object of a verb by a pronominal suffix. Thus in Jn. 19^{13} Pal. Syr. renders ܐܝܬܝ ܠܗ ܠܡܪܢ ܝܫܘܥ 'he brought Him (viz.) the Lord Jesus', 19^{16} ܕܒܪܘ ܠܗ ܠܡܪܢ ܝܫܘܥ 'they led Him the Lord Jesus', 19^{34} ܢܘܚ ܠܗ ܠܟܠܟܠܗ 'he pierced it His side'.* An example of this idiom is seen in the Greek of Jn. 9^{13} Ἄγουσιν αὐτὸν πρὸς τοὺς Φαρισαίους τόν ποτε τυφλόν = Pal. Syr. ܐܝܬܝܘ ܠܗ ܠܘܬ ܦܪ̈ܝܫܝ ܠܗܘ ܕܗܘܐ ܡܢ ܩܘܕܡ ܡܟܡܘܪ.

* No cases of the direct object of a verb so anticipated are found in Biblical Aramaic. We find the anticipatory pronoun, however, in such phrases as השתכחת בה בדניאל 'was found in him in Daniel' (Dan. 5^{12}), בה בליליא 'in it in the night', i. e. 'in the same night' (Dan. 5^{30}), שלחו עלוהי על ארתחששתא 'they sent to him to Artaxerxes' (Ezr. 4^{11}). A few cases of the construction are found in Hebrew: cf. Brockelmann, *Vergleich. Gramm. der semit. Sprachen*, ii. 227.

CHAPTER V

THE VERB

The Historic Present = Aramaic use of the Participle.

The Historic Present is extremely frequent in Jn. The occurrences are as follows:

ἄγουσιν, 9^{13}, 18^{28}.
ἀποκρίνεται, 12^{23}, $13^{26.38}$.
βάλλει, 13^{5}.
βλέπει, 1^{29}, $20^{1.5}$, 21^{20}; *βλέπουσιν*, 21^{9}.
δίδωσιν, 13^{26}, 21^{13}.
ἐγείρεται, 13^{4}.
ἔρχεται, $4^{5.7}$, 11^{38}, $12^{22\,\mathit{bis}}$, 13^{6}, 18^{3}, $20^{1.2.6.18.26}$, 21^{13}.
εὑρίσκει, $1^{41.43.45}$, 5^{14}.
θεωρεῖ, $20^{6.12.14}$; *θεωροῦσιν*, 6^{19}.
λαμβάνει, 13^{26}, 21^{13}.
λέγει, $1^{21.29.36.38.39.41.43.45.46.47.48.51}$, $2^{3.4.5.7.8.9}$, 3^{4}, $4^{7.9.11.15.16.17.19.21.25.26.28.34.49.50}$, $5^{6.8}$, $6^{5.8.12.20}$, $7^{6.50}$, 8^{39}, 9^{12}, $11^{7.11.23.24.27.39\,\mathit{bis}.40.44}$, $12^{4.22}$, $13^{6.8.9.10.24.25.27.31.36.37}$, $14^{5.6.8.9.22}$, $18^{4.5.17\,\mathit{bis}.26.38\,\mathit{bis}}$, $19^{4.5.6.9.10.14.15.26.27.28}$, $20^{2.13.15\,\mathit{bis}.16\,\mathit{bis}.17.19.22.27.29}$, $21^{3.5.7.10.12.15\,\mathit{ter}.16\,\mathit{ter}.17\,\mathit{bis}.19.21.22}$; *λέγουσιν*, 9^{17}, $11^{8.34}$, 12^{22}, 16^{29}, 20^{13}, 21^{3}.
μαρτυρεῖ, 1^{15}.
νεύει, 13^{24}.
τίθησιν, 13^{4}.
τρέχει, 20^{2}.
φαίνει, 1^{5}.
φησιν, 18^{29}.
φωνεῖ, 2^{9}.

This list gives a total of 164 occurrences.* The figures for the Synoptists, as given by Sir John Hawkins (*HS.*[2] pp. 143 ff.), are,

* Sir John Hawkins gives the figure as 162 (besides two cases preserved in Tischendorf in 11^{29}). He has, however, kindly lent his MS. list to the present writer, who has added *φαίνει* 1^{5} (which may be open to dispute) and *δίδωσιν* 21^{13}.

Mt. 78 (21 of which are derived from Mk.: in addition there are 15 Presents in Parables); Mk. 151; Lk. only 4 [or 6]; Acts 13. It thus appears that Jn. closely resembles Mk. in fondness for this usage. If Mk. were as long as Jn., the former would show proportionately 195 occurrences. The higher proportionate figure in Mk. is explained by the higher proportion of narrative to discourse in this Gospel. There are comparatively few cases of the Historic Present in Jn. 5—10 and 14—17.*

The use of the Historic Present in Mk. and Jn. strongly resembles a common Aramaic idiom in which in a description of past events the Participle is employed to represent the action described as in process of taking place. The following instances of this participial usage are found in the Aramaic chapters of the Book of Daniel. Theodotion sometimes renders it by an Historic Present or (more frequently) by an Imperfect; and when this is the case his rendering is added. In other cases he employs an Aorist.

עָנֵה '(was) answering' (always followed by וְאָמַר 'and (was) saying'), $2^{5.8.15.20.26.27.47}$, $3^{14.19.24.26.28}$, $4^{16b\ s.27}$, $5^{7.13.17}$, $6^{13.17.21}$, 7^{2} (this verb is frequently omitted in Theodotion's rendering).† עָנַיִן '(were) answering', 3^{24}.

אָמַר '(was) saying', $2^{5.8.15.20.26.27.47}$, $3^{14.19.24.26.28}$, $4^{4.11.16\,bis.20.27}$, $5^{7.13.17}$, $6^{13.17.21}$, 7^{2}. אָמְרִין '(were) saying', $2^{7.10}$, $3^{9.16.24}$, $6^{6.7.13.14.16}$, 7^{5}. Theodotion, *λέγει* in 2^{27}, *λέγουσιν* in 2^{10}, $6^{13.14.16}$, *ἔλεγον* in 7^{5}.

מִתְכַּנְּשִׁין '(were) gathering together', 3^{3}; קָאמִין '(were) standing', 3^{3}; קָרֵא '(was) crying' (*ἐβόα*), 3^{4}; שָׁמְעִין '(were) hearing' (*ἤκουον*), 3^{7}; נָפְלִין . . . וְסָגְדִין '(were) falling down . . . and (were) worshipping' (*πίπτοντες . . . προσεκύνουν*), 3^{7}; נָפְקִין '(were) coming forth', 3^{26}; מִתְכַּנְּשִׁין '(were) gathering together' (*συνάγονται*) 3^{27}; חָזַיִן '(were)

* Cf. *HS.*² pp. 143 f.

† It is remarkable that, though we constantly find עָנֵה (participle) coupled with וְאָמַר (participle) in the *singular*—'he (was) answering and (was) saying', we do not (with the single exception 3^{24}) find the participle *plural* עָנַיִן coupled with the participle plural וְאָמְרִין. In the plural the regular usage is the coupling of the *perfect* עֲנוֹ with the participle וְאָמְרִין—'they answered and (were) saying'. This fact suggests the possibility that the singular form should be vocalized, not עָנֵה *'ānē* (Participle), but עֲנָה *'ănā* (Perfect).

seeing' (ἐθεώρουν), 3[27]; נָחִת '(was) descending', 4[10]; קָרֵא '(was) crying', 4[11]; שָׁתֵה '(was) drinking', 5[1]; וְכָתְבָן 'and (were) writing' (καὶ ἔγραφον), 5[5]; חָזֵה '(was) seeing' (ἐθεώρει), 5[6]; מִשְׁתָּרַיִן '(were) being loosed' (διελύοντο), 5[6]; נָקְשָׁן '(were) knocking' (συνεκροτοῦντο), 5[6]; קָרֵא '(was) crying', 5[7]; עללין, K'ré עָלִּין '(were) entering' (εἰσεπορεύοντο), 5[8]; לָא־כָהֲלִין '(were) not being able' (οὐκ ἠδύναντο), 5[8]; מִתְבָּהַל '(was) being terrified', 5[9]; שָׁנַיִן '(were) being changed', 5[9]; מִשְׁתַּבְּשִׁין '(were) being perplexed' (συνεταράσσοντο), 5[9]; לָא־כָהֲלִין '(were) not being able', 5[15]; שָׁתַיִן '(were) drinking' (ἐπίνετε), 5[23]; הוּא בָּרֵךְ עַל־בִּרְכוֹהִי וּמְצַלֵּא וּמוֹדֵא 'he (was) kneeling on his knees and (was) praying and (was) giving thanks' (ἦν κάμπτων ἐπὶ τὰ γόνατα αὐτοῦ, καὶ προσευχόμενος καὶ ἐξομολογούμενος), 6[11]; מְגִיחָן '(were) bursting forth' (προσέβαλλον), 7[2]; סָלְקָן '(were) coming up' (ἀνέβαινεν), 7[3]; אָכְלָה וּמַדֱּקָה . . . רָפְסָה '(was) eating and (was) breaking in pieces . . . (was) trampling' (ἐσθίον καὶ λεπτῦνον . . . συνεπάτει), 7[7.19]; נָגֵד וְנָפֵק '(was) issuing and (was) coming forth' (εἷλκεν), 7[10]; מְמַלְּלָא '(was) speaking' (ἐλάλει), 7[11]; עָבְדָא '(was) making' (ἐποίει), 7[21]; יָכְלָה '(was) prevailing', 7[21].

The fact that in the 199½ Aramaic *vv.* of Dan. we thus find no less than 99 instances of this participial usage describing a past action shows how highly characteristic of the language the idiom is. That the usage naturally lends itself to representation in Greek by the Historic Present or Imperfect is obvious to an Aramaic scholar. If those who are unacquainted with Aramaic will read a passage of the book in English, substituting the literal renderings given above for those of R.V., and remembering that the time-determination (*was* or *is*) is absent from the original and can only be inferred from the context, they can hardly fail to come to the same conclusion.

It will be noticed that, out of the 99 examples, 23 are found with the verb 'answer', and no less than 36 with the verb 'say', leaving 40 (or considerably less than half the total) to verbs bearing other meanings. In Syriac the use of the Participle under discussion is practically confined to the verb ܐܡܪ 'say'.* In the 151 instances of the Historic Present in Mk., 72 are cases of λέγει, λέγουσιν. In the 164 instances in Jn. the proportion borne by λέγει, λέγουσιν to

* See, however, Burkitt, *Evangelion da-Mepharreshe*, ii, pp. 63 ff., for instances of its use with other verbs in Sin.

the whole number is considerably higher, viz. 120, or nearly three-fourths.

That the frequent use of the Historic Present in Mk. is due to Aramaic influence is maintained by Allen (*Expositor*, 1900, pp. 436 ff.; *Expository Times*, xiii, p. 329; Oxford *Studies in the Synoptic Problem*, p. 295) and by Wellhausen (*Einleitung in die drei ersten Evangelien*², p. 17). It can hardly be doubted that in Jn. also the same theory offers an adequate explanation of the same phenomenon.

The Imperfect = Aramaic use of the Participle coupled with the Substantive verb.

Instances of the Imperfect in Jn. (excluding the Substantive verb) are as follows:

διεγείρετο, 6^{18}.
διέτριβεν, 3^{22}.
διηκόνει, 12^{2}.
ἐβάπτιζεν, 3^{22}, 4^{2}; ἐβαπτίζοντο, 3^{23}.
ἐβάσταζεν, 12^{6}.
ἔβλεπον, 13^{22}.
ἐγίνωσκεν, 2^{25}.
ἐγόγγυζον, 6^{41}.
ἔδει, 4^{4}.
ἐδίδασκεν, 7^{14}.
ἐδίδοσαν, 19^{3}.
ἐδίωκον, 5^{16}.
ἐδόκουν, 13^{29}.
ἐζήτει, 19^{12}; ἐζήτουν, 5^{18}, $7^{1.11.30}$, 10^{39}, $11^{8.56}$.
ἐζώννυες, 21^{18}.
ἐθαύμαζον, 4^{27}, 7^{15}.
ἐθερμαίνοντο, 18^{18}.
ἐθεώρουν, 6^{2}.
εἶχον, 17^{5}; εἶχες, 19^{11}; εἶχεν, 2^{25}, 13^{29}; εἴχετε, 9^{41}; εἴχοσαν, $15^{22.24}$.
ἐκαθέζετο, 4^{6}, 11^{20}.
ἐκάθητο, 6^{3}.
ἔκειτο, 19^{29}, 20^{12}.

ἔκλαιεν, 20^{11}.

ἐκραύγαζον, 12^{13}.

ἐλάλει, 4^{27}, 7^{13}, 10^{6}.

ἔλεγεν, $2^{21.22}$, $5^{18.19}$, $6^{6.65.71}$, $8^{23.27.31}$, 9^{9}, $12^{29.33}$; ἔλεγον, $4^{33.42}$, 5^{10}, $6^{14.42}$, $7^{11.12\,bis.25.31.40.41\,bis}$, $8^{19.22.25}$, $9^{8.9.10\,bis.16\,bis}$, $10^{20.21.24.41}$, $11^{36.47.56}$, 12^{29}, 16^{18}, $19^{3.21}$, 20^{25}.

ἔλυε, 5^{18}.

ἐμάχοντο, 6^{52}.

ἐμαρτύρει, 12^{17}.

ἔμελεν, 12^{6}.

ἔμελλεν (ἤμ.), 4^{47}, $6^{6.71}$, 11^{51}, 12^{33}, 18^{32}; ἔμελλον, 7^{39}.

ἔμενεν (*v. l.* ἔμεινεν), 10^{40}.

ἐπίστευεν, 2^{24}; ἐπιστεύετε, $5^{46\,bis}$; ἐπίστευον, 7^{5}, $12^{11.37}$.

ἐπέκειτο, 11^{38}.

ἐποίει, 2^{23}, 5^{16}, 6^{2}.

ἐπορεύετο, 4^{50}.

ετήρουν, 17^{12}.

ἐτόλμα, 21^{12}.

ἔτρεχον, 20^{4}.

ἔφη, 1^{23}, 9^{38}.

ἐφοβοῦντο, 9^{22}.

ἐφίλει, 11^{36}, 15^{19}, 20^{2}.

ἠγάπα, 11^{5}, 13^{23}, 19^{26}, $21^{7.20}$; ἠγαπᾶτε, 8^{42}, 14^{28}.

ἠγωνίζοντο, 18^{36}.

ἠδύνατο (ἐδ.), 9^{33}, 11^{37}; ἠδύναντο, 12^{39}.

ἤθελες, 21^{18}; ἤθελεν, 7^{1}; ἤθελον, $6^{11.21}$, 7^{44}, 16^{19}.

ἠκολούθει, 6^{2}, 18^{15}.

ἤρχετο, 11^{29}; ἤρχοντο, 4^{30}, 6^{17}, 19^{3}, 20^{3}.

ἠρώτα, 4^{47}; ἠρώτων, $4^{31.40}$, 9^{15}, 12^{21}.

ἠσθένει, 4^{46}, 11^{2}.

ἴσχυον, 21^{6}.

κατέκειτο, 5^{3}.

παρεγίνοντο, 3^{23}.

περιεπάτεις, 21^{18}; περιεπάτει, 5^{9}, 7^{1}, 10^{23}, 11^{54}; περιεπάτουν, 6^{66}.

ὑπῆγον, 6^{21}, 12^{11}.

ὡμολόγουν, 12^{42}.

The total is 167. In Mt. the Imperfect occurs 94 times; in Mk. 228 times; in Lk. 259 times; in Acts 329 times.* If Jn. were as long as Mt., there would be proportionately 212 occurrences; if as long as Lk., 225; if as short as Mk., 133. Thus Jn.'s use of the tense, though more than twice as frequent as that of Mt., is considerably less than Lk.'s, and very much less than Mk.'s. The large amount of discourse in Jn. affords little opportunity for the use of the Imperfect. The last discourses, *chs.* 14–17, offer only 8 cases; while the bulk of the examples occur in *chs.* 4–12, where there are 118 cases.

Among Jn.'s Imperfects, the great frequency of ἔλεγεν, ἔλεγον attracts notice, and forms a bond of connexion with Mk.'s usage. Jn. has 46 occurrences, and Mk. 50; while in Mt. there are only 10, in Lk. 23, and in Acts 11.† It may be remarked that ἔλεγεν, ἔλεγον are very rare in LXX; Sir John Hawkins enumerating but 40 cases.

A frequent Aramaic usage, closely akin to the single use of the Participle above noticed, is the coupling of a Participle with the Substantive verb in description of past events. Thus, in place of saying 'he did' some action, Aramaic frequently says 'he *was doing*' it, thus pictorially representing the action as in process. The instances of this usage in the Aramaic of Dan. are commonly rendered both by LXX and Theodotion by a Greek *Imperfect*; though occasionally the rendering exactly copies the Aramaic by employing the Participle and Substantive verb. The following are the instances of the usage in description of past events:

	Aramaic.	*Literal rendering.*	*LXX.*	*Theodotion.*
2[31]	חָזֵה הֲוַיְתָ	'Thou wast seeing'.	ἑώρακας.	ἐθεώρεις.
2[34]	*id.*	*id.*	*id.*	*id.*
4[7]	חָזֵה הֲוֵית	'I was seeing'.	ἐκάθευδον.	ἐθεώρουν.
4[10]	*id.*	*id.*	ἐθεώρουν.	*id.*
5[19]	הֲווֹ זָאְעִין וְדָחֲלִין	'They were trembling and fearing'.	*vacat.*	ἦσαν τρέμοντες καὶ φοβούμενοι.

* Cf. *HS.*[2] p. 51, where the figure 163 for Jn. requires correction, as also the printer's error 12 for the occurrences of ἔφη, which should be 2.

† Cf. *HS.*[2] p. 12.

Aramaic.		*Literal rendering.*	*LXX.*	*Theodotion.*
5^{19}	דִּי־הֲוָא צָבֵא הֲוָה קָטֵל וְדִי־ הֲוָה צָבֵא הֲוָה מָחֵא וְדִי־הֲוָה צָבֵא הֲוָא מָרִים וְדִי־הֲוָה צָבֵא הֲוָא מַשְׁפִּל	'Whom he was willing he was killing, and whom he was willing he was smiting, and whom he was willing he was raising up, and whom he was wil- ling he was abasing'.	*om.*	οὓς ἠβούλετο αὐτὸς ἀνῄρει, καὶ οὓς ἠβού- λετο αὐτὸς ἔτυπτεν, καὶ οὓς ἠβούλετο αὐτὸς ὕψοι, καὶ οὓς ἠβού- λετο αὐτὸς ἐταπείνου.
6^{4}	הֲוָה מִתְנַצַּח עַל	'he was presiding over'.	*om.*	ἦν . . . ὑπέρ.
6^{5}	הֲווֹ בָעַיִן	'they were seeking'.	*diff.*	ἐζήτουν.
6^{11}	הֲוָא עָבֵד	'he was doing'.	ἐποίει.	ἦν ποιῶν.
6^{15}	הֲוָה מִשְׁתַּדַּר	'he was striving'.	*diff.*	ἠγωνίσατο.
7^{2}	חָזֵה הֲוֵית	'I was seeing'.	ἐθεώρουν.	ἐθεώρουν.
7^{4}	*id.*	*id.*	*id.*	*id.*
7^{6}	*id.*	*id.*	*id.*	*id.*
7^{7}	*id.*	*id.*	*id.*	*id.*
7^{8}	מִשְׁתַּכַּל הֲוֵית	'I was considering'.	*diff.*	προσενόουν.
7^{9}	חָזֵה הֲוֵית	'I was seeing'.	ἐθεώρουν.	ἐθεώρουν.
7^{11a}	*id.*	*id.*	*id.*	*id.*
7^{11b}	*id.*	*id.*	θεωρῶν ἤμην	*deest.*
7^{13}	*id.*	*id.*	ἐθεώρουν.	ἐθεώρουν.
7^{19}	הֲוָת שָׁנְיָה	'it was differing'.	διαφθείροντος (*sic*)	ἦν διαφέρον.
7^{21}	חָזֵה הֲוֵית	'I was seeing'.	κατενόουν.	ἐθεώρουν.

The use of the Substantive verb with the Participle of אמר 'he was saying' is frequent in Aramaic, and especially in Syriac, just as ἔλεγεν, ἔλεγον are particularly frequent in Mk. and Jn. אָמַר הֲוָא does not occur in Dan., the writer preferring the simple Participle אָמַר (cf. p. 88).

The Present sometimes = the Aramaic Participle as 'Futurum instans'.

The use of a Present to denote the *Futurum instans* is particularly frequent in Jn. with the verb ἔρχομαι. We may note the following instances:

$1^{15.27}$ ὁ ὀπίσω μου ἐρχόμενος.
1^{30} ὀπίσω μου ἔρχεται ἀνήρ.
$4^{21.23}$, $5^{25.28}$, $16^{2.25.32}$ ἔρχεται ὥρα.
4^{25} οἶδα ὅτι Μεσσίας ἔρχεται.
4^{35} τετραμηνός ἐστι καὶ ὁ θερισμὸς ἔρχεται.
5^{24} εἰς κρίσιν οὐκ ἔρχεται.
6^{14} ὁ προφήτης ὁ ἐρχόμενος εἰς τὸν κόσμον.
7^{27} ὁ δὲ Χριστὸς ὅταν ἔρχηται.
7^{41} Μὴ γὰρ ἐκ τῆς Γαλιλαίας ὁ Χριστὸς ἔρχεται;
7^{42} ἀπὸ Βηθλεὲμ . . . ἔρχεται ὁ Χριστός.
9^{4} ἔρχεται νύξ, ὅτε οὐδεὶς δύναται ἐργάζεσθαι.
11^{27} ὁ Χριστός, . . . ὁ εἰς τὸν κόσμον ἐρχόμενος.
14^{3} πάλιν ἔρχομαι.
$14^{18.28}$ ἔρχομαι πρὸς ὑμᾶς.
14^{30} ἔρχεται γὰρ ὁ τοῦ κόσμου ἄρχων.
21^{3} Ἐρχόμεθα καὶ ἡμεῖς σὺν σοί.
$21^{22.23}$ Ἐὰν αὐτὸν θέλω μένειν ἕως ἔρχομαι.

This use of ἔρχομαι is found also in the Synoptists, though with not nearly such frequency:—Mt. 3^{11} (Mk. 1^{7}, Lk. 3^{16}), Mt. 11^{3} (Lk. 7^{20}), Mt. 17^{11} (ἐλθών Mk. 9^{12}), Mt. 21^{5} (quotation), Mt. 24^{42} (Mk. 12^{35}), Mt. $24^{43.44}$ (Lk. $12^{39.40}$), Mt. 27^{49}, Lk. $17^{20\,bis}$, 23^{29}. As might be expected, it is particularly frequent in the Apocalypse—$1^{4.7.8}$, $2^{5.16}$, 3^{11}, 4^{8}, 9^{12}, 11^{14}, 16^{15}, $22^{7.12.20}$.

Instances of other Presents so used in Jn. are:

1^{29} Ἴδε ὁ ἀμνὸς τοῦ θεοῦ ὁ αἴρων τὴν ἁμαρτίαν τοῦ κόσμου.

12^{25} ὁ φιλῶν τὴν ψυχὴν αὐτοῦ ἀπολλύει αὐτήν (contrast Mt. 16^{25}, Mk. 8^{35}, Lk. 9^{24}, 17^{33}, ἀπολέσει αὐτήν).

17^{20} περὶ τῶν πιστευόντων διὰ τοῦ λόγου αὐτῶν εἰς ἐμέ.

In Aramaic (as also in Hebrew) the Participle is used as a *Futurum instans* with great frequency. In all cases cited above in which ἔρχομαι has the sense of a *Futurum instans*, Pesh. represents it by the Participle, except in 14[3], 16[2], where the future sense is expressed by the Imperfect. Moreover, in the only cases in Jn. where the Greek uses the Future ἐλεύσομαι, we find that Pesh. represents this by the Participle; 11[48] *ἐλεύσονται οἱ Ῥωμαῖοι καὶ ἀροῦσιν* = ܘܐܬܝܢ ܪܗܘܡܝܐ ܫܩܠܝܢ, lit. 'and the Romans coming, taking away'; 14[23] *πρὸς αὐτὸν ἐλευσόμεθα* = ܘܠܘܬܗ ܐܬܝܢ, lit. 'and to him we coming'; 16[7] *ὁ παράκλητος οὐ μὴ ἔλθῃ* (TR. *οὐκ ἐλεύσεται*) = ܦܪܩܠܛܐ ܠܐ ܐܬܐ, lit. 'the Paraclete not coming'. Cf. elsewhere, Mt. 9[15] *ἐλεύσονται δὲ ἡμέραι* = ܐܬܝܢ ܕܝܢ ܝܘܡܬܐ, lit. 'but days coming'; 25[31] *Ὅταν δὲ ἔλθῃ ὁ υἱὸς τοῦ ἀνθρώπου* = ܡܐ ܕܐܬܐ ܕܝܢ ܒܪܗ ܕܐܢܫܐ, lit. 'When the Son of man coming'; Mk. 8[38] *ὅταν ἔλθῃ ἐν τῇ δόξῃ τοῦ πατρὸς αὐτοῦ* = ܡܐ ܕܐܬܐ ܒܫܘܒܚܐ ܕܐܒܘܗܝ, lit. 'when He coming in the glory of His Father' (so Lk. 9[26]). Instances of the usage in the Aramaic of Dan. are, 2[13] וְדָתָא נֶפְקַת וְחַכִּימַיָּא מִתְקַטְּלִין 'So the decree went forth and the wise men being killed' (i.e. 'were about to be killed'); 4[22] וְלָךְ טָרְדִין מִן־אֲנָשָׁא 'And they driving thee from men' (i.e. 'they shall drive thee'); so *v.* [29]; 4[22] לָךְ מְצַבְּעִין 'they wetting thee' (i.e. 'they shall wet thee').

Verbal sequences.

1[39] *Ἔρχεσθε καὶ ὄψεσθε* 'Come, and ye shall see'. A similar sequence is idiomatic in Hebrew. Cf. Gen. 6[14], '*Make* (עֲשֵׂה) thee an ark . . . and *thou shalt pitch* (וְכָפַרְתָּ) it within and without with pitch'; so Targ. Onk., עִיבֵיד לָךְ . . . וְתִיחְפֵי יָתַהּ. 1 Sam. 15[3] לֵךְ וְהִכִּיתָה אֶת־עֲמָלֵק '*Go*, and *thou shalt smite* Amalek'; so Targ. Jon. אִיזֵיל וְתִימְחֵי יַת דְּבֵית עֲמָלֵק. See for further instances in Hebrew, Driver, *Tenses*, § 112. Cf. further in Aramaic, Ezr. 7[19.20], 'And the vessels that are given thee for the service of the house of thy God, *deliver thou* (הַשְׁלֵם) before the God of Jerusalem; and whatsoever more is needful . . . *thou shalt bestow* (תִּנְתֵּן) out of the king's treasure house'. *Acta Thomae* (p. ܪܨܒ), 'But *conduct yourselves* (ܐܬܕܒܪܘ ܐܢܬܘܢ) in all humility and temperance and purity, and in hope in God, and *ye shall become* (ܘܗܘܘ ܐܢܬܘܢ) His household-servants'. This form of sequence is not (apart from translations from the Hebrew) so characteristic of Aramaic as it is of Hebrew, except where the sequence is clearly to be regarded (as in the last instance) as the *result* of the preceding Imperative. This, however, is clearly implied in the expression Ἔρχεσθε καὶ ὄψεσθε. So 16^{24}, αἰτεῖτε καὶ λήμψεσθε.

Change of construction after a Participle is seen in two passages in Jn.—1^{32} Τεθέαμαι τὸ πνεῦμα καταβαῖνον . . . καὶ ἔμεινεν ἐπ' αὐτόν, and 5^{44} λαμβάνοντες, καὶ . . . οὐ ζητεῖτε. These are exactly analogous to a frequently-used Hebrew idiom; e.g. Ezek. 22^{3} עִיר שֹׁפֶכֶת דָּם . . . וְעָשְׂתָה גִלּוּלִים, lit. 'a city shedding blood . . . and makes idols' (i.e. 'that sheds . . . and makes', or 'shedding . . . and making'); Ps. 18^{34} מְשַׁוֶּה רַגְלַי כָּאַיָּלוֹת וְעַל בָּמֹתַי יַעֲמִידֵנִי, lit. 'Making my feet like the harts', and on my heights He sets me' (i.e. 'Who makes . . . and sets'); Gen. 27^{33} הַצָּד צַיִד וַיָּבֵא, lit. 'the one hunting venison and brought it' (i.e. 'who hunted . . . and brought'). See other cases in Driver, *Tenses*, § 117. In accordance with this usage, we should render καταβαῖνον . . . καὶ ἔμεινεν in Jn. 1^{32}, not as R.V. 'descending . . .; and it abode', but 'descending . . ., and *abiding*'; and λαμβάνοντες, καὶ . . . οὐ ζητεῖτε in 5^{44}, 'receiving . . . and *seeking not*', or 'who receive . . . and seek not'. This usage is remarkably frequent in the Apocalypse, and the cases have been collected and discussed by Dr. Charles in his Commentary i, p. cxlv; cf. 1^{5} τῷ ἀγαπῶντι ἡμᾶς . . . καὶ ἐποίησεν ἡμᾶς 'Unto Him that loved us . . . and hath made us, &c.' (not as R.V. 'and He made us', after semi-colon); $15^{2.3}$ ἑστῶτας . . . ἔχοντας κιθάρας . . . καὶ ᾄδουσιν 'standing . . . having harps . . . and *singing*' (A.V., R.V. 'And they sing', after full stop, are incorrect). Other cases may be seen in $2^{2.9.20.23}$, 3^{9}, 7^{14}, 13^{11}, $14^{2.3}$.*

The construction is rather Hebrew than Aramaic, though we may note Dan. 4^{22} וְלָךְ טָרְדִין מִן־אֲנָשָׁא . . . וְעִשְׂבָּא כְתוֹרִין לָךְ יְטַעֲמוּן

* Not, however, (with Dr. Charles) 1^{18} καὶ ὁ ζῶν· καὶ ἐγενόμην νεκρός, or 20^{4} (with rejection of οἵτινες as an editorial gloss) τὰς ψυχὰς τῶν πεπελεκισμένων . . . καὶ οὐ προσεκύνησαν τὸ θηρίον. An essential element in the Hebrew construction is that the finite verb expresses *the proper sequence of the Participle*, which may be actually a sequence in time, so that the ו connecting the finite verb with its antecedent expresses the sense '*and then*', or as introducing the direct result, '*and so*'; or a sequence in description in which, though the fact described may properly speaking be coeval with its antecedent, it follows naturally in the gradual unfolding of the picture (especially frequent in description of types of character). We do *not* find cases in which the sequence describes an event *actually prior in time to its antecedent*, as would be the case in the two passages in question. For these quite a different construction would be employed in Hebrew.

'And they shall drive thee (lit. driving thee) from men . . . and with grass like oxen they shall feed thee'. We have it in Jn. 1[32] Pal. Syr. . . . ܚܙܝܬ . . . ܘܫܪܐ ܥܠܘܗܝ, Pesh. ܕܚܙܝܬ . . . ܘܩܘܝܡܬ ܥܠܘܗܝ. In 5[44] ζητεῖτε is represented by the Participle; Pal. Syr. ܐܢܬܘܢ ܕܡܩܒܠܝܢ . . . ܒܥܝܢ ܐܢܬܘܢ ܩܒܠܝܢ, Pesh. ܡܩܒܠܝܢ ܐܢܬܘܢ . . . ܠܐ ܒܥܝܢ ܐܢܬܘܢ. In the O.T. passages it is usual, both in Targ. and Pesh., to resolve the opening Hebrew Participle into a Perfect or Imperfect preceded by the relative דְּ, and then to follow it by another Perfect or Imperfect.

CHAPTER VI

NEGATIVES

THE Semitic languages do not for the most part possess negative expressions such as *none, never*, but express them by using the corresponding positives coupled with the simple negative *not*. Thus e.g. Hebrew כֹּל . . . לֹא, Aramaic כֹּל . . . לָא, ܟܠ . . . ܠܐ 'any . . . not' = 'none'; or, since Heb. אִישׁ, Aram. אֱנָשׁ, ܐܢܫ, 'a man' is commonly used in the sense 'any one', '*none*' may be expressed by this term with preceding negative. So in Heb., Gen. 2^{5} כֹּל שִׂיחַ הַשָּׂדֶה טֶרֶם יִהְיֶה בָאָרֶץ, lit. '*any* plant of the field was *not* yet in the earth' (i.e. '*no* plant . . . was yet, &c.'); Gen. 4^{15} לְבִלְתִּי הַכּוֹת־אֹתוֹ כָּל־מֹצְאוֹ, lit. 'for the *not*-smiting him of *all* finding him' (i.e. 'that *none* finding him should smite him'); Ex. 12^{16} כָּל־מְלָאכָה לֹא־יֵעָשֶׂה, lit. '*all* work shall *not* be done' (i.e. '*no* work shall be done'); Gen. 31^{50} אֵין אִישׁ עִמָּנוּ, lit. 'there is *not a man* with us' (i.e. '*no one* is with us'); Gen. 41^{44} בִּלְעָדֶיךָ לֹא־יָרִים אִישׁ אֶת־יָדוֹ 'independently of thee *a man* shall *not* lift up his hand' (i.e. '*none* shall lift up, &c.'). In Aram., Dan. 2^{35} כָּל־אֲתַר לָא הִשְׁתְּכַח לְהוֹן '*any* place was *not* found for them' (i.e. '*no* place was found'); Dan. 4^{6} כָּל־רָז לָא אָנֵס לָךְ, lit. '*every* secret does *not* trouble thee' (i.e. '*no* secret troubles thee'); Dan. 2^{10} לָא־אִיתַי אֱנָשׁ עַל־יַבֶּשְׁתָּא דִּי מִלַּת מַלְכָּא יוּכַל לְהַחֲוָיָה, lit. 'there is *not a man* on earth that can show the king's matter' (i.e. '*no one* on earth can show, &c.').

We find the Semitism *πᾶς* (*πᾶν*) . . . *μή* = '*none*', '*nothing*', in Jn. in two passages: 6^{39} *ἵνα πᾶν ὃ δέδωκέν μοι μὴ ἀπολέσω ἐξ αὐτοῦ*, 12^{46} *ἵνα πᾶς ὁ πιστεύων εἰς ἐμὲ ἐν τῇ σκοτίᾳ μὴ μείνῃ*. *πᾶς . . . οὐ* (*μή*) is also found in Mt. 24^{22} = Mk. 13^{20} *οὐκ ἂν ἐσώθη πᾶσα σάρξ*, Lk. 1^{37} *οὐκ ἀδυνατήσει παρὰ τοῦ Θεοῦ πᾶν ῥῆμα*, Rom. 3^{20}, Gal. 2^{16} (both quotations of Ps. 143^{2}), Eph. 4^{29}, 5^{5}, 2 Pet. 1^{20}, 1 Jn. 2^{21} (cf. 2^{23}, $3^{6\,bis.\,9}$, 4^{3}, 5^{18}, where the renderings 'every one . . . not', 'no one' are equally legitimate), Apoc. 7^{16}, 18^{22}, 21^{27}, 22^{3}.

'*No one*' is expressed by οὐ . . . ἄνθρωπος in Jn. 3[27] Οὐ δύναται ἄνθρωπος λαμβάνειν οὐδὲν ἐὰν μὴ κτλ., 5[7] ἄνθρωπον οὐκ ἔχω ἵνα . . . βάλῃ με εἰς τὴν κολυμβήθραν, 7[46] Οὐδέποτε ἐλάλησεν οὕτως ἄνθρωπος.* In Mk. 11[2] we find ἐφ' ὃν οὐδεὶς οὔπω ἀνθρώπων ἐκάθισεν, 12[14] οὐ γὰρ βλέπεις εἰς πρόσωπον ἀνθρώπων (but here there is a sense of antithesis to τὴν ὁδὸν τοῦ Θεοῦ following), but elsewhere in the Synoptists there seems to be no case of οὐ . . . ἄνθρωπος.

'*Never*' is expressed in Heb. and Aram. 'not . . . for ever'; cf. in Heb. Ps. 30[7] בַּל־אֶמּוֹט לְעוֹלָם 'I shall never be moved'; Ps. 31[2], 71[1] אַל־אֵבוֹשָׁה לְעוֹלָם 'let me never be put to shame'; Ps. 119[93] לְעוֹלָם לֹא אֶשְׁכַּח פִּקּוּדֶיךָ 'I will never forget Thy commandments'; Isa. 25[2] לְעוֹלָם לֹא יִבָּנֶה 'it shall never be rebuilt'; in Aram., Dan. 2[44] דִּי לְעָלְמִין לָא תִתְחַבַּל 'which shall never be destroyed'; *Acta Thomae* (p. ܡܟܕ) ܘܢܗܘܘܢ ܒܡܠܟܘܬܐ ܕܥܡܗ ܠܥܠܡ ܠܐ ܥܒܪܐ 'and they shall be with Him in the kingdom which never passes away'; *id.* (p. ܪ̈ܝ) ܗܢܐ ܕܝܢ ܡܫܬܘܬܐ ܠܥܠܡ ܠܐ ܥܒܪܐ 'but this banquet shall never pass away'.

Similarly, οὐ μὴ . . . εἰς τὸν αἰῶνα occurs several times in Jn. in the sense '**never**': 4[14] οὐ μὴ διψήσει εἰς τὸν αἰῶνα, 8[51] θάνατον οὐ μὴ θεωρήσῃ εἰς τὸν αἰῶνα, 8[52] οὐ μὴ γεύσηται θανάτου εἰς τὸν αἰῶνα, 10[28] οὐ μὴ ἀπόλωνται εἰς τὸν αἰῶνα, 11[26] οὐ μὴ ἀποθάνῃ εἰς τὸν αἰῶνα, 13[8] οὐ μὴ νίψῃς μου τοὺς πόδας εἰς τὸν αἰῶνα. Cf. also 9[32] ἐκ τοῦ αἰῶνος οὐκ ἠκούσθη. The phrase is only found elsewhere in N.T. in Mt. 21[19] Οὐ μηκέτι ἐκ σοῦ καρπὸς γένηται εἰς τὸν αἰῶνα = Mk. 11[14], Mk. 3[29] οὐκ ἔχει ἄφεσιν εἰς τὸν αἰῶνα, 1 Cor. 8[13] οὐ μὴ φάγω κρέα εἰς τὸν αἰῶνα.

To express '*lest*' Hebrew has the single term פֶּן. To this in Aramaic corresponds the compound term דִּילְמָא (Syr. ܕܰܠܡܳܐ), formed from דִּי + לְמָא, Targ. דִּלְמָא from דְּ + לְמָא, i.e. lit. 'since why?' This properly introduces a rhetorical question deprecating the taking of a certain course (cf. *Oxford Heb. Lex.*, p. 554 *a*; אֲשֶׁר לָמָּה Dan. 1[10], שַׁלָּמָה Song 1[7], are instances of the equivalent Heb. phrase in late style). This expression occurs once in Biblical Aram., Ezr. 7[23], and is the regular equivalent of Heb. פֶּן in the Targg. דִּי לָא 'that . . . not' = 'lest' in the Aram. of Dan. 2[18], 6[9.18]; and in Pesh. ܕܠܐ 'that . . . not' is used indifferently with ܕܰܠܡܳܐ 'since why?' in the sense '*lest*' as the equivalent of Heb. פֶּן.

* ἄνθρωπος = τις, like indefinite אנש, is also found in Jn. 3[1.4], 7[23.51].

We have already remarked that in Jn. ἵνα μή is regularly employed to the exclusion of μήποτε. The occurrences, 18 in all (as against Mt. 8, Mk. 5, Lk. 8), are as follows: $3^{16.20}$, 4^{15}, 5^{14}, $6^{12.39.50}$, 7^{23}, $11^{37.50}$, $12^{35.40.42.46}$, 16^{1}, $18^{28.36}$, 19^{31}. These occurrences of 'that . . . not' do not all carry the sense '*lest*'; but this force is clear in the following:

3^{20} οὐκ ἔρχεται πρὸς τὸ φῶς, ἵνα μὴ ἐλεγχθῇ τὰ ἔργα αὐτοῦ.

5^{14} μηκέτι ἁμάρτανε, ἵνα μὴ χεῖρόν σοί τι γένηται.

7^{23} εἰ περιτομὴν λαμβάνει ἄνθρωπος ἐν σαββάτῳ ἵνα μὴ λυθῇ ὁ νόμος Μωυσέως.

12^{35} περιπατεῖτε ὡς τὸ φῶς ἔχετε, ἵνα μὴ σκοτία ὑμᾶς καταλάβῃ.

12^{40} ἵνα μὴ ἴδωσιν τοῖς ὀφθαλμοῖς.

12^{42} ἀλλὰ διὰ τοὺς Φαρισαίους οὐχ ὡμολόγουν ἵνα μὴ ἀποσυνάγωγοι γένωνται.

16^{1} ταῦτα λελάληκα ὑμῖν ἵνα μὴ σκανδαλισθῆτε.

18^{28} αὐτοὶ οὐκ εἰσῆλθον εἰς τὸ πραιτώριον, ἵνα μὴ μιανθῶσιν.

18^{36} οἱ ὑπηρέται οἱ ἐμοὶ ἠγωνίζοντο ἄν, ἵνα μὴ παραδοθῶ τοῖς Ἰουδαίοις.

19^{31} ἵνα μὴ μείνῃ ἐπὶ τοῦ σταυροῦ τὰ σώματα.

μήποτε, which never occurs in Jn., is found in Mt. 8 times, Mk. *twice*, Lk. 6 times.

A striking proof that Jn.'s ἵνα μή = 'lest' represents the Aramaic דְּלָא is to be seen in the quotation from Isa. 6^{10} which occurs in Jn. 12^{40}. In this quotation the Heb. uses פֶּן 'lest', and this is represented in LXX by μήποτε, but in Pesh. by ܕܠܐ 'that . . . not'.

Heb.	פֶּן־יִרְאֶה בְעֵינָיו
LXX	μήποτε ἴδωσιν τοῖς ὀφθαλμοῖς
Pesh.	ܕܠܐ ܢܚܙܘܢ ܒܥܝܢܝܗܘܢ

The quotation is given in Mt. 13^{15} in the *ipsissima verba* of LXX; while Mk. 4^{12}, quoting more freely, yet has the μήποτε of LXX, μήποτε ἐπιστρέψωσιν καὶ ἀφεθῇ αὐτοῖς (i.e. פֶּן . . . שָׁב וְרָפָא לוֹ). Jn., however, rendering ἵνα μὴ ἴδωσιν τοῖς ὀφθαλμοῖς, departs from the Heb. and LXX phrases in order to use an Aramaic phrase which is actually employed in the rendering of Pesh. What evidence could prove more cogently that his Greek translates an Aramaic original?

CHAPTER VII

MISTRANSLATIONS OF THE ORIGINAL ARAMAIC OF THE GOSPEL

The most weighty form of evidence in proof that a document is a translation from another language is the existence of difficulties or peculiarities of language which can be shown to find their solution in the theory of mistranslation from the assumed original language. There are a considerable number of such in the Fourth Gospel, and some of them have already been noticed in the preceding discussion. These may first be summarized.

The particle דְ with a relative sense mistranslated by *ἵνα* or *ὅτι*.

> *ἵνα* for דְ = 'who, which', 1^{8}, 5^{7}, $6^{30.50}$, 9^{36}, 14^{16} (cf. p. 75).
> *ὅτι* for דְ = 'who', 8^{45}, 9^{17}; less certainly in 1^{16} (cf. p. 76).
> *ἵνα* for דְ = 'when' (properly 'which . . . in it'), 12^{23}, 13^{1}, $16^{2.32}$ (cf. p. 77).
> *ὅτι* for דְ = 'when', 9^{8}, 12^{41} (cf. p. 78).

דְ = 'because, inasmuch as', mistranslated as a relative, $1^{4.13}$ (cf. pp. 29. 34).

1^{5}, 12^{35}. *καταλαμβάνειν* = קַבֵּיל 'take, receive', a misunderstanding of אַקְבֵּיל 'darken' (cf. p. 29).

1^{9}. *ἦν* = subst. verb הֲוָא, probably a misreading of הוּא = *ἐκεῖνος* (cf. p. 33).

The ambiguity of the particle דְ has, as we have seen in the cases noted above, caused difficulty to the translator. There are several other passages in which, though the relative force of the particle is clear, the fact that it lacks expression of gender and number has led to misapprehension. These may conveniently be taken together.

10^{29}. *ὁ πατήρ μου ὃ δέδωκέν μοι πάντων μεῖζόν ἐστιν.* This reading has the support of B* 𝔏 𝔈 (boh) 𝔊, and is therefore adopted by

WH. It can only be rendered, 'As for My Father, that which He hath given Me is greater than all'. This is explained by Westcott to mean that 'the faithful regarded in their unity, as a complete body, are stronger than every opposing power. This is their essential character, and "no one is able . . ." Cf. 1 Jn. 5[4].' The whole context cries out against the falsity of this exegesis. Stress has been laid in the parable upon the weakness of the sheep, their liability to be scattered and injured by the powers of evil, and their utter dependence upon the Good Shepherd. In the parallel clause their safeguard is stated to consist in the fact that 'no one is able to snatch them out of My Father's hand'. But, if Westcott is correct, this would seem to be merely supplementary to the thought of the power of the flock regarded as a unity—which is incredible. Again, the phrase 'greater than all' has, on this text, to be explained as 'stronger than every opposing power'; yet what authority is afforded by the context for thus limiting its scope? Clearly the expression, as it stands without limitation, is applicable to God alone. There can be no doubt that the sense intended is that which is given by the less authenticated reading, adopted by R.V., *ὁ πατήρ μου ὃς δέδωκέν μοι μείζων πάντων ἐστίν*, which supplies the reason for the parallel clause which follows. Yet there can be little doubt that WH. are correct in regarding the more difficult reading as original, and the more natural one as a correction of it; since, had the latter been original, it is inconceivable that the former could have arisen out of it. Its origin may be traced to an unintelligent rendering of the Aramaic אָבִי דִיהַב לִי רַבָּא מִן־כֹּלָּא, in which דְּ . . . רַבָּא may be taken to mean either ὃς . . . *μείζων* or ὃ . . . *μεῖζον*. Possibly the first draft of the translation rendered דְּ only as a neuter (ὃ . . . *μείζων*, ℵ L Ψ), and the other readings are corrections dictated by regard for grammar.

This explanation of the anomaly offered by the Greek might be regarded as less than convincing if the passage stood alone. There are, however, other passages in which the text is similarly and obviously at fault. In 17[11] we read, *τήρησον αὐτοὺς ἐν τῷ ὀνόματί σου ᾧ δέδωκάς μοι, ἵνα ὦσιν ἓν καθὼς ἡμεῖς*, and similarly in *v.*[12], *ἐγὼ ἐτήρουν αὐτοὺς ἐν τῷ ὀνόματί σου ᾧ δέδωκάς μοι.* Is it possible to believe that the sense intended is, 'Thy name which Thou hast given Me'? Westcott may well observe on *v.*[11], 'The phrase is very remarkable, and has no exact parallel except in *v.*[12]. Clearly the object of δέδωκας is established by *v.*[2] ἵνα πᾶν ὃ δέδωκας αὐτῷ δώσει αὐτοῖς ζωὴν αἰώνιον, *v.*[6] Ἐφανέρωσά σου τὸ ὄνομα τοῖς ἀνθρώποις οὓς ἔδωκάς μοι ἐκ τοῦ κόσμου, *v.*[24] Πατήρ, ὃ δέδωκάς μοι, θέλω ἵνα ὅπου εἰμὶ ἐγὼ κἀκεῖνοι ὦσιν μετ' ἐμοῦ, the whole burden of the prayer being the commendation of the disciples to the Father on the ground that it is He who has given them to the Son. Thus οὓς δέδωκάς μοι, the less well attested reading in both *v.*[11] and *v.*[12], certainly gives the meaning originally intended; yet in the Greek it must be regarded as a correction of the much more strongly attested reading ᾧ κτλ. (ℵ A B C L Y Ψ, &c.). The solution is again found in the ambiguity of the relative דְּ. There is another reading ὃ (D* U X 157 *al. pauc.*), which may, like ὃ in 10[29], be conjectured to be the original rendering of the genderless דְּ by a neuter, which easily lent itself to correction into ᾧ.

That the translator was capable of reproducing דְּ by a neuter, and then completing the relative by a masculine, is proved by 17[24], Πατήρ, ὃ δέδωκάς μοι, θέλω ἵνα ὅπου εἰμὶ ἐγὼ κἀκεῖνοι ὦσιν μετ' ἐμοῦ, where ὃ, representing 'those whom', is reinforced by κἀκεῖνοι. Similarly, we read in 17[2], ἵνα πᾶν ὃ δέδωκας αὐτῷ δώσει αὐτοῖς ζωὴν αἰώνιον. Here πᾶν ὃ = the neutral כֹּלָּא דְּ, which may stand in Aramaic for 'all (*or* every one) who', or 'all which'. The same phrase is to be seen again in 6[37], πᾶν ὃ δίδωσίν μοι ὁ πατὴρ πρὸς ἐμὲ ἥξει, and here the sense intended is 'every one who' (cf. the following καὶ τὸν ἐρχόμενον πρός με κτλ.), not, 'everything which'. In 6[39] the neutral collective conception is continued throughout the sentence—ἵνα πᾶν ὃ δέδωκέν μοι μὴ ἀπολέσω ἐξ αὐτοῦ ἀλλὰ ἀναστήσω αὐτὸ τῇ ἐσχάτῃ ἡμέρᾳ. In Hebrew there is a similar usage of כֻּלּוֹ with neutral suffix—'*the whole of it*' = 'all of them', 'every one'. So Isa. 1[23], 'Thy princes are rebellious, and companions of thieves; *all of it* loveth bribes, &c.'; Jer. 6[13], 'For from their least unto their greatest *all of it* maketh unjust gain'; cf. Ex. 14[7], Isa. 9[16], 15[3], Jer. 8[6.10], &c.

Besides these instances of mistranslation we may notice the following passages:

1[15]. Ὁ ὀπίσω μου ἐρχόμενος ἔμπροσθέν μου γέγονεν, ὅτι πρῶτός μου ἦν. Dr. Ball (*Expos. Times*, xxi, p. 92) remarks that 'This testimony, virtually repeated in *vv.*$^{27.30}$, is most naturally understood as a reference to the fact that our Lord's influence was to displace, or was already displacing, that of His Forerunner (cf. 3^{30}). Instead of *hath become*, we should rather have expected *will become* or *is to become*.' He suggests therefore that the Greek γέγονεν may be due to the translator's having supplied a wrong vowel to the Aramaic הוי, reading it as הֲוֵי *hăwê* (a by-form of the Perfect הֲוָה *hăwā*) instead of הָוֵי *hāwê* (the Participle) which would bear the sense 'is becoming' or 'is about to become'. Further, ὅτι πρῶτός μου ἦν 'because He was before me' may be due to a misreading קֳדָמַי *ḳodāmay* of an original קַדְמַי *ḳadmay*, 'first'. Thus the original text may have run—

דְּאָתֵי בַּתְרַי קֳדָמַי הֲוֵי
מְטוּל דְּקַדְמַי הוּא

'He who is coming after me, before me will become;
Because He was the first (of all)':

i.e. because He existed 'in the Beginning'. The assonance between the kindred words קֳדָמַי 'before me' and קַדְמַי 'first' offers a characteristic Semitic word-play.

1^{29} Ἴδε ὁ ἀμνὸς τοῦ Θεοῦ ὁ αἴρων τὴν ἁμαρτίαν τοῦ κόσμου. Dr. Ball (*op. cit. supra*), while making some valuable remarks about the Aramaic original of the phrase ὁ ἀμνὸς τοῦ θεοῦ, questions whether the statement 'which taketh away (*or* beareth) the sins of the world' is original, on the ground that it 'antedates that doctrine of the suffering Messiah, which only came home to the Apostles themselves after the Resurrection (Lk. 24$^{21.26}$)', and 'does not well harmonize with the general tone of the Baptist's teaching about the Messiah, as reported by the Synoptists (Mt. 3)'. He therefore conjectures that the words 'may be supposed to have been added by some editor of the Greek text who recollected Isa. 53^{7}, and who wrote in the light of a later stage of Christian knowledge'.

It may be argued, on the contrary, that the whole of Jn.'s presentation of the Baptist's witness, including these words, is fully in accord with the Synoptic narrative. It is agreed that the reference of ὁ αἴρων κτλ. is to Isa. 53, i.e. the culminating passage referring to the mission of the righteous Servant of Yahweh which forms the main theme of the prophecy of Deutero-Isaiah, *chs.* 40–55, with which *ch.* 61 (the opening passage of which is applied by our Lord to Himself in Lk. $4^{16\text{ff.}}$), though probably the work of a later prophet, stands in close association as further drawing out the mission of the ideal Servant. The Baptist's description of his own function, 'I am the voice of one crying, &c.' (common to Jn. and the Synoptists) is drawn from Isa. 40^3; and it is therefore reasonable to assume that in preparing for his mission he had made a special study of Isa. 40 ff., and was impressed with the conception of the ideal Servant of Yahweh which these chapters contain. That he regarded himself as but the forerunner of a greater One is a second fact common to all four Gospels; and the relation of Isa. 40^3 to its sequel might in itself serve to justify the conjecture that this greater One was pictured by him as fulfilling the ideal of the Servant. We are not, however, limited to conjecture. Our Lord's reply to the disciples of the Baptist whom he sent to inquire whether He was really ὁ ἐρχόμενος (Mt. 11^{2-6} = Lk. 7^{18-23}) took the practical shape of performing acts of mercy in their presence; and His answer, based on the things which they had seen and heard, leaves us in no doubt that the evidence suited to carry conviction to the Baptist's mind was *His fulfilment of the acts which had been predicted of the ideal Servant.* We may compare especially τυφλοὶ ἀναβλέπουσιν with Isa. 42^7 'to open blind eyes' (part of the Servant's mission),* 61^1 'to proclaim . . . the opening (of eyes) to them that are blind', 35^5 'Then the eyes of the blind shall be opened'†; χωλοὶ περιπατοῦσιν with Isa. 35^6 'then shall the lame man leap as an hart'; πτωχοὶ εὐαγγελίζονται with 61^1 'Yahweh hath anointed me to preach good tidings to the poor'. The gentle words of reproof with which the message ends—καὶ μακάριός ἐστιν ὃς ἐὰν μὴ σκανδαλισθῇ ἐν ἐμοί—would naturally remind the Baptist not to range himself with those of whom it had been written, 'Like as many were appalled at thee, &c.' (Isa. 52^{14}), and 'as one

* The reference in Isa. is of course to the removal of *moral* blindness; but it should be unnecessary to recall the fact that our Lord's physical miracles had always their moral analogue, and depended for their performance upon faith in the recipient.

† Isa. 35, which is late, is based upon Isa. 40 ff., and develops its thought.

from whom men hide their face, he was despised and we esteemed him not' (Isa. 53^{3}).

From these considerations we deduce the conclusion that the fact that our Lord was to fulfil the rôle of the ideal Servant, though not understood by the Apostles, *was in some measure realized by the Baptist.* If this was so, since the atoning work pictured in Isa. 53 formed the culmination of that rôle, can it be maintained that the words *ὁ αἴρων τὴν ἁμαρτίαν τοῦ κόσμου* are improbable in the Baptist's mouth? In the verses which follow, Jn. 1^{30-34}, he states that he had no previous knowledge of Him Whose coming he was heralding, and did not know how to recognize Him till it was Divinely revealed to him that the sign would be the descent of the Spirit upon Him. This revelation was surely deduced from Isa. 42^{1} (the first great passage descriptive of the Servant's mission), where Yahweh states, 'I have put My Spirit upon him'; and Isa. 61^{1} where the Servant is represented as saying, 'The Spirit of the Lord Yahweh is upon me'.* Thus evidence unites in indicating that it was the coming of the ideal Servant of Yahweh that the Baptist believed himself to be heralding.†

* Cf. the way in which the heavenly announcement at the Baptism, Mt. 3^{17} and parallels, is modelled on Isa. 42^{1} as quoted in Mt. 12^{18} (noted by Allen, *ad loc.*).

† It is perhaps significant that (apart from Jn. 3^{28}) the title *Χριστός* 'Messiah' is not employed by the Baptist. His titles are *ὁ ὀπίσω μου ἐρχόμενος* Mt. 3^{11}, Jn. 1^{27}, *ὁ ἐρχόμενος* simply Mt. 11^{3} = Lk. 7^{20}, *ὁ ἀμνὸς τοῦ Θεοῦ* Jn. $1^{29.36}$, *ὁ υἱὸς τοῦ Θεοῦ* Jn. 1^{34}. The fact is evident that Deutero-Isaiah's conception of the suffering Servant did not enter into the popular Messianic expectation of the time (cf. a sermon by the writer on *The Old Testament Conception of Atonement fulfilled by Christ*, published by the Oxford University Press, pp. 10 f.). Very possibly the Baptist avoided the title 'Messiah' in order that he might not mistakenly be supposed to be heralding the political Messiah of popular expectation. That he was not alone in fixing his hopes upon the ideals of Deutero-Isaiah rather than upon those associated with the Messianic King is proved by the Birth-narrative of Lk., where Simeon is described (2^{25}) as *προσδεχόμενος παράκλησιν τοῦ Ἰσραήλ*—a clear reference to 'Comfort ye, comfort ye my people', which forms the burden of Deutero-Isaiah's prophecy (Isa. 40^{1}; cf. also 49^{13}, 51^{3}, and in Trito-Isaiah 57^{18}, 61^{2}, $66^{11,13}$). Thus, when this latter holds the infant Saviour in his arms and uses the words, *εἶδον οἱ ὀφθαλμοί μου τὸ σωτήριόν σου . . . φῶς εἰς ἀποκάλυψιν ἐθνῶν*, he has clearly in mind the passage in the second great description of the ideal Servant where the words occur, 'I will give thee for *a light to the Gentiles*, that thou mayest be *My salvation* (*or*, that My salvation may be) unto the end of the earth' (cf. also *καὶ δόξαν λαοῦ σου Ἰσραήλ* with Isa. 46^{13}, 'and I will place *salvation* in Zion *for Israel My glory*'). His knowledge of the third and fourth Servant-passages, where the Servant is pictured as meeting opposition, persecution, and death (Isa. 50^{4-7},

What, however, is the origin of the expression 'Lamb *of God*' as used by the Baptist, and what is its precise force? The phrase does not occur in Isa. 53, where *v.* 7, which brings in the simile of a lamb, simply says that the Servant was 'like a lamb that is led to the slaughter (not, 'to the sacrifice'), and like a ewe (LXX ἀμνός) that before her shearers is dumb'. The words ὁ αἴρων κτλ. are based, not on this verse but on *v.* 11, 'and their iniquities *he* shall bear', where the simile is dropped and 'My righteous Servant' preceding forms the back-reference of the emphatic '*he*'. 'The Lamb *of God*' suggests the sense, 'the Lamb *provided by* God' as a fitting offering, which reminds us of Gen. 22⁸, 'God shall provide Himself a lamb for a burnt offering'; and combining *v.* 7 and *v.* 11 of Isa. 53 with *v.* 10 which states that it was Yahweh who was pleased to bruise him, and allowing for the influence of Gen. 22⁸, we may perhaps consider that we have accounted for the use of the phrase.

A more probable solution, however, is suggested by Dr. Ball's remark that Heb. טְלֵה *ṭālê* 'lamb' has come in its Aram. form טַלְיָא *ṭalyā* to mean 'child', 'boy', 'young man', 'servant'.* In the last sense it denotes in Pesh. e.g. Abraham's 'young men' (Gen. 22³; so also in Targ. Jerus.), the priest's 'servant' (1 Sam. 2^13.15), and the centurion's 'servant' (Mt. 8^6.13). Thus ὁ ἀμνὸς τοῦ Θεοῦ may stand for טַלְיָא דֵּאלָהָא, intended primarily to bear the sense, 'the *Servant* of God', i.e. Yahweh's righteous Servant who, according to Isa. 53^11.12, was to bear the sins of many. If this is so, there may well be a word-play in the choice of the term טַלְיָא, suggesting as it does the *lamb-like* or sinless character of the ideal Servant; thus, 'the *Lamb* of God' is a rendering by no means excluded by this new interpretation. Further, since טַלְיָא also bears the sense 'child', it is not unlikely that the thought of 'the *Child* of God' is also present.† In *vv.* 31–34 the sign by which

52^13—53^12), obliges him, moreover, to warn the holy Mother that the child is destined to become a σημεῖον ἀντιλεγόμενον, and to predict καὶ σοῦ δὲ αὐτῆς τὴν ψυχὴν διελεύσεται ῥομφαία. Anna the prophetess and her circle seem also to have rested in the same hope (cf. Lk. 2^36–38). All this is not a later invention; it bears upon its face the unmistakable stamp of historical truth.

* The fem. of this word, *ṭ^elîthā* 'maiden', is familiar to every one from Mk. 5^41.

† Dr. Ball renders the assumed Aram. original, 'Behold the Young Servant *or* Child of God', and does not bring the expression into connexion with Deutero-Isaiah.

the Baptist was to recognize ὁ ἐρχόμενος, viz. the descent and abiding on Him of the Spirit, was, as we have already remarked, the sign of Yahweh's ideal Servant. After witnessing this, the Baptist says, κἀγὼ ἑώρακα καὶ μεμαρτύρηκα ὅτι οὗτός ἐστιν ὁ υἱὸς τοῦ Θεοῦ. It is not impossible that ὁ υἱὸς τοῦ Θεοῦ may again represent the Aram. טַלְיָא דֶאלָהָא, interpreted as 'the *Child* of God' but intended primarily to mean 'the *Servant* of God'. A sufficient explanation for the translation of the same term by ἀμνός in *v.*[29] but by υἱός in *v.*[34] may be found in the difference of context, the first passage picturing the טַלְיָא as a sacrifice, the second as baptizing with the Holy Spirit.

If it be objected against this explanation of ἀμνός = טַלְיָא in the sense 'Servant' that the term used in Deutero-Isaiah to denote the ideal Servant is regularly Heb. עֶבֶד = Aram. עַבְדָּא, properly 'bond-servant', it may be replied that the choice of טַלְיָא rather than עַבְדָּא is sufficiently explained by the word-play involved. While עַבְדָּא = δοῦλος, טַלְיָא = παῖς. Both Greek terms are indifferently used in LXX to render the עֶבֶד of Deutero-Isaiah, but the preference is for παῖς (δοῦλος in 49[3,5]; παῖς in 42[1], 49[6], 50[10], 52[13]); and it is παῖς which is used of our Lord as the ideal Servant in Acts 3[13], 4[27,30].

2[22]. Ὅτε οὖν ἠγέρθη ἐκ νεκρῶν, ἐμνήσθησαν οἱ μαθηταὶ αὐτοῦ ὅτι τοῦτο ἔλεγεν. We note the curious use of the Imperfect, 'He was saying', where the context demands a Pluperfect, 'He had said'. In Aramaic an Imperfect sense is indicated by the coupling of the *Participle* אָמַר *'āmar* with the subst. verb, while a Pluperfect is commonly represented by use of the *Perfect* אֲמַר *'ămar* similarly coupled with the subst. verb. Thus אֲמַר הֲוָא *'ămar hăwā* 'He had said' may easily have been misinterpreted as אָמַר הֲוָא *'āmar hăwā* 'He was saying', an unvocalized text in W. Aramaic affording (so far as we know) no distinction between the Perfect and the Participle beyond that which is indicated by the context. In a carefully written unvocalized Syriac text the distinction is marked by use of a diacritic point, below for the Perfect, above for the Participle. Thus ܐܡܪ ܗܘܐ = 'He had said', ܐܡܪ ܗܘܐ = 'He was saying'.

6[63]. τὰ ῥήματα ἃ ἐγὼ λελάληκα ὑμῖν seems to mean, 'The things about which I have been speaking to you' (viz. the eating of My flesh and the drinking of My blood).* So perhaps in *v.*[68] ῥήματα ζωῆς αἰωνίου should mean, 'the things of eternal life'. Aramaic מִלָּה, like Hebrew דָּבָר, means both, 'word' and 'thing'. Cf. for the latter sense, Dan. $2^{8.10.11.15.17.23}$, $5^{15.26}$, $7^{1.16.28}$. It is ordinarily rendered ῥῆμα or λόγος by Theodotion; cf. 2[8] ἀπέστη ἀπ' ἐμοῦ τὸ ῥῆμα. Similarly Hebrew דָּבָר 'thing' is often rendered ῥῆμα in LXX; e.g. 2 Sam. 12[6] ἀνθ' ὧν ὅτι ἐποίησεν τὸ ῥῆμα τοῦτο.

$7^{37.38}$. Ἐν δὲ τῇ ἐσχάτῃ ἡμέρᾳ τῇ μεγάλῃ τῆς ἑορτῆς ἱστήκει ὁ Ἰησοῦς, καὶ ἔκραξε λέγων Ἐάν τις διψᾷ ἐρχέσθω πρός με καὶ πινέτω. ὁ πιστεύων εἰς ἐμέ, καθὼς εἶπεν ἡ γραφή, ποταμοὶ ἐκ τῆς κοιλίας αὐτοῦ ῥεύσουσιν ὕδατος ζῶντος. The quotation which our Lord here refers to the Scriptures has caused great perplexity. The fact has rightly been recognized that it is a free combination of several O.T. passages which speak of a river of living waters which, in the Messianic age, is to issue from the Temple-mount, and to become the source of life and healing far and wide. The principal development of this conception is found in Ezek. 47^{1-12}. We may notice especially *v.*[9], where it is stated that 'it shall come to pass, that every living creature which swarmeth in every place whither *the rivers* come, shall live'. Ezekiel's conception has been taken up by two later prophets. Joel 3[18] (4[18] in the Heb.) predicts that '*a fountain shall come forth* of the house of the Lord, and shall water the valley of Shittim'; while in Zech. 14[8] we find the statement, 'It shall come to pass in that day, that *living waters shall go out* from Jerusalem; half of them toward the eastern sea, and half of them towards the western sea' (the latter statement is based upon the passage quoted from Ezek., where the word rendered 'the rivers' is vocalized as a dual, נַחֲלַיִם). We may believe that our Lord had all these passages in His mind; and in each of them the expressions which are most significant are italicized. In addition to these passages, it can hardly be doubted that, in using the words Ἐάν τις διψᾷ ἐρχέσθω πρός με καὶ πινέτω, He was dwelling on Isa. 55[1 ff.], 'Ho, every one that thirsteth, *come ye to the waters*. . . . Incline your ear and *come unto Me*; hear, and your soul shall live'; and Jer. 2[13], 'They have forsaken *Me, the source of living waters*'.

There still remains the outstanding difficulty, '*out of his belly*

* Cf. Gore, *Bampton Lectures*, note 60 (p. 275).

shall flow, &c.' Even if, as seems more than doubtful, the thought is of the distribution of the blessing 'in fuller measure' by its recipient (so Westcott, who compares 4^{14}, 6^{57}, 5^{26}), the fact remains that this conception as expressed cannot be connected with any O.T. passage; and though we can understand that our Lord may well have combined the sense of the passages noticed above, and that so doing His reference would be immediately apprehended by His hearers, we cannot believe that He would have imported, or that they would have accepted, an idea which is not found in any O.T. passage which speaks of the water of life.

The difficulty may at once be solved upon the hypothesis that the passage has been translated from Aramaic. As we have seen, Joel speaks of 'a fountain', Hebrew מַעְיָן *ma'yān**; and the word is the same in Aramaic (employed, e.g., in the Targum of Ps. 104^{10}, Prov. 5^{16}, 8^{28}). The Aramaic for 'belly' or 'bowels' is מְעִין *mĕ'in* (Hebrew מֵעִים); it is used, e.g., of the belly of the image in Dan. 2^{32}. It will at once be seen that, in an unvocalized text, מְעִין 'belly' and מַעְיָן 'fountain', would be absolutely identical. Adopting the word for 'fountain' our Lord's words would run in Aramaic, מַן דְּצָחֵי יֵיתֵי לְוָתִי וְיִשְׁתֵּי מַן דִּמְהֵימַן בִּי הֵיךְ דְּאָמַר כְּתָבָא נַחְלִין מִן־מַעְיָן דְּמַיִּין נָבְעִין יְהוֹן נָגְדִין. If 'fountain' is correct, however, how can we connect 'He that believeth in Me' with 'rivers from the fountain'? There can be little doubt that, as was recognized by the most ancient western interpreters, the clause really belongs to the offer preceding it. On this view the Aramaic yields the sense—

> 'He that thirsteth, let him come unto Me;
> And let him drink that believeth in Me.

As the Scripture hath said, Rivers shall flow forth from the fountain of living waters'.

* It is worthy of note that the Joel-passage with its allusion to the fountain is directly applied to the Messiah in Midrash Rabba on Ecclesiastes, par. i. 28: מה גואל ראשון העלה את הבאר אף גואל אחרון יעלה את המים שנא׳ ומעין מבית י״י יצא והשקה את נחל השטים 'Just as the first Redeemer (Moses) caused the well to spring up, so also shall the second Redeemer cause the waters to spring up, as it is said, "And a fountain shall come forth from the House of the Lord, &c."'. This passage follows directly upon a similar Midrashic deduction which was clearly in the minds of the people who witnessed our Lord's miracle

Our Lord, we are told, 'stood forth and cried aloud', like one of the prophets of old; and His words, like theirs, fall naturally into grand and impressive parallelism. The reference to Scripture which follows the parallel couplet summarizes the main conceptions of Ezekiel, Joel, and Zechariah. When the passage was translated from Aramaic into Greek, מן מעין was taken to mean, 'from the belly'; and this was connected with 'he that believeth in Me', and was therefore rendered, 'from *his* belly'.

8[56]. Ἀβραὰμ ὁ πατὴρ ὑμῶν ἠγαλλιάσατο ἵνα ἴδῃ τὴν ἡμέραν τὴν ἐμήν, καὶ εἶδεν καὶ ἐχάρη. This passage can hardly be preserved in its original form. No extension of the use of ἵνα seems adequate to explain ἠγαλλιάσατο ἵνα ἴδῃ, and moreover, if we grant that 'rejoiced to see' is the sense intended, the following clause καὶ εἶδεν καὶ ἐχάρη, instead of forming a climax, makes mere tautology. What we expect the first clause to say is, not that Abraham rejoiced to see the day, but that he *longed* to see it, and that the satisfaction of this longing was the cause of his gladness. After a verb meaning 'longed' the construction with ἵνα (Aramaic דְּ) would be natural; and this meaning is expressed both by Pal. Syr. ܐܬܪܓܓ and by Pesh. ܡܣܘܚ ܗܘܐ. In Syriac ܣܘܚ in Pe'al and Pa'el (the form used in Pesh.) means both 'wished, longed' and also 'exulted' (cf. Payne Smith, *s. v.*). The verb is not known to occur in W. Aramaic, but there is no reason why it should not have been in use; and the assumption that a wrong meaning has been given to it by the translator ('exulted' instead of 'longed') at once removes the difficulty.*

of the loaves and fishes, and, in asking a further sign, recalled the miracle of the Manna (6[14.30.31]): מה גואל הראשון הוריד את המן שנאמר הנני ממטיר לכם לחם מן השמים אף גואל אחרון יוריד את המן שנא׳ יהי פסת בר בארץ 'Just as the first Redeemer brought down the Manna, as it is said, "Behold, I am about to rain bread from heaven for you", so also the second Redeemer shall bring down the Manna, as it is said, "There shall be a handful of corn in the earth"'.

* (1) What is the basis of the statement that Abraham saw the day of our Lord, and (2) what precisely is to be understood by 'My day'? There is nothing in the text of Genesis, or elsewhere in the O.T., which seems adequately to answer these questions; yet we must suppose that our Lord's words, so far from being similarly obscure to His hearers, were in fact calculated to appeal to their knowledge of current Biblical exegesis. Perusal of the Rabbinic interpretation of the Covenant-scene in Gen. 15, as we find it set forth in the Jerusalem Targum, appears at once to shed a flood of light upon both questions; and lends, moreover,

9^{25}. *ἓν οἶδα*, i.e. חֲדָא יָדַע אֲנָה, may well be an error for הָדָא יָדַע אֲנָה '*This* I know'; and this is actually the reading of Pal. Syr. ܗܕܐ ܝܕܥ ܐܢܐ. The difference between חדא *ḥădā* 'one' and הדא *hādā* 'this' in an unvocalized text is merely the difference between ח and ה, which are very easily confused. It cannot be urged, however, that *ἓν οἶδα* yields an unsuitable sense.

20^{2}. The strange use of *οὐκ οἴδαμεν* in the mouth of Mary Magdalen, where we should expect *οὐκ οἶδα*, may be due to a

strong support to the reading '*longed* to see My day', which we have adopted above.

The Targum of this chapter opens by picturing Abraham in despondent frame of mind after his victory over the kings narrated in *ch.* 14;—'The righteous Abraham pondered in his heart and said, "Woe is me! perchance I have received the recompense of the commandment in this world, and there shall be for me no part in the world to come; or perchance the brethren and neighbours of those slain ones who fell before me shall come and be established in their cities and provinces, and there shall be associated with them many legions whom they will lead out against me: perchance the commands imposed upon me were but light in the former times when they fell before me, and they are spared as my opponents; or perchance merit was found in me in the former times when they fell before me, but perchance it shall not be found in me the second time, and the name of Heaven shall be profaned in me." Therefore there came a word of prophecy from before the Lord to righteous Abraham, saying, "Fear not, Abraham; although many legions shall be gathered together and shall come against thee, My *Mēmrā* shall be a protecting buckler to thee in this world, and a shield over thee continually in the world to come."' Coming to $v.^{12}$, we find the following paraphrase:—'And the sun was inclining towards setting, and a deep sweet sleep fell upon Abraham. And lo, Abraham saw four kingdoms which were to arise to enslave his sons, אֵימָה חֲשֵׁכָה גְדֹלָה נֹפֶלֶת עָלָיו "Terror Darkness Great Falling upon him". אֵימָה *Terror*, which is Babylon; חֲשֵׁכָה *Darkness*, which is Media; גְּדֹלָה *Great*, which is Greece; נֹפֶלֶת *Falling*, which is Edom (i.e. Rome), that is the fourth kingdom which is destined to fall, and shall not rise again for ever and ever. $v.^{17}$ And lo, the sun had set and it was dark; and lo, Abraham beheld until seats were ranged in order and thrones set; and lo, Gehenna which is prepared for the wicked in the world to come like an oven with glowing sparks surrounding it and flames of fire, into the midst of which the wicked fell because they had rebelled against the Law in their lifetime; but the righteous who kept it shall be delivered from affliction'.

The reference is to the four kingdoms of Dan. 7^{1-14} (cf. the same interpretation of 'Terror, &c.' in Midrash Bereshith Rabba, par. xliv. 20), whose career is terminated by the great world-judgement which ushers in the coming of the Son of Man ($v.^{13}$). If, then, this Rabbinic exegesis lies behind Jn. 8^{56}, 'My day' is 'the day of the Son of Man', a vision of which was granted to Abraham in response to his heart-searching and longing. This is in entire accordance with the eschatological background which we find to the conception of the Son of Man in the Synoptic Gospels.

misreading לָא יְדַעְנָא *lā yda'nā* (1st plur. Perfect) of an original לָא יָדְעָנָא *lā yād'ānā* (fem. sing. Participle combined with 1st pers. pronoun). Cf., for this latter form, Dalman, *Gramm.* p. 235. The same mistake, *yda'nā* for *yāda'nā* (masc. sing. Participle combined with 1st pers. pronoun), is made in the vocalization of ידענא Num. 22[6] in Walton's Polyglot. Possibly οἴδαμεν in the opening words of Nicodemus (3[2]) may likewise represent יָדְעָנָא 'I know'.

20[18]. ἔρχεται Μαριὰμ ἡ Μαγδαληνὴ ἀγγέλλουσα . . . ὅτι Ἑώρακα τὸν κύριον καὶ ταῦτα εἶπεν αὐτῇ. The change from direct to oblique oration is strange and awkward. Ἑώρακα = חֲמֵית *hămēth*, ἑώρακε = חַמְיַת *hamyath*.* The two forms are identical in the unvocalized text, and the latter may easily have been taken for the former by the translator under the influence of the ordinary construction with ὅτι *recitativum*. Thus we may conjecture that the original ran, 'announcing that she had seen the Lord, and that He had spoken, &c.'

* We have assigned the Galilaean verb חֲמָא to a native of Magdala. If חֲזָא was used in the narrative there might be a precisely similar confusion—1st pers. חֲזֵית, 3rd pers. חֲזָת.

CHAPTER VIII

OLD TESTAMENT QUOTATIONS IN THE FOURTH GOSPEL

THE question whether the writer of the Fourth Gospel cited the O. T. from the Hebrew Bible or the LXX is important in its bearing on the question of the original language of the Gospel. If the author was a Hellenist he would naturally have employed the LXX. If he was a Palestinian he would be more likely to make his citations from the Hebrew; and if he actually wrote in Aramaic he could hardly have done otherwise. Thus, though the question of the Johannine quotations has frequently received discussion, a fresh examination may possibly bring to light certain points which have hitherto passed unnoticed. This section of our examination gives therefore a tabulation of all O. T. citations and references, together with the Hebrew text of each passage and its translation compared with the LXX rendering.

1. 1[23] Ἐγὼ φωνὴ βοῶντος ἐν τῇ ἐρήμῳ Εὐθύνατε τὴν ὁδὸν Κυρίου, καθὼς εἶπεν Ἠσαίας ὁ προφήτης.

Isa. 40[3] קוֹל קוֹרֵא בַּמִּדְבָּר פַּנּוּ דֶּרֶךְ יְהוָה 'The voice of one crying, In the wilderness prepare ye the way of the Lord'.

LXX Φωνὴ βοῶντος ἐν τῇ ἐρήμῳ, Ἑτοιμάσατε τὴν ὁδὸν Κυρίου.

Jn. quotes from memory, and substitutes the verb of the parallel clause, יַשְּׁרוּ בָּעֲרָבָה מְסִלָּה לֵאלֹהֵינוּ 'make straight in the desert a highway for our God', for the verb פַּנּוּ 'prepare ye'. In doing this, he seems to be thinking, however, of the Hebrew and not of the LXX, since the latter renders יַשְּׁרוּ not by Εὐθύνατε, but by εὐθείας ποιεῖτε. The fact that the words 'in the wilderness' properly form in the Hebrew the opening of the proclamation (synonymous with 'in the desert' of the parallel clause), whereas LXX and Jn., as the text of these versions is punctuated, treat them as descriptive of the speaker's situation, is unimportant, since the punctuation is a secondary matter.

2. I[51] *Ἀμὴν ἀμὴν λέγω ὑμῖν, ὄψεσθε τὸν οὐρανὸν ἀνεῳγότα, καὶ τοὺς ἀγγέλους τοῦ Θεοῦ ἀναβαίνοντας καὶ καταβαίνοντας ἐπὶ τὸν υἱὸν τοῦ ἀνθρώπου.*

Gen. 28[12] וַיַּחֲלֹם וְהִנֵּה סֻלָּם מֻצָּב אַרְצָה וְרֹאשׁוֹ מַגִּיעַ הַשָּׁמָיְמָה וְהִנֵּה מַלְאֲכֵי אֱלֹהִים עֹלִים וְיֹרְדִים בּוֹ 'And he dreamed, and lo, a ladder set up on the earth, and its top reaching to the heaven ; and lo, the angels of God ascending and descending upon it'.

LXX *καὶ ἐνυπνιάσθη· καὶ ἰδοὺ κλίμαξ ἐστηριγμένη ἐν τῇ γῇ, ἧς ἡ κεφαλὴ ἀφικνεῖτο εἰς τὸν οὐρανόν, καὶ οἱ ἄγγελοι τοῦ Θεοῦ ἀνέβαινον καὶ κατέβαινον ἐπ' αὐτῆς.*

The quotation takes the form of a free reminiscence. It seems clear, however, that in the words, 'ascending and descending upon the Son of man', we have an interpretation of the final בּוֹ different from that which is generally accepted. בּוֹ is regularly taken to mean 'on it' (the ladder); but there is also the possibility of the interpretation 'on him' (Jacob), and this appears to be adopted in Jn.'s citation.* Jacob, as the ancestor of the nation of Israel, summarizes in his person the ideal Israel in *posse*, just as our Lord, at the other end of the line, summarizes it in *esse* as the Son of man. The Genesis-passage, in which 'the ladder is an image of the invisible, but actual and unceasing connexion in which God, by the ministry of His angels, stands with the earth, in this instance with Jacob' (Delitzsch), points forward to 'the constant and living intercourse ever maintained between Christ and the Father' (Driver). The point which concerns us here is that the interpretation put upon the passage depends on the Hebrew, in which, since סֻלָּם 'ladder' is masculine, the force of בּוֹ is ambiguous. In LXX, *ἐπ' αὐτῆς* can refer only to *κλίμαξ*. It may be added that Jn.'s *ἀναβαίνοντας καὶ καταβαίνοντας* literally

* We should of course expect עָלָיו in this sense, as in the following verse נִצָּב עָלָיו 'standing over him' (not 'standing upon it'—the ladder). We are not, however, concerned to argue the legitimacy of the interpretation, but merely its origin ; though it may be remarked that this interpretation of ב might be justified by the use of the preposition to denote *proximity* (see *Oxford Hebrew Lexicon*, ב § II).

represents the Hebrew participial construction עֹלִים וְיֹרְדִים, which is obscured in ἀνέβαινον καὶ κατέβαινον of LXX.*

3. 2[17] *Ἐμνήσθησαν οἱ μαθηταὶ αὐτοῦ ὅτι γεγραμμένον ἐστίν Ὁ ζῆλος τοῦ οἴκου σου καταφάγεταί με.*

Ps. 69[10] קִנְאַת בֵּיתְךָ אֲכָלָתְנִי 'The zeal of Thine house hath eaten me'.

LXX *ὁ ζῆλος τοῦ οἴκου σου καταφάγεταί με.*

Here Jn. and LXX are in verbal agreement against the Heb. 'hath eaten me'.

There is a *v. l.* κατέφαγεν which is found in LXX in B[b]א[ca]R, and in Jn. in (13) &c. 𝔏 𝔖 (vt.[s] vg.) 𝔈 (boh) Eus Epiph.

4. 6[31] *οἱ πατέρες ἡμῶν τὸ μάννα ἔφαγον ἐν τῇ ἐρήμῳ, καθώς ἐστιν γεγραμμένον Ἄρτον ἐκ τοῦ οὐρανοῦ ἔδωκεν αὐτοῖς φαγεῖν.*

Ex. 16[4] הִנְנִי מַמְטִיר לָכֶם לֶחֶם מִן־הַשָּׁמָיִם 'Behold, I will rain for

* This note stands as worked out by the writer before it occurred to him to consult the Midrash Bereshith Rabba for traces of the interpretation of בו which he has suggested as inherent in the Johannine reference. He now finds that such an interpretation was actually put forward and debated in early times in Rabbinic circles; cf. Bereshith Rabba, par. lxviii. 18: ר׳ חייא ור׳ ינאי ח״א עולים ויורדים בסלם. וח״א עולים ויורדים ביעקב. מ״ד עולים ויורדים בסלם ניחא. ומ״ד עולים ויורדים ביעקב. מעלים ומורידים בו. אפזים בו קפזים בו סונטים בו. שנא׳ ישראל אשר בך אתפאר את הוא שאיקונין שלך חקוקה למעלה. עולים למעלה ורואים איקונים שלו. ויורדים למטה ומוצאים אותו ישן. '(Interpretations of) Rabbi Ḥiya and Rabbi Yannai. The one scholar says, "Ascending and descending upon the ladder", and the other says, "Ascending and descending upon Jacob". The explanation, "Ascending and descending upon the ladder", is to be preferred. The explanation, "Ascending and descending upon Jacob", implies that they were taking up and bringing down upon him. They were leaping and skipping over him, and rallying him, as it is said, "Israel in whom I glory" (Isa. 49[3]). "Thou art he whose εἰκών is engraved on high." They were ascending on high and looking at his εἰκών, and then descending below and finding him sleeping'. The words translated 'they were taking up and bringing down upon him' are very obscure in meaning; but the following note by Dr. Ball offers an elucidation. 'I would ask why the Genesis text does not say *were coming down and going up thereon?* It seems rather strange that the Angels of God should start from the earth. But leaving that on one side, I am inclined to think that the Midrashic מעלים ומורידים בו is a sort of general reply to the unasked question, *Why were the angels going up and coming down?* the answer being, *They were taking up and bringing down*—acting as carriers between Earth and Heaven. In this case, apparently, they were taking up to Heaven the εἰκών of the sleeping Jacob (which

you bread from heaven'. LXX Ἰδοὺ ἐγὼ ὕω ὑμῖν ἄρτους ἐκ τοῦ οὐρανοῦ.

Ex. 16[15] הוּא הַלֶּחֶם אֲשֶׁר נָתַן יְהוָה לָכֶם לְאָכְלָה 'That is the bread which the Lord hath given you to eat'. LXX Οὗτος ὁ ἄρτος ὃν ἔδωκεν Κύριος ὑμῖν φαγεῖν.

Ps. 78[24] וּדְגַן שָׁמַיִם נָתַן לָמוֹ 'And corn of heaven He gave them'. LXX καὶ ἄρτον οὐρανοῦ ἔδωκεν αὐτοῖς.

In Ps. 78[24] LXX's rendering of דגן 'corn' by ἄρτον (only so rendered here) is dictated by recollection of Ex. 16[4]. Jn.'s quotation is a free reminiscence of Ex. 16[4,15], probably uninfluenced by recollection of the Ps. passage. In rendering Ἄρτον ἐκ τοῦ οὐρανοῦ it is nearer to the Heb. of Ex. 16[4] than is LXX plur. ἄρτους.

5. 6[45] ἔστιν γεγραμμένον ἐν τοῖς προφήταις Καὶ ἔσονται πάντες διδακτοὶ Θεοῦ.

is "fastened to the Throne of Glory"; Targ. Jon. *ad loc.*). As Jacob was in deep sleep, was this εἰκών his wraith or spirit—supposed to be separated from the body under conditions of trance? The case would then be parallel to that of St. Paul "caught up to the third Heaven" (2 Cor. 12[1ff.]) where he "heard" ἄρρητα, much as Jacob became conscious of Yahweh "standing by him", and heard His voice.'

It is difficult to resist the conclusion that the remarkable explanation of this Midrash throws further light upon the Johannine passage. Jacob's εἰκών (the Hebrew simply reproduces the Greek term) is already existent in Heaven (cf. also Targ. Jerus. and Targ. Jon. *ad loc.*); this εἰκών—inasmuch as Jacob embodies the national hope and ideal—represents the heavenly Man (cf. 1 Cor. 15[47–49] ὁ δεύτερος ἄνθρωπος ἐξ οὐρανοῦ, whose εἰκών we are in the future to bear) who is to come on the clouds of Heaven; if the heavens were opened Nathaniel might behold the angels exulting over him.

The same interpretation of בו as referring to Jacob is given a little further on (B.R. par. lxix. 1) in a comment on והנה י״י נצב עליו 'And, behold, the Lord stood over him' (Gen. 28[13]): א״ר אבהו משל לבן מלכים שהיה ישן על גבי עריסה והיו זבובים שכנים עליו. וכיון שבא מינקתו שחה עליו מינקתו וברחו מעליו. כך בתחלה והנה מלאכי אלהים עולים ויורדים בו. כיון שנתגלה עליו הקב״ה ברחו מעליו. 'Rabbi Abbahu said, It is like a royal child who was sleeping in a cradle and flies were settling on him; but when his nurse came, his nurse bent over him, and they flew away from off him. So at first, "And, behold, the angels of God ascending and descending upon him". When the Holy One (blessed be He) revealed Himself over him they flew away from off him'. We may note that Rabbi Ḥiya and Rabbi Yannai also differed as to the interpretation of the suffix of עליו, the one explaining that the Lord stood *on the ladder*, the other that He stood *over Jacob*.

Isa. 54^{13} וְכָל־בָּנַיִךְ לִמּוּדֵי יְהוָה 'And all thy sons shall be taught of the Lord'.

LXX (in connexion with *v.* [12] *καὶ θήσω τὰς ἐπάλξεις σου ἴασπιν, κτλ.*) *καὶ πάντας τοὺς υἱούς σου διδακτοὺς Θεοῦ.*

Clearly Jn., in treating the statement as an independent sentence, is dependent upon Heb. and not on LXX. Nevertheless, it is probable that the use of Θεοῦ—'taught of *God*' in place of 'taught of the Lord'—is due to LXX influence. If this is so, the natural inference is that the quotation was originally made directly from the Heb., and was afterwards modified by a copyist under LXX influence—possibly by the translator from Aramaic into Greek.

6. 7^{38} *καθὼς εἶπεν ἡ γραφή, ποταμοὶ ἐκ τῆς κοιλίας αὐτοῦ ῥεύσουσιν ὕδατος ζῶντος.*

This passage has already been discussed, and has been shown to involve a misunderstanding of an Aramaic original (cf. p. 109).

7. 7^{42} *οὐχ ἡ γραφὴ εἶπεν ὅτι ἐκ τοῦ σπέρματος Δαυείδ, καὶ ἀπὸ Βηθλεὲμ τῆς κώμης ὅπου ἦν Δαυείδ, ἔρχεται ὁ Χριστός;*

Based on Isa. 11^{1}, Jer. 23^{5}, &c. (Davidic descent), Mic. 5^{2} (5^{1} in Heb.; from Bethlehem). The references are general merely.

8. 8^{17} *ἐν τῷ νόμῳ δὲ τῷ ὑμετέρῳ γέγραπται ὅτι δύο ἀνθρώπων ἡ μαρτυρία ἀληθής ἐστιν.*

Deut. 19^{15} עַל־פִּי שְׁנֵי עֵדִים אוֹ עַל־פִּי שְׁלֹשָׁה יָקוּם דָּבָר 'At the mouth of two witnesses or at the mouth of three shall a word be established'.

LXX *ἐπὶ στόματος δύο μαρτύρων καὶ ἐπὶ στόματος τριῶν μαρτύρων στήσεται πᾶν ῥῆμα.*

A vague reference.

9. 10^{34} *Οὐκ ἔστιν γεγραμμένον ἐν τῷ νόμῳ ὑμῶν ὅτι Ἐγὼ εἶπα Θεοί ἐστε;*

Ps. 82^{6} אֲנִי אָמַרְתִּי אֱלֹהִים אַתֶּם 'I have said, Ye are gods'.

LXX *Ἐγὼ εἶπα Θεοί ἐστε.*

Heb. and LXX agree exactly, and the verbal agreement between Jn. and LXX has therefore no special significance, since Heb. could hardly be otherwise rendered.

10. 12^{13} *καὶ ἐκραύγαζον Ὡσαννά, εὐλογημένος ὁ ἐρχόμενος ἐν ὀνόματι Κυρίου.*

Ps. 118[25,26] אָנָּא יְהוָה הוֹשִׁיעָה נָּא

. . . . .

בָּרוּךְ הַבָּא בְּשֵׁם יְהוָה

'O Lord, save now!

. . . .

Blessed be he that cometh in the name of the Lord!'

LXX *ὦ Κύριε, σῶσον δή,*

. . . . .

εὐλογημένος ὁ ἐρχόμενος ἐν ὀνόματι Κυρίου.

Heb. and LXX agree exactly. *Ὡσαννά* represents the Heb. *hôšî'ā-nnā* 'Save now!' which, by substitution of the short form of the imperative for that with the cohortative termination, becomes *hôša'-nā*. *εὐλογημένος κτλ.* is verbally identical with LXX; but the Heb. could hardly be otherwise translated.

11. 12[14,15] *εὑρὼν δὲ ὁ Ἰησοῦς ὀνάριον ἐκάθισεν ἐπ' αὐτό, καθώς ἐστιν γεγραμμένον*

Μὴ φοβοῦ, θυγάτηρ Σιών·
ἰδοὺ ὁ βασιλεύς σου ἔρχεται,
καθήμενος ἐπὶ πῶλον ὄνου.

Zech. 9[9]
גִּילִי מְאֹד בַּת־צִיּוֹן
הָרִיעִי בַּת־יְרוּשָׁלַםִ
הִנֵּה מַלְכֵּךְ יָבוֹא לָךְ
צַדִּיק וְנוֹשָׁע הוּא
עָנִי וְרֹכֵב עַל־חֲמוֹר
וְעַל־עַיִר בֶּן־אֲתֹנוֹת

'Exult greatly, O daughter of Zion;
Shout, O daughter of Jerusalem.
Behold, thy king cometh unto thee;
Righteous and victorious is he;
Lowly, and riding upon an ass,
And upon a colt, an ass's foal'.

LXX *Χαῖρε σφόδρα, θύγατερ Σειών·*
κήρυσσε, θύγατερ Ἰερουσαλήμ·
ἰδοὺ ὁ βασιλεύς σου ἔρχεταί σοι
δίκαιος καὶ σώζων,
αὐτὸς πραῢς καὶ ἐπιβεβηκὼς ἐπὶ ὑποζύγιον
καὶ πῶλον νέον.

The quotation is abbreviated and somewhat free. It is clear, however, that πῶλον ὄνου is derived from Heb. and not from LXX.

12. 12^{34} Ἡμεῖς ἠκούσαμεν ἐκ τοῦ νόμου ὅτι ὁ Χριστὸς μένει εἰς τὸν αἰῶνα.

Ezek. 37^{25} וְדָוִד עַבְדִּי נָשִׂיא לָהֶם לְעוֹלָם 'And David my servant shall be their prince for ever'.

LXX καὶ Δαυεὶδ ὁ δοῦλός μου ἄρχων εἰς τὸν αἰῶνα.

Cf. also Isa. 9^7 (9^6 in Heb.), 2 Sam. 7^{13}, Ps. $89^{4f.}$, 110^4.

The reference is vague and general.

13. 12^{38}. ἵνα ὁ λόγος Ἠσαίου τοῦ προφήτου πληρωθῇ ὃν εἶπεν
Κύριε, τίς ἐπίστευσεν τῇ ἀκοῇ ἡμῶν;
καὶ ὁ βραχίων Κυρίου τίνι ἀπεκαλύφθη;

Isa. 53^1 מִי הֶאֱמִין לִשְׁמֻעָתֵנוּ
וּזְרוֹעַ יְהוָה עַל־מִי נִגְלָתָה

'Who hath believed our report;
And the arm of the Lord, to whom hath it been revealed'.

LXX Κύριε, τίς ἐπίστευσεν τῇ ἀκοῇ ἡμῶν;
καὶ ὁ βραχίων Κυρίου τίνι ἀπεκαλύφθη;

Heb. and LXX agree exactly, except that LXX has added the opening Κύριε, which is also found in Jn.'s quotation which agrees verbally with LXX. It is clear that the text of Jn. is influenced by LXX.

14. $12^{39.40}$ ὅτι πάλιν εἶπεν Ἠσαίας
Τετύφλωκεν αὐτῶν τοὺς ὀφθαλμοὺς
καὶ ἐπώρωσεν αὐτῶν τὴν καρδίαν,
ἵνα μὴ ἴδωσιν τοῖς ὀφθαλμοῖς
καὶ νοήσωσιν τῇ καρδίᾳ καὶ στραφῶσιν, καὶ ἰάσομαι αὐτούς.

Isa. 6^{10} הַשְׁמֵן לֵב־הָעָם הַזֶּה
וְאָזְנָיו הַכְבֵּד וְעֵינָיו הָשַׁע
פֶּן־יִרְאֶה בְעֵינָיו וּבְאָזְנָיו יִשְׁמָע
וּלְבָבוֹ יָבִין וָשָׁב וְרָפָא לוֹ

'Make the heart of this people gross,
And make their ears heavy, and blind their eyes;
Lest they see with their eyes, and hear with their ears,
And understand with their heart, and repent, and be healed'.

LXX ἐπαχύνθη γὰρ ἡ καρδία τοῦ λαοῦ τούτου,
καὶ τοῖς ὠσὶν αὐτῶν βαρέως ἤκουσαν καὶ τοὺς ὀφθαλμοὺς ἐκάμμυσαν,
μή ποτε ἴδωσιν τοῖς ὀφθαλμοῖς καὶ τοῖς ὠσὶν ἀκούσωσιν,
καὶ τῇ καρδίᾳ συνῶσιν καὶ ἐπιστρέψωσιν, καὶ ἰάσομαι αὐτούς.

Here Jn. is clearly independent of LXX; contrast Τετύφλωκεν αὐτῶν τοὺς ὀφθαλμούς with καὶ τοὺς ὀφθαλμοὺς ἐκάμμυσαν: ἵνα μή with μή ποτε: καὶ νοήσωσιν τῇ καρδίᾳ with καὶ τῇ καρδίᾳ συνῶσιν: στραφῶσιν with ἐπιστρέψωσιν. Jn. is not, however, merely a free reminiscence of the Hebrew, as might be supposed from the fact that the writer uses past tenses τετύφλωκεν, ἐπώρωσεν, while the Hebrew appears to use Imperatives (R.V. 'shut', 'make fat'). הַשְׁמֵן, הָשַׁע are either treated as Infinitives Absolute in place of Perfects—'blinding' (lit. 'smearing over'), 'making gross', standing for 'He hath blinded', 'hath made gross' (a normal and idiomatic usage); or the forms are read as Perfects, הִשְׁמִן, הֵשַׁע, as they might naturally be read in the unvocalized text.* Thus (allowing for omission of the reference to ears, and the transposition of a clause) Jn.'s reading is a reasonably accurate rendering of Heb., and is nearer to it than LXX in reading sing. τετύφλωκεν in place of plur. ἐκάμμυσαν which makes the people the subject.

15. 13[18] ἀλλ' ἵνα ἡ γραφὴ πληρωθῇ Ὁ τρώγων μου τὸν ἄρτον ἐπῆρεν ἐπ' ἐμὲ τὴν πτέρναν αὐτοῦ.

Ps. 41[10] אוֹכֵל לַחְמִי הִגְדִּיל עָלַי עָקֵב 'He that eateth my bread hath lifted up his heel against me'.

LXX ὁ ἐσθίων ἄρτους μου, ἐμεγάλυνεν ἐπ' ἐμὲ πτερνισμόν.

Jn. renders Heb. accurately, and is independent of LXX.

16. 15[25] ἀλλ' ἵνα πληρωθῇ ὁ λόγος ὁ ἐν τῷ νόμῳ αὐτῶν γεγραμμένος ὅτι Ἐμίσησάν με δωρεάν.

Ps. 35[19] and 69[4] ([5] in Heb.) שֹׂנְאַי חִנָּם 'my haters without cause'.

LXX in both passages, οἱ μισοῦντές με δωρεάν.

A free reminiscence.

* Symmachus took the Imperatives הַכְבֵּד, הָשַׁע as Perfects הִכְבִּד, הֵשַׁע, but, unlike Jn., made the people (not Yahweh) the subject—ὁ λαὸς οὗτος τὰ ὦτα ἐβάρυνε, καὶ τοὺς ὀφθαλμοὺς αὐτοῦ ἔμυσε.

17. 19[24] ἵνα ἡ γραφὴ πληρωθῇ

Διεμερίσαντο τὰ ἱμάτιά μου ἑαυτοῖς
καὶ ἐπὶ τὸν ἱματισμόν μου ἔβαλον κλῆρον.

Ps. 22[18] ([19] in Heb.) יְחַלְּקוּ בְגָדַי לָהֶם
וְעַל־לְבוּשִׁי יַפִּילוּ גוֹרָל

'They part (*or* parted) my garments among them,
And upon my vesture do (*or* did) they cast lots'.

LXX διεμερίσαντο τὰ ἱμάτιά μου ἑαυτοῖς
καὶ ἐπὶ τὸν ἱματισμόν μου ἔβαλον κλῆρον.

Heb. and LXX agree closely. The verbal agreement between Jn. and LXX points to LXX influence.

18. 19[28.29] Μετὰ ταῦτα εἰδὼς ὁ Ἰησοῦς ὅτι ἤδη πάντα τετέλεσται ἵνα τελειωθῇ ἡ γραφὴ λέγει Διψῶ. σκεῦος ἔκειτο ὄξους μεστόν· σπόγγον οὖν μεστὸν τοῦ ὄξους ὑσσώπῳ περιθέντες προσήνεγκαν αὐτοῦ τῷ στόματι.

Ps. 69[21] ([22] in Heb.) וְלִצְמָאִי יַשְׁקוּנִי חֹמֶץ 'and for my thirst they gave me vinegar to drink'.

LXX καὶ εἰς τὴν δίψαν μου ἐπότισάν με ὄξος.

The reference is general merely.

19. 19[36] ἐγένετο γὰρ ταῦτα ἵνα ἡ γραφὴ πληρωθῇ Ὀστοῦν οὐ συντριβήσεται αὐτοῦ.

Ex. 12[46] וְעֶצֶם לֹא־תִשְׁבְּרוּ־בוֹ 'and ye shall break no bone of it'.

LXX καὶ ὀστοῦν οὐ συντρίψετε ἀπ' αὐτοῦ.

Num. 9[12] וְעֶצֶם לֹא יִשְׁבְּרוּ־בוֹ 'and they shall break no bone of it'.

LXX καὶ ὀστοῦν οὐ συντρίψουσιν ἀπ' αὐτοῦ.

Ps. 34[20] ([21] in Heb.) שֹׁמֵר כָּל־עַצְמוֹתָיו
אַחַת מֵהֵנָּה לֹא נִשְׁבָּרָה

'He keepeth all his bones;
Not one of them is broken'.

LXX [Κύριος] φυλάσσει πάντα τὰ ὀστᾶ αὐτῶν,
ἓν ἐξ αὐτῶν οὐ συντριβήσεται.

The quotation is a free reminiscence.

20. 19[37] καὶ πάλιν ἑτέρα γραφὴ λέγει Ὄψονται εἰς ὃν ἐξεκέντησαν.

Zech. 12[10] וְהִבִּיטוּ אֵלַי אֵת אֲשֶׁר־דָּקָרוּ 'and they shall look on me whom they have pierced'.

LXX καὶ ἐπιβλέψονται πρὸς μὲ ἀνθ' ὧν κατωρχήσαντο.

Some fifty Heb. MSS. read אֵלָיו 'on him', and it is this text upon which Jn. is dependent; or—since אֵלָיו (אֵלַי) אֵת אֲשֶׁר is scarcely possible as a Hebrew construction—he may presuppose the more natural reading אֶל־אֲשֶׁר. The strange LXX rendering is based on a reading רָקְדוּ 'they danced', an erroneous transposition of the letters of דָּקְרוּ 'they pierced'.

Several LXX MSS., representing the Lucianic recension, read *καὶ ἐπιβλέψονται πρὸς μὲ εἰς ὃν ἐξεκέντησαν*, which is the rendering of Theodotion. Aquila . . . *σὺν ᾧ ἐξεκέντησαν*, Symmachus . . . *ἔμπροσθεν ἐπεξεκέντησαν*.

It is obvious that Jn. is independent of LXX, whose rendering destroys the point of the quotation. The connexion with Theodotion in the rendering *εἰς ὃν ἐξεκέντησαν* appears to be fortuitous merely, and does not imply that Jn. and Theodotion were dependent upon an earlier non-Septuagintal rendering (as suggested by Swete, *Introd. to the O. T. in Greek*, p. 398). Ἐκκεντεῖν is the natural rendering of דקר (used by LXX in Judg. 9[54], 1 Chr. 10[4], Jer. 44 (37)[10], Lam. 4[9], and by Aquila and Symmachus in Isa. 13[15]); and the variation between Jn.'s *ὄψονται εἰς ὃν* and Theodotion's *ἐπιβλέψονται πρὸς μὲ εἰς ὃν* is decisive against common borrowing from an earlier Greek source. In the LXX MS. 240 we find the rendering *ὄψονται πρὸς μὲ εἰς ὃν ἐξεκέντησαν as a doublet*, and this no doubt is a Christian marginal variant influenced by Jn. The Apocalypse, which is thoroughly Hebraic, has an echo of the O.T. passage in 1[7] *καὶ ὄψεται αὐτὸν πᾶς ὀφθαλμὸς καὶ οἵτινες αὐτὸν ἐξεκέντησαν.* Here we notice that the two verbs are the same as those employed in Jn.

Thus the following classification of Jn.'s O.T. quotations may be made:

(*a*) Quotations dependent on the Hebrew; Nos. 1, 2, 4, 5, 11, 14, 15, 20.

(*b*) Quotations agreeing with LXX where this is an accurate rendering of the Hebrew; 9, 10, 17.

(*c*) Quotations agreeing with LXX where this differs from the Hebrew; 3, (5), 13.

(*d*) Free reminiscences; 4, 7, 8, 12, 16, 18, 19.

(*e*) Misreading of an Aramaic original; 6.

Under (*a*) we notice that, while in 4 and 11 the points of agreement with Heb. against LXX are slight, all the other cases are weighty and preclude any other theory than a first-hand knowledge of the Heb. text.

Under (*b*) the agreement with LXX in 9 and 10 might be accidental, since the Heb. could scarcely be translated in other words. This, however, is a point not to be pressed, since 17 and the three cases under (*c*) show a connexion with LXX which cannot be accidental.

Under (*c*) we observe that the variations of Jn. and LXX from Heb. are very slight, and that the point of the quotations in no way depends upon them. In 3 (2^{17}) the Heb. reading 'hath eaten me' is represented by Jn.'s *v. l.* κατέφαγεν which has considerable attestation. In 5 the variation from Heb. consists only in the substitution of Θεοῦ for 'the Lord', and in 13 only in the prefixing of Κύριε.

We have now to seek an explanation of the fact that, while a considerable number of the quotations in Jn. presuppose direct use of the Hebrew Bible, certain others are as clearly conformed to LXX. We may rule out the possibilities that the writer was familiar with both Heb. and LXX, and quoted from both indiscriminately; or that the Gospel is composite, the use of Heb. and LXX marking different strands of authorship. There remains the theory that the writer used either Heb. or LXX solely, and that the variations from his regular usage are the work of a later hand. Now it is obvious that the agreements with Heb. cannot be due to alteration, since e.g. 2 and 20 exhibit points of connexion vital to the quotation which are absent from LXX. On the other hand, all the quotations which now agree verbally with LXX might very well have been quoted from Heb. and subsequently modified so as to agree with LXX, since the variation between Heb. and LXX is in every case slight and unimportant. This inference, which emerges from a consideration of the quotations as a whole, seems to be raised to a certainty by the fact that 5 has points of connexion with both Heb. *and* LXX. The words 'And they shall be all taught of God' agree with Heb. as being an independent sentence, and can hardly depend upon LXX, 'And I will make . . . all thy sons to be taught of God'; while the point of connexion with LXX—'taught of *God*' instead of Heb. 'taught of *the Lord*'—is just the kind of alteration which might subsequently be made under LXX influence. If this be granted, the fact that the writer of the Gospel was a Palestinian Jew employing the Heb., and not a Hellenist dependent on LXX, is proved. Further, it must surely be admitted that slight modifications of passages originally quoted from Heb. into verbal agreement with LXX, though they might very possibly be made by a reviser or copyist of the Greek text, would be far more likely to arise in process of translation into Greek from another language, such as Aramaic. And in 6 (7^{38}) we have very striking evidence that the language in which the O.T. reference was originally cast *was* Aramaic.

CHAPTER IX

EPILOGUE

At the close of this discussion the writer may be expected to offer some remarks as to the influence which his theory should, if it gains acceptance, exercise upon current historical criticism of the Fourth Gospel. This is a task which for two reasons he feels somewhat loth to essay. Firstly, the question has been mainly if not wholly linguistic, and ought at the outset to be presented for consideration uncomplicated by ulterior issues. And secondly, the writer is conscious that in attempting to touch upon such larger issues he is in danger of getting outside his province; for, while to the best of his ability he has made a minute study of the Gospel itself, and can claim some knowledge of the external criteria bearing upon the question of authorship, he cannot claim conversance with more than a small portion of the gigantic mass of modern literature which has been directed towards the solution of the Johannine problem.

Still, it goes without saying that in the course of the linguistic investigation the question of its bearing upon the authorship of the Gospel has been constantly in his mind. If the theory is soundly based, it must surely affect something like a revolution in current Johannine criticism; for, while cutting at the roots of the fashionable assumptions of a particular school of critics, it may be held to go even farther, and to demand a re-examination, if not a reconstruction, of certain fundamental postulates which have hitherto been accepted by all schools of criticism. Thus it may be thought fitting that the author of the theory should indicate in brief the results to which he believes that it points.

In the first place, it should establish beyond question the fact that the Gospel is a product of Palestinian thought. This is a conclusion which emerges with no less clearness even if it be held that the evidence which has been offered is insufficient to prove actual translation from Aramaic; for at least it cannot be disputed that the case for virtual translation is irrefragable. The author's language is cast throughout in the Aramaic mould. He is thoroughly familiar with Rabbinic speculation. He knows his Old Testament, not through the medium of the LXX, but in the original language.

If this be granted, the figment of Alexandrine influence upon the author must be held finally to be disproved. His Logos-doctrine is the development of conceptions enshrined in the Targums, and is not derived from Philo. This can hardly be disputed in face of the evidence adduced on pp. 35 ff. Could New Testament scholars ever have arrived at any other conclusion if they had approached the subject with an adequate Semitic, as well as a Greek, equipment? Not, indeed, that Palestinian Rabbinism was wholly uninfluenced by Greek thought; the Midrashim prove the contrary. Yet, when this is admitted, Palestinian Jewish thought is one thing, Alexandrine Hellenistic thought another. It may be true that there is an ultimate connexion between the Logos-conception of Philo and that of the Gospel-prologue; but this connexion is no closer than is implied by a common parentage. Philo's doctrine was in no sense the moulding influence of our author's thought.

It may be observed that the theory that the Gospel was written in Aramaic fits in admirably with other well-ascertained results of internal evidence—the author's intimate knowledge of Palestinian topography, of Jewish festivals and customs, and of the current Messianic expectations at the time of our Lord. On all these questions, in which in time past his accuracy has in one way or another been impugned, he has been triumphantly vindicated. If, in addition, it is proved that he actually wrote in Aramaic, we have added the coping-stone which harmoniously completes the building.

Here, however, we find that our theory seems to call for the re-opening of a question which is generally supposed to be settled. If the Gospel was written in Aramaic, it must surely have been written in Palestine or Syria; it could hardly have been written at Ephesus. This conclusion is by no means necessarily at variance with the tradition that the author spent the latter part of his life at

Ephesus; for obviously we have the possibility that he may have written the Gospel at an earlier period. It may be observed that, while tradition generally assigns the writing of the Gospel to Ephesus, there are traces of a different opinion. The Muratorian Canon seems to state that the Gospel was written before the breaking up of the Apostolic circle,* therefore, presumably, in Palestine.

The assignment of a Palestinian or Syrian origin to the Gospel would seem to carry with it an earlier date for its composition than that which is commonly accepted (A.D. 90 or somewhat later); possibly even a considerably earlier one. But this is by no means at variance with the facts of internal evidence. Even apart from a full acceptance of the theory propounded in the present volume, it must surely be admitted that the facts which have been brought together greatly strengthen the case for holding that the Gospel is the work of an eye-witness. The view that it represents the mature Christian experience of that witness is doubtless sound; but if we are to assume that he was a man of eighty or more when he took up his pen, we are postulating for him a mental vigour quite exceptional in one so old. Opinions may differ as to the impression of the author's personality conveyed by the Gospel; but the present writer feels that, while the First Epistle might fairly be regarded as the product of extreme old age, the planning and execution of the Gospel is hardly consistent with such a theory. The age of sixty-five or seventy would at any rate be more normal for the composition of a work which exhibits so markedly a maturity which is as yet unimpaired. Assuming that the author was about twenty at the Crucifixion, this would lead us to date the Gospel A.D. 75-80. The question whether it would be reasonable to place it even earlier demands an expert knowledge of its relation to the Synoptic Gospels and a first-hand conclusion as to the dates of these latter; and on these points the writer does

* The Fourth Gospel is said to be the work of 'Ioannis ex discipulis'. The occasion of its composition is given as follows: 'Cohortantibus condiscipulis et episcopis suis dixit, Conieiunate mihi hodie triduo et quid cuique fuerit revelatum alterutrum nobis enarremus. Eadem nocte revelatum Andreae ex apostolis ut recognoscentibus cunctis Ioannes suo nomine cuncta discriberet.' Since John himself is named 'one of the disciples', it seems to follow that 'his fellow-disciples' (one of whom is Andrew) are the other Apostles.

not feel qualified to venture an opinion. We may note, however, that there seem to be no indications pointing to a date prior to the destruction of Jerusalem in A.D. 70; the evidence of 5^2, Ἔστιν δὲ ἐν τοῖς Ἱεροσολύμοις ἐπὶ τῇ προβατικῇ κολυμβήθρα . . . πέντε στοὰς ἔχουσα, which has been thought to imply that the city was still standing intact, being of doubtful validity if the Greek is regarded as a translation from Aramaic.*

On the other hand, there *are* a number of indications which suggest a certain remoteness, both in time and place, from the scenes described, and also seem to imply that the author was not writing, at least primarily, *for Jews*, but for a larger circle of Christians. What Jew, or indeed what Gentile inhabitant of *Palestine*, would need to be informed that the Jews have no dealings with the Samaritans, that Tabernacles was the feast of the Jews, or that the festival of the Dedication took place in winter?† Of course it might be maintained that the author, writing not merely for his contemporaries but for posterity to whom such details would not be obvious, took care to insert them; but such a theory can hardly claim probability.

We arrive, then, at the impression that the Gospel was not written at an earlier date than A.D. 75–80, nor from Palestine; yet on the other hand our theory of an Aramaic original seems to demand that it should have originated in an Aramaic-speaking country. Thus Syria is indicated, and if Syria, then Antioch.

* The meaning '*was*' or '*is*' might be left in Aramaic to be inferred from the context, or at any rate expressed in such a way that confusion would be easy in translation. For Ἔστιν . . . ἔχουσα Cur. has ܐܝܬ ... ܘܐܝܬ ܒܗ, lit. 'Existing *was* . . . and existing in it'; Pesh. ܐܝܬ ܗܘܐ ... ܘܐܝܬ ܗܘܐ ܒܗ 'Existing *was* . . . and existing *was* in it'; while in Pal. Syr. we find ܐܝܬ ܗܳܘܶܐ ... ܘܗܳܘܶܐ ܒܗ 'Existing *is* . . . and *is* in it'. Here, however, the only time-determining factor is the dot above ܗܳܘܶܐ, which marks it as the Participle *hāwē*, not the Perfect *hăwā*. In W. Aramaic there would probably have been no mark of distinction.

† Instances of such touches may be seen in $2^{6.13.23}$, $4^{5.9}$, 5^2, $6^{1.4}$, $7^{2.37}$, 10^{22}, 11^{18}, $19^{31.40}$. Two of these passages, viz. 2^{23} ἐν τῷ πάσχα ἐν τῇ ἑορτῇ, 6^1 πέραν τῆς θαλάσσης τῆς Γαλιλαίας τῆς Τιβεριάδος, convey the impression of conflation. Of course it must be assumed, on the hypothesis of translation, that in 4^{25} (ὁ λεγόμενος Χριστός), 5^2 (Ἑβραϊστί), 19^{13} (Λιθόστρωτον, Ἑβρ. δέ), 19^{17} (Κρανίου Τόπον, ὃ λέγεται Ἑβρ.), 20^{16} (Ἑβρ. . . . ὃ λέγεται Διδάσκαλε) the translator has glossed the text for the benefit of his readers. It is possible that some of the touches in the first set of passages given in this note may be translator's glosses.

Though Antioch was a Greek city, it stood not far from the heart of the district whence from the earliest times the Aramaic speech was diffused, eastward into Mesopotamia and southward through Syria and Palestine. The city must have been bilingual, and though Greek was doubtless the language of the upper classes, there must have been a large substratum of population to whom Aramaic was the more familiar language. This follows necessarily from the exigencies of trade—both the regularly organized caravan-trade from beyond the Euphrates, and the local trade which brought the country people into the metropolis to sell their food-stuffs, and to add new blood to the population. As we learn from Acts, the natural line of expansion for the infant-Church at Jerusalem was northward to Antioch. If the writer of the Fourth Gospel really spent the last part of his life at Ephesus, then we have in Antioch a half-way house between this and Jerusalem; and if the line of his missionary activity was Jerusalem—Antioch—Ephesus he was following in the footsteps of St. Paul.

It is interesting to note that we are not entirely without external indication that St. John was at Antioch and wrote the Gospel there. Mr. F. C. Conybeare has quoted a statement translated from a Syriac fragment appended to the Armenian translation to the commentary of St. Ephrem on Tatian's Diatessaron: 'Iohannes scripsit illud [evangelium] graece Antiochiae, nam permansit in terra usque ad tempus Traiani'.* There exists a wide-spread (though not very early) tradition that St. Ignatius was a disciple of St. John. The Μαρτύριον Ἰγνατίου (5th or 6th century A.D.) so describes him at its opening, and adds later on the scarcely credible statement that he and Polycarp (born A.D. 69) had together been disciples of the Apostle.†

The facts which lead the present writer to suggest the theory that the Fourth Gospel may have been written at Antioch are as follows:

1. The Epistles of St. Ignatius (*c.* A.D. 110) are full of Johannine Theology. It is true that there is only one passage in them which approximates to an actual verbal quotation, but reminiscences of the teaching of the Gospel are more numerous than is generally

* *ZNTW*. 1902, p. 193.

† Cf. Lightfoot, *Apostolic Fathers*, II. ii, pp. 473 f., who argues against the historical value of the statement and seeks to explain how it may have arisen.

recognized. Dr. Inge's conclusion is that 'Ignatius' use of the Fourth Gospel is highly probable, but falls some way short of certainty'.* One of his reasons for this doubtful verdict is 'our ignorance how far some of the Logia of Christ recorded by John may have been current in Asia Minor before the publication of the Gospel'. This is met if it can be shown that Ignatius was probably also acquainted with the First Epistle of St. John; and this seems to be the case.† The Ignatian expressions, ὁ ἄρχων τοῦ αἰῶνος τούτου and τέκνα φωτὸς ἀληθείας may actually imply acquaintance with the original Aramaic of the Gospel.

2. Drs. Rendel Harris and Mingana, in their recent edition of the Odes and Psalms of Solomon (1920), have made a case for a connexion between the Odes and the Letters of Ignatius, and have shown that the dependence is almost certainly on Ignatius's side. There is a tradition recorded by the historian Socrates that Ignatius instructed the Antiochenes in the composition and singing of hymns.‡ Theophilus of Antioch was also familiar with the

* *The New Testament in the Apostolic Fathers*, by a committee of the Oxford Society of Historical Theology, p. 83.

† Cf. especially the group of passages reflecting the teaching of 1 Jn. quoted from the letter to the Ephesians on p. 154.

‡ 'We must also tell whence the custom of the Church of singing antiphonal hymns had its origin. Ignatius, the third bishop after Peter of the Syrian Antioch, who also had personal intercourse with the Apostles themselves, saw a vision of angels praising the Trinity in antiphonal hymns, and delivered the fashion of the vision to the church in Antioch: from whence also the same tradition was transmitted to other churches.'—Socrates, *HE.* vi. 8, quoted by Harris and Mingana, p. 43. These editors also aptly call attention (p. 47) to two passages in Ignatius's letters in which he uses chorus-singing as a metaphor for Christian harmony; Ephes. 4, '*In your* concord and harmonious *love* Jesus Christ *is sung.* And do ye, *each and all*, form yourselves into a chorus, that, being harmonious in concord, and taking the key-note of God, ye may *in oneness sing* with one voice through Jesus Christ unto the Father, that He may both hear you *and acknowledge you* by your good deeds to be the members of His Son' (i. e. *His children*); Rom. 2, 'Forming yourselves into a *chorus, in love sing* to the Father in Jesus Christ.' These passages find a striking parallel in Ode 41, which begins as follows:

> 'Let *all of us* who are the Lord's bairns, praise Him:
> And let us appropriate the truth of His faith:
> *And His children shall be acknowledged by Him*:
> Therefore *let us sing in His love.*
> . . . .
> Let us, therefore, *all of us unite together* in the name of the Lord.'

The italics draw attention to the parallelism in thought.

Odes.* It seems clear that they were originally composed in Syriac.† The conclusion of these editors is that they were probably written at Antioch in the first century.‡

Now the fact that the writer of the Odes was acquainted with the Fourth Gospel can be proved fairly clearly; though here again the evidence takes the form of reminiscence of the teaching rather than actual verbal quotation. Surprising as this may seem in view of the very early date which is assigned to the Odes, it is the less surprising if, as on our theory, the date of the Gospel is earlier than is commonly supposed; and it becomes quite comprehensible if the Gospel was actually composed at Antioch and first circulated there in Aramaic. It is noteworthy that a great part of the connexions with the thought of the Gospel, both in Ignatius's Letters and in the Odes, are with the Last Discourses, Jn. 13—17.

The evidence for all this appears so highly important that it is given in detail in an Appendix.

The supposed influence of Pauline Theology upon the Fourth Gospel in no way conflicts with our new theory as to the date and place of the Gospel. A period of twenty years or so allows ample time for the principal epistles of St. Paul to have become well known at Antioch. The present writer has, however, put forward suggestions (pp. 45 ff.) which may indicate a somewhat different conclusion, viz. that both St. Paul and the author of the Gospel may have been influenced by a common earlier source of teaching. Both of them were Rabbinists; and the course of the present discussion has revealed several instances of a knowledge of Rabbinic speculation on the part of the Gospel-author which is independent of St. Paul. Both again were mystics; but there is no reason for assuming that the mysticism of the Gospel was a development of Pauline teaching. Mysticism is one of the characteristics of the Rabbinic method of treating Scripture; and the question how far this trait in the two Christian writers is based on Jewish Haggada is one which calls for further investigation. The inclusion within the early Church at Jerusalem of a large contingent from the priestly class (Acts 6^7) must almost

* *op. cit.* ch. iii. † *op. cit.* ch. xiii. ‡ *op. cit.* ch. iv.

certainly have resulted in the application of Rabbinic speculation to the service of the new Faith.

As to the author of the Gospel—while the conclusion that he wrote his Gospel in Aramaic strongly confirms the opinion that he was an actual eye-witness of the events which he describes, it must be admitted that the clear traces which we have noticed of his acquaintance with Rabbinic learning * seem to diminish the probability that he was St. John the Apostle. St. Peter and St. John impressed the priestly authorities at Jerusalem as ἄνθρωποι ἀγράμματοι καὶ ἰδιῶται (Acts 4[13]); and though the phrase is used in connexion with their unexpected eloquence, the paradox consisted, not in the fact that having previously been ἀγράμματοι—i.e. untrained in Rabbinic methods of exegesis—they now appeared so to be trained; but in the fact that, though still ἀγράμματοι, they were able to speak and argue eloquently and convincingly. It is of course conceivable that the Galilaean fisherman, especially if a young man, may have had a natural aptitude for assimilating the Rabbinic methods of argument; and that, his interest being whetted through listening to our Lord's discussions with the Rabbinists at Jerusalem, he may subsequently have carried his studies farther in this direction, e.g. through intercourse with the Christian members of the Jewish priesthood. It is clear, however, that if we had reason to think that, like St. Paul, he had actually undergone a thorough Rabbinic training, much light would be thrown upon the Gospel. We should then understand how it was that the author was able to retain the substance of our Lord's arguments with his former teachers, and why these arguments appealed to him more than the simple parabolic teaching which was adapted to the Galilaean peasantry. His first-hand use of the Hebrew Bible would be explained; and, supposing that he may also have been the author of the Apocalypse, we should understand how he was able to construct this work upon a Biblical Hebrew model.

Now, as Prof. Delff was the first to remark,† there are details in

* Cf. especially pp. 35 ff., 43 ff., 110 n., 111 n., 116 n.

† *Gesch. d. Rabbi Jesus v. Nazareth* (1899). pp. 67 ff.; *Das vierte Evangelium* (1890), pp. 1 ff. Delff's theory was followed by Bousset in the 1st ed. of his *Offenbarung Johannis* (1896), but dropped by him in the 2nd ed. (1906); cf. p. 46, n. 2. It is regarded with considerable favour by Dr. Sanday, *Criticism of the Fourth Gospel*, pp. 17 f., 90, 99 ff.

the Gospel which, taken together, strongly suggest that the author had some connexion with priestly circles. He (on the assumption that he is the unnamed disciple) was known to the high priest and gained ready admission to his house, which was denied to Peter until he intervened ($18^{15.16}$). He alone of the Evangelists mentions the name of the high priest's servant, Malchus, whose ear Peter cut off (18^{10}), and also the fact that one of those who questioned Peter was a kinsman of Malchus (18^{26}). He has special knowledge of persons like Nicodemus and Joseph of Arimathaea, who were both members of the Sanhedrin ($3^{1\,ff.}$, 7^{50}, $19^{38\,ff.}$), and seems to have gained inside information as to what went on at meetings of the Sanhedrin (7^{15-52}, 11^{47-53}, 12^{10}), which may have come to him through Nicodemus. The fact that, when our Lord commended His Mother to his care, he took her *εἰς τὰ ἴδια* 'from that hour' suggests that he had a house at or near Jerusalem (19^{27}).

The deduction based on these internal indications serves further to explain the remarkable statement of Polycrates of Ephesus that John, who reclined on the breast of the Lord, was a priest wearing the sacerdotal frontlet (*ὃς ἐγενήθη ἱερεὺς τὸ πέταλον πεφορεκώς*), which otherwise is an insoluble enigma. Moreover, if Polycrates supposed that John the author of the Gospel was the Apostle St. John, it is in the highest degree anomalous that he should mention him subsequently to Philip, whom he defines as *τῶν δώδεκα ἀποστόλων*, and the daughters of Philip, and should then describe him, not as an Apostle, but as *μάρτυς καὶ διδάσκαλος* simply—this too in spite of the fact that 'he sleeps at Ephesus' where Polycrates himself was bishop, while Philip 'sleeps at Hierapolis' (Eusebius, *HE.* v. 24). If one of the most famous members of the original Apostolic band had actually preceded him in his own see, he would surely have named him first of all.

The familiar quotation from Papias (Eusebius, *HE.* iii. 39) seems likewise to indicate that the celebrated John of Ephesus was not the Apostle. Papias tells us that 'if any one chanced to come my way who had been a follower of the presbyters, I would inquire as to the sayings of the presbyters—what Andrew or Peter said (*εἶπεν*), or Philip or Thomas or James or John or Matthew, or any other of the Lord's disciples; and also what

Aristion and John the presbyter, the Lord's disciples, say (λέγουσιν)'. Unless we adopt the view that the Apostles mentioned are termed 'the presbyters'* (a view both improbable in itself and also apparently excluded by the distinctive application of the term to the second John), it is clear from this passage that Papias only claims to have learned the Apostles' sayings *at third hand,* i.e. he learned from his informants what the presbyters said that the Apostles said. On the other hand, the obvious deduction from the statement 'also what Aristion and John the presbyter, the Lord's disciples, *say*', is that Papias learned the sayings of these disciples *at second hand*; and since the change of tense from εἶπεν to λέγουσιν is clearly intentional, it is natural to infer that Aristion and the second John were still living, and that Papias might have heard them *at first hand* if he had had the opportunity.†

If this conclusion is sound, and if the title 'the Lord's disciples' implies—as in the first occurrence, where it is applied to the Apostles—actual knowledge of our Lord during His earthly life, then the date at which Papias collected his materials cannot be later than A.D. 100—a conclusion which fits in with the statement of Irenaeus that he was a companion of Polycarp (A.D. 69-155) and 'one of the ancients' (ἀρχαῖος ἀνήρ).‡ It follows that *c.* A.D. 100 Papias knew of a John whom he termed 'the presbyter' (apparently in distinction from John the Apostle before mentioned), who, though an actual disciple of our Lord, was still living at that date, and must therefore have been of a very advanced age. On the other hand, all that he claims to have learned (or to have

* This is the view of Eusebius (see foot-note following), and it is taken e. g. by Lightfoot, *Essays on Supernatural Religion*, p. 145, and by Westcott, *Canon of the N.T.* p. 70, n. 1. On the contrary, see Moffatt, *Introd. to Literature of N.T.*[3] p. 599.

† Papias *does not state* in this passage that he was an actual hearer of Aristion and John the presbyter, as is unwarrantably assumed by Eusebius; Καὶ ὁ νῦν δὲ ἡμῖν δηλούμενος Παπίας τοὺς μὲν τῶν ἀποστόλων λόγους παρὰ τῶν παρηκολουθηκότων ὁμολογεῖ παρειληφέναι, Ἀριστίωνος δὲ καὶ τοῦ πρεσβυτέρου Ἰωάννου αὐτήκοον ἑαυτόν φησι γενέσθαι. Why Dr. Lightfoot (*Essays on Supern. Rel.* p. 146) should accept Eusebius's opinion on this point against the plain sense of the passage is incomprehensible.

‡ *Haer.* V. xxxiii. 4; Eusebius, *HE.* iii. 39. A.D. 100 is adopted by Dr. Sanday (*Criticism of the Fourth Gospel*, pp. 250 f.), as against the extreme date adopted by Harnack (*c.* A.D. 145-60). Eusebius (*HE.* iii. 36) states that his episcopate was contemporary not only with Polycarp's, but also with Ignatius's (d. A.D. 110).

endeavoured to learn) by word of mouth about the Apostolic son of Zebedee is what others said that the presbyters said that he said; and so far is he from attaching any special prominence to him that he mentions him only sixth in a list of seven of the Apostles.

Now Irenaeus tells us that John, 'the disciple of the Lord', who wrote the Gospel, survived at Ephesus until the times of Trajan,* i.e. until after A.D. 98. If this John was the son of Zebedee, would Papias—who must certainly have been born long before his death, and who was probably collecting his information, if not before, at any rate not long after that event, and who was bishop of a Church which was close to Ephesus—have been reduced to learning at third hand as to his teaching? And since, for one man who could give him authentic information as to what Andrew or Peter had said, there must (on this hypothesis) have been ten who could give him fuller and more recent information as to what John the son of Zebedee had said, is it at all likely that the vastly superior importance to Papias of John as a witness to our Lord's acts and teaching, involved in the fact of his nearness to him both in time and in place, should be ignored to such an extent that he only mentions the Apostle sixth in a list of seven?

The inference is clear that Papias did not claim to have any better knowledge of John the son of Zebedee than he possessed of Andrew, Peter, and the rest who had died years before he began to collect his materials. The absence of such a claim fits in with the statement attributed to him by Philippus Sidetes (5th cent.) and Georgius Hamartolus (9th cent.) that John and James his brother were slain by the Jews, which certainly seems to imply that John the son of Zebedee did not survive to a ripe old age in Asia, but lost his life through Jewish persecution, and therefore probably in Palestine and prior to the destruction of Jerusalem in A.D. 70.† There exists, however, yet another statement attributed to Papias in an argument prefixed to a Vatican MS. of the Fourth Gospel (9th cent.):—'Evangelium Iohannis manifestatum et datum est ecclesiis ab Iohanne adhuc in corpore constituto, sicut Papias

* *Haer.* II. xxii. 5; III. i. 1; III. iii. 4.

† On further evidence as to the martyrdom cf. Moffatt, *Introd. to Lit. of N.T.*[3] pp. 601 ff.; and most recently, Charles, *Revelation*, i, pp. xlv ff.

nomine Hierapolitanus, discipulus Iohannis carus, in exotericis, id est in extremis [externis] quinque libris retulit. Descripsit vero evangelium dictante Iohanne recte'.* Confused and improbable as this statement seems in detail, we have no grounds for questioning the main facts, viz. that Papias may have stated that the author of the Gospel was John of Asia who survived into his own times.

If, however, the other statement referred to Papias means that John the son of Zebedee suffered martyrdom in Palestine prior to A.D. 70, the statement as to the writing of the Gospel can only be squared with it on the assumption that the references are to two different Johns—in the first case to the Apostle, in the second to John of Asia, i.e. the presbyter.

Now the writer of the Second and Third Epistles of St. John actually describes himself as ὁ πρεσβύτερος, and the inference from the contents of the Epistles is that they were not intended to be anonymous, but that this title was sufficient to mark the writer's identity. If they are rightly ascribed to John, the inference that this is the Ἰωάννης ὁ πρεσβύτερος of Papias is obvious.† Dr. Charles in his *Commentary on Revelation* (i, pp. xxxiv ff.) has argued from a careful linguistic study that the Fourth Gospel and the three Epistles of St. John are by the same author. It follows that the Gospel is the work of John the presbyter, and that the tradition that it was composed at Ephesus is wrapped up with the fact of his authorship. Thus the earliest Asian tradition, as represented by Papias and Polycrates and confirmed by the testimony of the Second and Third Epistles, points to the presbyter and not the son of Zebedee as the author of the Gospel.

* Cf. Lightfoot, *Essays on Supern. Rel.* pp. 210 ff.; Westcott, *Canon of N.T.* p. 77, n. 1. Lightfoot (p. 214) has an ingenious suggestion as to the way in which the statement may have arisen that Papias was actually the amanuensis of John. 'Papias may have quoted the Gospel "delivered by John to the Churches, which *they* wrote down from his lips" (ὃ ἀπέγραφον ἀπὸ τοῦ στόματος αὐτοῦ); and some later writer, mistaking the ambiguous ἀπέγραφον, interpreted it "*I* wrote down", thus making Papias himself the amanuensis.'

† This seems to be hinted by Eusebius, *HE.* iii. 25: Τῶν δ' ἀντιλεγομένων, γνωρίμων δ' οὖν ὅμως τοῖς πολλοῖς . . . ἡ ὀνομαζομένη δευτέρα καὶ τρίτη Ἰωάννου, εἴτε τοῦ εὐαγγελιστοῦ τυγχάνουσαι, εἴτε καὶ ἑτέρου ὁμωνύμου ἐκείνῳ. The view is definitely taken by Jerome, *de viris illust.* cc. 9 and 18.

Our evidence, however, is incomplete without examination of the testimony of St. Irenaeus, which is important because, in the well-known passage from his letter to Florinus (Eusebius, *HE.* v. 20), he states that in his boyhood (*παῖς ἔτι ὤν*) he was a hearer of Polycarp and could remember his description of 'his intercourse with John and with the rest who had seen the Lord'. Irenaeus appears unjustly to have suffered considerable misrepresentation. While claimed on the one hand as a conclusive witness to the fact that the John of Ephesus was the Apostle St. John, he is commonly accused, on the other hand, by the opponents of this theory of having mistaken the meaning of his teacher Polycarp, and supposed that he was referring to the Apostle when all the time he was speaking of the presbyter. Similarly, he is taken to task by Eusebius (*HE.* iii. 39) because he describes Papias as *ὁ Ἰωάννου μὲν ἀκουστής, Πολυκάρπου δὲ ἑταῖρος γεγονώς.* Eusebius's comment on this statement is *Αὐτός γε μὴν ὁ Παπίας κατὰ τὸ προοίμιον τῶν αὐτοῦ λόγων, ἀκροατὴν μὲν καὶ αὐτόπτην οὐδαμῶς ἑαυτὸν γενέσθαι τῶν ἱερῶν ἀποστόλων ἐμφαίνει, παρειληφέναι δὲ τὰ τῆς πίστεως παρὰ τῶν ἐκείνοις γνωρίμων.* The error of which he is accused by Eusebius is cited by modern critics as enhancing the probability that he made the additional error of mistaking Polycarp's reminiscences of the presbyter as referring to the Apostle.

In reality, it is doubtful whether Irenaeus makes any mistake at all. The true state of affairs may best be gathered by tabulating all his references to the author of the Fourth Gospel, whom he also regarded as author of the Apocalypse.*

	Occurrences.
'John the disciple of the Lord'	
In references to the Gospel	9
In references to the Apocalypse . . .	3
In references to incidents at Ephesus . .	2
Total	14

* These computations are as complete as the writer could make them; but he cannot claim that they are more than approximately so. They cover the fragments as well as the *Contra Haer.* Under 'John' a few Gospel references referring to the son of Zebedee have not been reckoned.

'The disciple of the Lord'	1
'His disciple John'	1
'John'	
In references to the Gospel	20
In references to the Apocalypse	10
In references to incidents at Ephesus	1
Total	31
'The Apostle'	2

With these references we may compare Irenaeus's references to other Evangelists and Apostles:

'Matthew the Apostle'	1
'Matthew' elsewhere.	
'Mark the interpreter and disciple of Peter'	1
'Mark the disciple and interpreter of Peter'	1
'Mark' elsewhere.	
'Luke the follower and disciple of the Apostles'	1
'Luke the disciple and attendant of the Apostles'	1
'Luke the attendant of Paul'	1
'Luke' elsewhere.	
'Peter the Apostle'	1
'Peter' elsewhere.	
'Paul the Apostle'	17
'Paul, being the Apostle of the Gentiles'	1
'Paul His Apostle'	1
'Paul'	64
'The Apostle'	74

Here we notice the extraordinary care which Irenaeus takes accurately to define the position and authority of his witnesses. This comes out especially in his description of Mark and Luke; while Matthew alone of the Synoptists is correctly given the title of Apostle.

We notice again that, while Matthew, Peter, and Paul are defined as Apostles, John *is never so defined by name.* It is true that in two passages which come near together (*Haer.* I. ix. 2, 3) he is mentioned as 'the Apostle' simply, having just previously been cited as 'John'; but this is different from the direct attachment of the title to his name. Irenaeus, when not specially defining the rank of his witnesses, uses the term 'Apostle' in a wider sense. Thus in *Haer.* III. xi. 9, after a summary of the teaching and scope of the four Gospels, he remarks, 'Having thus ascertained the opinion of those who delivered the Gospel to us . . . let us proceed to the remaining Apostles'; and again in IV. *pref.* 1, 'Accordingly, in the book before this we have set forth the sentence of the Apostles upon them all'. There are several passages in which John is included by inference among the Apostles; II. xxii. 5, 'And all the elders testify, who in Asia conferred with John the disciple of the Lord, that John had handed down these facts; for he abode with them until the times of Trajan. And some of them saw not only John, but also other Apostles'; III. iii. 4, 'And Polycarp too, who had not only been trained by the Apostles, and had conversed with many of those who had seen Christ, but also had been constituted by the Apostles bishop over Asia in the church of Smyrna . . . having always taught these things, which he had learned from the Apostles'; 'And there are some who have been told by him (Polycarp) that John the disciple of the Lord, when he had gone to have a bath at Ephesus . . . and Polycarp too himself. . . . Such pious care had the Apostles and their disciples, &c.'; 'Yea, and the church at Ephesus, having had both Paul for its founder, and John to abide among them until the times of Trajan, is a true witness of the tradition of the Apostles'; Letter to Victor (Eusebius, *HE.* v. 24), 'For neither could Anicetus persuade Polycarp not to observe (the Quartodeciman practice), inasmuch as he had always observed it with John the disciple of our Lord and the rest of the Apostles with whom he had associated'.

Let us attach full weight to these passages (which the writer believes are all which come into question), and we are still brought to a standstill by the fact that, if Irenaeus believed John of Ephesus to have been *one of the Twelve Apostles*, it is most remarkable that he never styles him 'John the Apostle', but always 'John the disciple of the Lord'. We note specially the fact that even where the four Evangelists are most carefully described in III. ix. 1; x. 1, 6; xi. 1, and the first of them figures as 'Matthew the Apostle', John is still simply 'John the disciple of the Lord'. Had Irenaeus taken him for the Apostle John, it would have been so natural in this case to have added 'who was one of the twelve Apostles'. We are bound also to contrast the way in which he is only twice referred to unnamed as 'the Apostle', with the 74 occasions on which St. Paul is so styled.

Now arises the question—Whence did Irenaeus obtain this distinctive title, 'the disciple of the Lord'? It is not derived from the Fourth Gospel; for, had this been so, we should have expected 'the disciple whom Jesus loved'. Looking at the titles of other witnesses, we observe that 'Mark the interpreter and disciple of Peter' seems clearly to depend upon Papias's statement, Μάρκος μὲν ἑρμηνευτὴς Πέτρου γενόμενος . . . Οὔτε γὰρ ἤκουσε τοῦ Κυρίου, οὔτε παρηκολούθησεν αὐτῷ· ὕστερον δέ, ὡς ἔφην, Πέτρῳ (Eusebius, *HE.* iii. 39). In the same way, we observe that Papias styles Aristion and John the presbyter οἱ τοῦ Κυρίου μαθηταί. It is true that in the same paragraph he subjoins ἤ τις ἕτερος τῶν τοῦ Κυρίου μαθητῶν to the names of the seven Apostles whom he mentions, and so may be taken to include them as μαθηταί. Here, however, we mark a difference; since the sense obviously is that Papias was anxious to gain information coming from any (presumably deceased) μαθητὴς Κυρίου (i.e. direct associate of the Lord), whether Apostle or otherwise. But in the cases of Aristion and John the presbyter οἱ τοῦ Κυρίου μαθηταί is *their distinctive title*, i.e. they were not Apostles, but they were (presumably) associates of our Lord who fell into a class by themselves as still living when Papias was collecting his information.

On the basis of these facts we conclude without hesitation that by 'John the disciple of the Lord' Irenaeus means John the presbyter, and that when he refers to Papias as ὁ Ἰωάννου μὲν ἀκουστής, he is at any rate as correct as Eusebius when he says ὁ νῦν δὲ ἡμῖν δηλούμενος Παπίας . . . τοῦ πρεσβυτέρου Ἰωάννου αὐτήκοον ἑαυτόν φησι γενέσθαι. It is Eusebius who, jumping to the conclusion that John the Apostle (mentioned sixth by Papias in his list of seven Apostles) must be the Evangelist (σαφῶς δηλῶν τὸν εὐαγγελιστήν), attaches to Irenaeus the charge of misconstruing Papias's evidence which has stuck to him ever since. In reality Irenaeus appears to be an impeccable witness as to the early Asian tradition in regard to John; and he completes our evidence that John the Evangelist and disciple of the Lord, who survived to old age at Ephesus, was not the son of Zebedee, but the presbyter.

Thus all the early Asiatic evidence, i.e. all the external evidence that matters, unites in indicating that the only John of Ephesus was John the presbyter, and that he wrote the Fourth Gospel. This, as we have seen, fits in wonderfully well with the internal evidence which favours the view that the author was not John the son of Zebedee, but a Jerusalemite of priestly family. There are, however, other internal considerations which may seem to tell against this view. If there were not, then surely there would be no problem of authorship remaining.

The first difficulty is the finding of a place among the companions of our Lord for a young man of priestly family who was not one of the twelve Apostles. This is largely based, it seems, upon the presupposition that the Apostles were our Lord's only openly-confessed adherents and regular companions. This of course is not the case. There were others from whom the seventy (or, according to the alternative reading of WH., seventy-two) missioners were drawn, who must, we may conjecture, have companied with Him not a little before they were fit to be entrusted with their mission. Yet of these we should know nothing apart from Lk. $10^{1\text{ff}}$. There were, again, the women who accompanied Him during a part at least of His evangelistic tours, and ministered to Him and His Apostles out of their substance. Of this fact too we should have been ignorant but for Lk. $8^{1\text{ff}}$. According to St. Paul in 1 Cor. 15^{6}, one of our Lord's Resurrection-appearances was 'to above five hundred brethren at once'. After the Ascension the number of 'the brethren' at Jerusalem is given in Acts 1^{15} as about one hundred and twenty, all of whom, apparently (perhaps with the addition of other disciples who had come up to Jerusalem for the Feast), received the outpouring of the Spirit at Pentecost.

Thus, if it were necessary to suppose that the young priestly disciple regularly accompanied our Lord upon His travels, this would not constitute an insuperable difficulty. But it is not so necessary; and indeed the probability is against such a theory.

Let us ask ourselves—How is it probable that our Lord would have dealt with a young man of good family and priestly connexions whom we may assume to have been a mere youth (perhaps not more than sixteen), who was keenly desirous of joining Him and becoming His disciple? Is it not likely that, while reading his heart and recognizing the great sincerity of his desire, He would—just because of his youth and the great renunciation of home and prospects which He knew that the step would entail—have refused with all tenderness to allow him at once to throw in his lot with the Apostolic band, and commanded him for the time to remain at home at Jerusalem? Meanwhile, whenever our Lord came up to Jerusalem and engaged in discussion with the Rabbinists, the young disciple would be there, making as much as he could of the great Teacher's temporary presence, keenly following the debates which his scholastic training so well enabled him to appreciate, drinking in every word of the subtle arguments of which the Galilaean Apostles could make nothing.*

Thus may well be explained the fact that the great bulk of the Gospel has to do with scenes and discourses at or near Jerusalem, the Galilaean episodes taking a comparatively subordinate part. And, in assessing the qualities in the young disciple which made him pre-eminently 'the disciple whom Jesus loved', shall we be wrong in attaching full weight to the *intellectual bond*—the fact that the youth's upbringing enabled him, in a far fuller measure than the untrained and more slow-witted Galilaean Apostles (at least before Pentecost), to enter into our Lord's point of view, to follow

* It is important to notice that the opinion of Jewish scholars distinctly favours the general historical character of the discourses in the Fourth Gospel, as representing one aspect of our Lord's teaching. Cf. the words of Dr. Abrahams in his essay 'Rabbinic aids to exegesis', *Cambridge Biblical Essays*, p. 181. 'One of the most remarkable facts about the writings of recent Jewish critics of the New Testament has been that they have tended on the whole to confirm the Gospel picture of external Jewish life, and where there is discrepancy, these critics tend to prove that the blame lies not with the New Testament originals but with their interpreters. Dr. Güdemann, Dr. Büchler, Dr. Schechter, Dr. Chwolson, Dr. Marmorstein, have all shown that the Talmud makes credible details which many Christian expositors have been rather inclined to dispute. Most remarkable of all has been the cumulative strength of the arguments adduced by Jewish writers favourable to the authenticity of the discourses in the Fourth Gospel, especially in relation to the circumstances under which they are reported to have been spoken. Much more may be expected in this direction, for Jewish scholars have only of late turned themselves to the close investigation of the New Testament.'

His expositions of the inner meaning of the Old Testament, and to grasp the fact that He was in the highest sense the embodiment of its ideals?

It is only natural that such a disciple should have been present at the Last Supper, and that the Apostles should not have grudged him a place next his Lord to which his deep affection and high gifts entitled him.* Nor is it surprising, even apart from his

* It would, however, not be strange if the position of privilege granted by our Lord to the young disciple should have excited the disapproval of some members at least of the Apostolic Twelve. Lk. 22^{21-34}—a passage of extraordinary interest as appearing to offer a summary of the events of the fuller narrative contained in Jn. 13—states in *v.*[24], *'Εγένετο δὲ καὶ φιλονεικία ἐν αὐτοῖς, τὸ τίς αὐτῶν δοκεῖ εἶναι μείζων*. This is met by our Lord's words of reproof, in which *ἐγὼ δὲ ἐν μέσῳ ὑμῶν εἰμὶ ὡς ὁ διακονῶν* is the verbal summary with which the foot-washing of Jn. 13 corresponds as the acted parable. Occasion for the Apostles' strife as to precedence may, as Dr. Plummer suggests, have arisen respecting the places at the Last Supper; but when we consider that the Twelve must presumably have sat at meals alone with their Master on many other occasions, the reason why the strife should have arisen on *this* occasion of all others is not apparent. Supposing, however, that this time the circle was enlarged by admission of the young disciple, and that he was placed by our Lord next to Himself, it may be that we have found the cause of this outbreak of *φιλονεικία*. Adopting this hypothesis, we seem to read our Lord's words of reproof with a new understanding. In the injunction *ἀλλ' ὁ μείζων ἐν ὑμῖν γινέσθω ὡς ὁ νεώτερος* the young disciple John becomes the concrete example of *ὁ νεώτερος*, which seems almost to acquire the meaning, 'this youth' (cf. Mk. 9^{33-41} and parallels). Again, the point of *v.*[28] appears to stand out more clearly: 'But *ye* (Apostles, in contrast to this young disciple) are they which have continued with Me in My temptations; and I appoint unto you a kingdom, even as My Father hath appointed unto Me, that ye may eat and drink at My table in My kingdom, and sit on thrones judging the twelve tribes of Israel'. These words, with all the fullness of promise which they undoubtedly contain, seem to be cast—with something like a touch of irony—in language adapted to appeal to the then-condition of the Apostles' ideals.

If our theory be true, the relation of the Twelve to St. John presents a close analogy to that of Martha to Mary (Lk. 10^{38-42}). Like Martha they were eager to spend and be spent in the service of their Master; but they were not, at that stage, endowed with the religious insight and spiritual (as distinct from practical) devotion possessed by Mary and the young disciple John. John, like Mary, had chosen the good part, which was not to be taken away from him.

If such was the occasion which led to the sublime example of the foot-washing, we see at once why the Fourth Evangelist gives no hint of the special circumstances which led up to it. As elsewhere, he suppresses his own personality as far as possible; and would, we may think, be the more careful to do so if it was his own position at the Supper which excited the envy of the Twelve. It may be added that the words *μετὰ τῶν δώδεκα* Mk. 14^{17}, *μετὰ τῶν δώδεκα [μαθητῶν]* Mt. 26^{20}, *καὶ οἱ ἀπόστολοι σὺν αὐτῷ* Lk. 22^{14}, by no means exclude the presence of a non-Apostolic guest at the Supper. The presence of John (as we picture him) might well have devotion, that when the Galilaeans fled in panic at the arrest, he should have followed on and entered boldly into the high priest's house.

We have now, it may be observed, further explained the bond of union between St. John and St. Paul to which allusion has already been made. Similarity of social position, a common Rabbinic training, common ideals and pride of race and enthusiasm for Judaism in its higher developments, account for much. We seem here to find explained the remarkable double attitude towards the Jews which characterizes both the Christian converts. If from one point of view the unbelieving Jews excite St. Paul's keenest antipathy, as those 'who both killed the Lord Jesus and the prophets, and drave out us, and please not God, and are contrary to all men; forbidding us to speak to the Gentiles that they may be saved; to fill up their sins alway: but the wrath is come upon them to the uttermost' (1 Thess. $2^{15.16}$); from another he can assert with all earnestness, 'I could wish myself anathema from Christ for my brethren's sake, my kinsmen according to the flesh: who are Israelites; whose is the adoption, and the glory, and the covenants, and the giving of the law, and the cultus, and the promises; whose are the fathers, and of whom is Christ after the flesh' (Rom. 9^{3-5}), and can speak not without satisfaction of the privileges which he inherited as 'a Hebrew of Hebrew parents' and the recipient of a thorough training in the strictest principles of Judaism (Phil. 3^{4-6}). So to St. John 'the Jews' from one point of view stand as the embodiment of unbelief and hardened opposition to the Embodiment of Light and Truth; yet from another he can record (with certainly a strong touch of national feeling) our Lord's words to the Samaritan woman, 'Ye worship that which ye know not: we worship that which we know: for salvation is from the Jews' (Jn. 4^{22}), and can refer, with a glow of enthusiasm, to 'the last day, the great day of the feast' of Tabernacles (Jn. 7^{37}).

It was precisely the grasp of Judaism from the inside only

seemed not to call for record. He may have counted for no more to the Apostles *at that time* than would nowadays a young scholar and thinker in the minds of men of practical ability holding high official positions in the Church.

possible to a trained Rabbinic scholar which emphasized the sense of its privileges and opened out the vista of its lofty possibilities in the light of the teaching of Him who was seen to be both its supreme exponent and its ultimate goal; while at the same time strengthening the recoil from those its professed teachers and practitioners who resolutely shut their ears to and resisted the Truth, and would not come to Him that they might have life. Such scholars were St. Paul and the Fourth Evangelist.

The other difficulty which may be urged against our view lies in the fact that there are indications in the Gospel which undoubtedly may be taken to point to John the son of Zebedee as the author. This conclusion, however, is largely bound up with the line of reasoning with which Dr. Westcott has familiarized us, in which we first take our stand upon the indubitable indications that the author of the Gospel was an eye-witness, and then argue—if an eye-witness, then an Apostle; if an Apostle, then John the son of Zebedee. If, however, the inference from eye-witness to Apostle may be questioned (as the present writer has questioned it in the preceding argument), and if the grounds upon which it is questioned be held to be valid, then the case for the authorship of John the son of Zebedee is clearly weakened. The fact that John the son of Zebedee is not mentioned by name is weighty if the author must needs be an Apostle. If there are grounds for holding that he was not an Apostle, then this omission falls into the same category as the omission of the names of James the son of Zebedee, Matthew, James the son of Alphaeus, Simon Zelotes, and possibly Bartholomew, i.e. it may be due to accident. We may feel surprise that two of the Apostles who so frequently in the Synoptic Gospels accompany Peter as special attendants of our Lord should not receive mention; but we should hardly be justified in arguing from this that one of these unnamed Apostles must be the author, even in the absence of strong indications to the contrary. From the opening of *ch.* 21 it is clear that the disciple whom Jesus loved is included under οἱ τοῦ Ζεβεδαίου on the ordinary view, but under ἄλλοι ἐκ τῶν μαθητῶν αὐτοῦ δύο upon the view which we are maintaining; and it is legitimate to argue that, since the author always elsewhere deliberately conceals his identity, the latter conclusion is (apart from evidence to the contrary) more probable than the former.*

The argument from the fact that the disciple whom Jesus loved is brought into connexion with Peter three times in rather special circumstances ($13^{23\,\text{ff.}}$, $20^{2\,\text{ff.}}$, $21^{20\,\text{ff.}}$) is weakened when we reflect that Peter stood in a special relation to our Lord as leader of the Apostolic band, and therefore any one else who, for any reason likewise stood in a special relation was bound to come into close connexion with Peter. In $13^{23\,\text{ff.}}$ all that the connexion amounts to is that a privileged Apostle of greater boldness than the others suggested a question to a disciple whom he recognized as still more intimate with our Lord than himself; in $21^{20\,\text{ff.}}$ that, having heard a prediction as to his own future, he inquired as to the fate of that other who was similarly united to his Master by a special tie of devotion. The remaining passage, $20^{2\,\text{ff.}}$, suggests indeed that the two disciples were lodging together—or it may have been, keeping vigil—in the same abode; but this is natural in the circumstances. The very facts that the younger disciple had witnessed Peter's denial, and at the same time was animated by a kindred affection for our Lord which would make him understand the better the dreadful grief of the repentant Apostle, would undoubtedly draw him close to him in the hour of need.

We are left, then, with the account in Jn. $1^{35\,\text{ff.}}$ of the first meeting with Jesus of the two disciples of St. John Baptist, one of whom we are told was Andrew the brother of Simon Peter, and the other, we infer, was the author of the Gospel. In *v.* [41] it is said of Andrew, *εὑρίσκει οὗτος πρῶτον τὸν ἀδελφὸν τὸν ἴδιον Σίμωνα*, and from this Dr. Westcott draws the deduction—'The words imply that some one else was afterwards found; and from the form of the sentence we may conclude that this is James the brother of John'.

This narrative is not a duplicate of the account of the call of the two pairs of Apostles in Mk. 1^{16-20} = Mt. 4^{18-22}, for (not to speak of the difference in detail) the scene is different—in Jn. Bethabara (or Bethany) beyond Jordan, where John was baptizing; in the Synoptists, the sea of Galilee. The two accounts may quite well

* Notice the similarity of the phrase to *ἐκ τῶν μαθητῶν αὐτοῦ δύο* 1^{35}, *ὁ ἄλλος μαθητής* $20^{2.3.4.8}$.

L 2

be harmonized if we suppose that the definite call (Δεῦτε ὀπίσω μου) of the Synoptic narrative came subsequently to the virtual call described by Jn.; and on this view the readiness of the disciples at once to leave their occupations and follow Christ receives considerable elucidation—they came at once without question because they had already been prepared for the call by the meeting described in Jn.

It must be remarked, however, that while this conclusion is clear as regards Andrew and Peter, the question as to the second disciple mentioned in Jn. 1[35 ff.] is involved in considerable obscurity. In the first place, we cannot be quite sure that the author of the Gospel is referring to himself; though this assumption is natural, and explains the author's detailed knowledge of the circumstances, both here and in the preceding *vv.* [29 ff.]. Secondly, Dr. Westcott's deduction from the statement εὑρίσκει οὗτος πρῶτον κτλ. is surely much too categorical. Why should πρῶτον imply that some one else was afterwards found? Comparing the use of the adverb in Mt. 6[33] ζητεῖτε δὲ πρῶτον τὴν βασιλείαν καὶ τὴν δικαιοσύνην αὐτοῦ, we may say rather that it implies that Andrew *made it his first business* to find his brother—'found him *then and there*'. If, then, the author of the Gospel is describing his own first interview with our Lord, there is nothing in the narrative which really conflicts with the theory that he was not the son of Zebedee but a member of a priestly family from Jerusalem. It is quite likely that such a one may have joined the multitudes who flocked to hear the Baptist, may have attached himself to him as a disciple and so have formed a friendship with Andrew, from whom incidentally he may at a later time have learned the details of the feeding of the five thousand (cf. 6[8]), if, as on our view, he was not permitted to become a constant follower of our Lord, but was an actual eye-witness of the Jerusalem-scenes only.

In endeavouring thus to strike a balance between the two views of authorship which we have been discussing—Apostle or young priestly disciple—we find that, while there is much both in internal and external evidence which is difficult to harmonize with the former view, the latter view seems wholly to be supported by the earliest external evidence, and to have the preponderant support of internal evidence; such internal indications as may seem, at first sight, to tell against it, being amenable to a reasonable solution.

A last point to which reference must briefly be made is the bearing of our theory of an Aramaic original for the Fourth Gospel upon the question of the authorship of the Apocalypse. In making the few remarks which he has to offer on this subject, the writer would guard against the impression that he has come to a fixed opinion. He has not studied the Apocalypse sufficiently thoroughly to do this. All that he has to put forward are certain obvious considerations which seem necessarily to arise out of his new theory as to the Gospel.

The case against the view that the Gospel and Apocalypse are by the same author has always been based chiefly upon the difference in Greek style. It is held that the extraordinary solecisms of the Apocalypse find no parallel in the Gospel, in which the language 'flows along smoothly from the prologue to the end; there is no startling phrase, no defiance of syntax; if it is obviously the work of one who was more familiar with the construction of the Semitic than of the Greek sentence, yet the author seldom or never offends against definite laws. In these respects he not only differs from the Apocalyptist, but stands at the opposite pole to the eccentricities, the roughnesses, the audacities of the latter'.*

It is obvious that, if the Gospel is a translation from Aramaic, the criterion of Greek style as differentiating the two books at once falls to the ground. On the other hand, if the Gospel was written in Aramaic prior to the author's arrival in Ephesus somewhat late in his life, and he then adopted Greek owing to the exigencies of his new surroundings, such Greek as we find in the Apocalypse would not be surprising.†

* Swete, *Apocalypse*[2], p. cxxviii. It may be remarked that this estimate of the smoothness of the Greek of the Gospel is perhaps somewhat exaggerated in face e.g. of the group of passages which the present writer has brought together on pp. 101 ff.

† It may be urged that, if the Gospel is a translation, the Epistles still remain; and they, though presumably written in Greek, do not display the solecisms of the Apocalypse. But the Epistles may well have been dictated to an amanuensis, who was in some degree responsible for the correctness of the Greek; and possibly this amanuensis may have been the translator of the Gospel.

Again, we have to notice that, as Dr. Charles has ably pointed out, the author of the Apocalypse frames his style upon a Biblical Hebrew model. Such a knowledge of Biblical Hebrew, though unexpected in a Galilaean fisherman, would be natural in a trained Rabbinic scholar. We have found reason to believe that the author of the Gospel was such a scholar; and it seems necessary to hold that the author of the Apocalypse, who must likewise have been a Palestinian, was similarly equipped.*

It is a remarkable fact that, though Dr. Charles holds that the author of the Apocalypse was not the author of the Gospel, the description which he gives (i, p. xliv) of the characteristics of the former is applicable, in its main details, to the latter according to the conclusions which we have formed in the present discussion. Thus we are told that the author of the Apocalypse 'was a Palestinian Jew. He was a great spiritual genius, a man of profound insight and the widest sympathies'. He had an 'intimate acquaintance with the Hebrew text of the O.T.' 'The fact that he thought in Hebrew and translated its idioms literally into Greek, points to Palestine as his original home.' 'His extraordinary use of Greek appears to prove not only that he never mastered the ordinary Greek of his own times, but that he came to acquire whatever knowledge he had of this language when somewhat advanced in years.' All these characteristics are precisely those which we should expect that the author of the Fourth Gospel would display if he turned himself to the composition of a book like the Apocalypse. Is this coincidence merely accidental?

The following is a rough list of Semitisms common to the Fourth Gospel and the Apocalypse:

Asyndeton (cf. p. 49), which is an Aramaic characteristic, is naturally not to be expected in a work which conforms itself to Biblical Hebrew style. The author of Apoc. slips into it, however,

* Dr. Charles is hardly accurate in speaking (i, p. xliv) of 'his use of Hebrew practically as his mother tongue (for Hebrew was still the language of learned discussions in Palestine)'. The language of learned discussion in Palestine was New Hebrew, which is in many respects more closely akin to Aramaic than to the classical Hebrew in which this writer correctly finds the author's model (cf. p. 17, foot-note). Rabbinic scholars were, however, naturally skilled in their knowledge of the O.T. in the original; and the author is deliberately modelling his style upon the O.T. and not upon New Hebrew.

not infrequently towards the end of his book, possibly owing to the fact that Aramaic was his mother-tongue. It may be noted that Aramaic has influenced New Hebrew in this respect (cf. p. 50). Cf. Apoc. 16^{6}, 19^{20}, $20^{3.5.6.14}$, 21^{4}, $22^{15.17}$.

Parataxis (cf. p. 56). The co-ordination of sentences by καί . . . καί is so frequent in Apoc. that it needs no illustration.

Non-use of Aorist Participle describing action anterior to Finite verb. There seems to be only one instance, viz. ἐπιστρέψας εἶδον 1^{12}. In Jn. the usage is far less frequent than in the Synoptists (cf. p. 56).

Avoidance of the Genitive absolute construction. This construction is totally absent from Apoc. Though used occasionally in Jn., it is far less frequent than in the Synoptists (cf. p. 57).*

Use of Casus pendens (cf. p. 63). See Swete, p. cxviii; Charles, i, pp. cxlix, 53. This construction is more frequent in Jn. than in Apoc.

καί *linking contrasted statements* (cf. p. 66). Cf. Apoc. $2^{13.21}$, $3^{1.5.8}$.

Great rarity of δέ. There seem to be 5 occurrences only in Apoc., viz. 1^{14}, 2^{24}, 10^{2}, 19^{12}, 21^{8}. δέ in Jn. is proportionately slightly less frequent than in Mk., and less than half as frequent as in Mt. and Lk. (cf. p. 69).

Infrequency of γάρ (cf. p. 69). Only about 17 occurrences.

ἵνα μή *frequent*, μήποτε *never*. There are 11 occurrences of ἵνα μή in Apoc., and none of μήποτε. μήποτε never occurs in Jn. in sense 'that . . . not', 'lest', its place being regularly taken by ἵνα μή (cf. pp. 69 f., 100).

The Relative completed by a Pronoun (cf. p. 84). Cf. Apoc. 3^{8}, $7^{2.9}$, $12^{6.14}$, $13^{8.12}$, 17^{9}, 20^{8}.

ὄνομα αὐτῷ = '*Whose name was*'. Jn. 1^{6}, 3^{1}, Apoc. 6^{3}, 9^{11}. Never elsewhere in N.T. (cf. p. 30).

ἔρχεται *Present used as Futurum instans* (cf. p. 94). Cf. Apoc. $1^{4.7.8}$, $2^{5.16}$, 3^{11}, 4^{8}, 9^{12}, 11^{14}, 16^{15}, $22^{7.12.20}$. The same usage is seen with other verbs in 11^{5} (ἐκπορεύεται, κατεσθίει), $11^{9.10}$ (βλέπουσιν, ἀφίουσιν, χαίρουσιν, εὐφραίνονται), 14^{9} (προσκυνεῖ, λαμβάνει).

* Dr. Charles (i, p. xxxv) states that the Genitive absolute 'occurs often' in Jn. As a matter of fact the occurrences are 17, as against Mt. 48, Mk. 36, Lk. 59, i. e. it is proportionately about $2\frac{1}{2}$ times as frequent in the Synoptists as in Jn.

Change of construction after Participle (cf. p. 96, where the cases in Apoc. are noted).

πᾶς (πᾶν) . . . οὐ = '*none*' (p. 98). Cf. Apoc. 7[16], 28[22], 21[27], 22[3].

Thus it appears that the case against identity of authorship of the Gospel and Apocalypse can certainly not be maintained upon the ground of style. The evidence is all in the other direction.

A few words may be added as to the claim to authorship made by the Apocalyptist. He describes himself as 'John' simply in 1[1,4], 22[8]; in 1[9] with the addition of 'your brother and companion in the tribulation and kingdom and endurance (which is) in Jesus'. In 18[20], 21[14] he seems to distinguish himself from the Twelve Apostles. In 22[9] he is ranked among the prophets. Though the tone of authority in which he delivers his message is bound up with the fact that he is the mouthpiece of the glorified Christ, it is clear that he recognizes that his name carries the authority of a *true* mouthpiece, i.e. he is a man well known and of important standing in the churches of Asia. His work, though apparently utilizing older sources, must almost certainly be dated towards the end of the reign of Domitian, i.e. shortly before A.D. 96.

Now the evidence which we have already reviewed points to the conclusion that there was but *one* John of great note in Asia at this period, viz. John the presbyter, who was known as 'the disciple of the Lord'. Evidence also indicates that this John was the author of the Fourth Gospel. Unless, therefore, the Apocalypse is pseudonymous (against which see Dr. Charles, i, pp. xxxviii f.), the conclusion is certainly cogent that the author who signs himself 'John' is John the presbyter.

Thus the evidence of claim to authorship combines with that of Semitic style in suggesting that the author of the Apocalypse is one with the author of the Fourth Gospel and Epistles. Whether there exist criteria of Theological thought or other internal characteristics which are sufficient to disprove this inference is a question which the writer must leave to others to decide.

APPENDIX

1. *Reminiscences of the teaching of the Fourth Gospel (and 1 Jn.) in the Epistles of St. Ignatius.*

To the Ephesians.

2. πρέπον οὖν ἐστιν κατὰ πάντα τρόπον δοξάζειν Ἰησοῦν Χριστὸν τὸν δοξάσαντα ὑμᾶς· ἵνα ἐν μιᾷ ὑποταγῇ κατηρτισμένοι . . . κατὰ πάντα ἦτε ἡγιασμένοι.	Jn. 17^{22} κἀγὼ τὴν δόξαν ἣν δέδωκάς μοι δέδωκα αὐτοῖς, ἵνα ὦσιν ἓν καθὼς ἡμεῖς ἕν. Jn. 17^{19} ἵνα ὦσιν καὶ αὐτοὶ ἡγιασμένοι ἐν ἀληθείᾳ.
4. διὰ τοῦτο ἐν τῇ ὁμονοίᾳ ὑμῶν καὶ συμφώνῳ ἀγάπῃ Ἰησοῦς Χριστὸς ᾄδεται.	Jn. 13^{35} ἐν τούτῳ γνώσονται πάντες ὅτι ἐμοὶ μαθηταί ἐστε, ἐὰν ἀγάπην ἔχητε ἐν ἀλλήλοις.
5. πόσῳ μᾶλλον ὑμᾶς μακαρίζω τοὺς ἀνακεκραμένους οὕτως, ὡς ἡ ἐκκλησία Ἰησοῦ Χριστῷ καὶ ὡς Ἰησοῦς Χριστὸς τῷ πατρί, ἵνα πάντα ἐν ἑνότητι σύμφωνα ᾖ.	Jn. 17^{21} ἵνα πάντες ἓν ὦσιν, καθὼς σύ, πατήρ, ἐν ἐμοὶ κἀγὼ ἐν σοί, ἵνα καὶ αὐτοὶ ἐν ἡμῖν [ἓν] ὦσιν.
7. Christ is ἐν θανάτῳ ζωὴ ἀληθινή. Cf. 11. μόνον ἐν Χριστῷ Ἰησοῦ εὑρεθῆναι εἰς τὸ ἀληθινὸν ζῆν. Trall. 9. ἐν Χριστῷ Ἰησοῦ, οὗ χωρὶς τὸ ἀληθινὸν ζῆν οὐκ ἔχομεν.	Jn. $11^{25,26}$ Ἐγώ εἰμι . . . ἡ ζωή· ὁ πιστεύων εἰς ἐμὲ κἂν ἀποθάνῃ ζήσεται· κτλ. Cf. also 1 Jn. 5^{21}.

We may note that the adj. ἀληθινός is specially characteristic of Jn. (9 times), 1 Jn. (4 times), and Apoc. (10 times), occurring but 5 times besides in the whole remainder of the N.T.

11. Ἔσχατοι καιροί.	1 Jn. 2^{18} ἐσχάτη ὥρα ἐστίν.

14. Ὧν οὐδὲν λανθάνει ὑμᾶς, ἐὰν τελείως εἰς Ἰησοῦν Χριστὸν ἔχητε τὴν πίστιν καὶ τὴν ἀγάπην· ἥτις ἐστὶν ἀρχὴ ζωῆς καὶ τέλος· ἀρχὴ μὲν πίστις, τέλος δὲ ἀγάπη· τὰ δὲ δύο ἐν ἑνότητι γενόμενα Θεός ἐστιν.

1 Jn. $4^{8.16}$ ὁ Θεὸς ἀγάπη ἐστίν.

1 Jn. 2^{5} ἀληθῶς ἐν τούτῳ ἡ ἀγάπη τοῦ Θεοῦ τετελείωται. Cf. $4^{12.17.18}$.

The Johannine teaching is here combined with that of St. Paul in 1 Cor. 13.

14. οὐδεὶς πίστιν ἐπαγγελλόμενος ἁμαρτάνει οὐδὲ ἀγάπην κεκτημένος μισεῖ.

1 Jn. 3^{6} πᾶς ὁ ἐν αὐτῷ μένων οὐχ ἁμαρτάνει.

1 Jn. 4^{20} ἐάν τις εἴπῃ ὅτι Ἀγαπῶ τὸν Θεόν, καὶ τὸν ἀδελφὸν αὐτοῦ μισῇ, ψεύστης ἐστίν. Cf. also $2^{9.11}$.

15. πάντα οὖν ποιῶμεν, ὡς αὐτοῦ ἐν ἡμῖν κατοικοῦντος, ἵνα ὦμεν αὐτοῦ ναοὶ καὶ αὐτὸς ᾖ ἐν ἡμῖν Θεός.

1 Jn. 3^{24} καὶ ὁ τηρῶν τὰς ἐντολὰς αὐτοῦ ἐν αὐτῷ μένει καὶ αὐτὸς ἐν αὐτῷ.

17. Διὰ τοῦτο μύρον ἔλαβεν ἐπὶ τῆς κεφαλῆς [αὐτοῦ] ὁ Κύριος, ἵνα πνέῃ τῇ ἐκκλησίᾳ ἀφθαρσίαν.

Jn. 12^{3} ἡ δὲ οἰκία ἐπληρώθη ἐκ τῆς ὀσμῆς τοῦ μύρου.

The words ἐπὶ τῆς κεφαλῆς αὐτοῦ prove that St. Ignatius has in mind the narrative of the anointing as recorded in Mk. 14^{3-9} = Mt. 26^{6-13}. According to Jn. $12^{1\,ff.}$ our Lord's *feet* were anointed; yet it is difficult to resist the conclusion that Ignatius's words ἵνα πνέῃ κτλ. are based on recollection of the passage from Jn. which we have placed as a parallel, 'the house' being allegorized as referring to the Church.

17, 19. The phrase ὁ ἄρχων τοῦ αἰῶνος τούτου occurs six times in St. Ignatius's letters (the other occurrences are Magn. 1; Trall. 4; Rom. 7; Phil. 6). In the Syriac version the equivalent is ܐܪܟܘܢܗ ܕܥܠܡܐ ܗܢܐ (Eph. 19). In Jn. 12^{31}, 16^{11} we have the phrase ὁ ἄρχων τοῦ κόσμου τούτου, which is rendered by Sin. ܐܪܟܘܢܗ (ܡܕܒܪܢܗ 12^{31}) ܕܥܠܡܐ ܗܢܐ, and by Pesh. ܐܪܟܘܢܐ ܕܥܠܡܐ ܗܢܐ; in 14^{30} ὁ τοῦ κόσμου [τούτου] ἄρχων is rendered by Sin. and Pesh. ܐܪܟܘܢܐ ܕܥܠܡܐ. In Jn., as in Ignatius, the thought is of the spiritual ruler of *the present age* or *world-period* (properly τοῦ αἰῶνος τούτου), just as in 1 Cor. $2^{6.8}$ τῶν ἀρχόντων τοῦ αἰῶνος τούτου denotes the earthly rulers of the present age. Aramaic has but one term עָלְמָא (Syr. ܥܳܠܡܳܐ) to denote *αἰών* and *κόσμος*, and the Johannine rendering *τοῦ κόσμου τούτου* is less accurate than *τοῦ αἰῶνος τούτου*, and mistranslates the original which must have been אַרְכּוֹנָא דְעָלְמָא הָדֵין. It can hardly be doubted, then, that Ignatius drew his phrase from Jn., and the form in which he gives it suggests that he may have known the Aramaic original of the Gospel.

To the Magnesians.

1. ἐν αἷς [ἐκκλησίαις] ἕνωσιν εὔχομαι σαρκὸς καὶ πνεύματος Ἰησοῦ Χριστοῦ τοῦ διὰ παντὸς ἡμῶν ζῆν, πίστεώς τε καὶ ἀγάπης ἧς οὐδὲν προκέκριται, τὸ δὲ κυριώτερον, Ἰησοῦ καὶ πατρός.

Jn. 17^{21} (quoted above on Eph. 5).

5. ὥσπερ γάρ ἐστιν νομίσματα δύο, ὃ μὲν Θεοῦ ὃ δὲ κόσμου, καὶ ἕκαστον αὐτῶν ἴδιον χαρακτῆρα ἐπικείμενον ἔχει, οἱ ἄπιστοι τοῦ κόσμου τούτου, οἱ δὲ πιστοὶ ἐν ἀγάπῃ χαρακτῆρα Θεοῦ πατρὸς διὰ Ἰησοῦ Χριστοῦ . . .

Jn. 15^{19} εἰ ἐκ τοῦ κόσμου ἦτε, ὁ κόσμος ἂν τὸ ἴδιον ἐφίλει· ὅτι δὲ ἐκ τοῦ κόσμου οὐκ ἐστέ, ἀλλ' ἐγὼ ἐξελεξάμην ὑμᾶς ἐκ τοῦ κόσμου, διὰ τοῦτο μισεῖ ὑμᾶς ὁ κόσμος.

5. τὸ ζῆν αὐτοῦ οὐκ ἔστιν ἐν ἡμῖν.

1 Jn. 1^{8} ἡ ἀλήθεια οὐκ ἔστιν ἐν ἡμῖν.

1 Jn. 1^{10} ὁ λόγος αὐτοῦ οὐκ ἔστιν ἐν ἡμῖν.

Jn. 8^{37} ὁ λόγος ὁ ἐμὸς οὐ χωρεῖ ἐν ὑμῖν.

1 Jn. 3^{15} οὐκ ἔχει ζωὴν αἰώνιον ἐν αὐτῷ μένουσαν.

6. πάντες οὖν ὁμοήθειαν Θεοῦ λαβόντες ἐντρέπεσθε ἀλλήλους . . . ἐν Ἰησοῦ Χριστῷ ἀλλήλους διὰ παντὸς ἀγαπᾶτε.

Jn. 13^{35} (quoted above on Eph. 4).

7. Ὥσπερ οὖν ὁ Κύριος ἄνευ τοῦ πατρὸς οὐδὲν ἐποίησεν [ἡνωμένος ὤν], . . .

Jn. 5^{19} οὐ δύναται ὁ υἱὸς ποιεῖν ἀφ' ἑαυτοῦ οὐδὲν ἂν μή τι βλέπῃ τὸν πατέρα ποιοῦντα.

Jn. 8^{28} ἀπ' ἐμαυτοῦ ποιῶ οὐδέν,

	ἀλλὰ καθὼς ἐδίδαξέν με ὁ πατὴρ ταῦτα λαλῶ.
	Jn. 10^{30} ἐγὼ καὶ ὁ πατὴρ ἕν ἐσμεν. Cf. also $10^{25.37.38}$.
7. ἐπὶ ἕνα Ἰησοῦν Χριστὸν τὸν ἀφ' ἑνὸς πατρὸς προελθόντα καὶ εἰς ἕνα ὄντα καὶ χωρήσαντα.	Jn. 16^{28} ἐξῆλθον ἐκ τοῦ πατρὸς καὶ ἐλήλυθα εἰς τὸν κόσμον· πάλιν ἀφίημι τὸν κόσμον καὶ πορεύομαι πρὸς τὸν πατέρα. Cf. 8^{42}, 13^{3}.
εἰς ἕνα ὄντα.	Jn. 1^{18} ὁ ὢν εἰς τὸν κόλπον τοῦ πατρός. Cf. $14^{10.11.20}$.
καὶ χωρήσαντα.	Cf. $14^{12.28}$, $16^{10.17}$.
8. ὅτι εἷς Θεός ἐστιν ὁ φανερώσας ἑαυτὸν διὰ Ἰησοῦ Χριστοῦ τοῦ υἱοῦ αὐτοῦ,	Jn. 17^{6} Ἐφανέρωσά σου τὸ ὄνομα.
ὅς ἐστιν αὐτοῦ λόγος ἀπὸ σιγῆς προελθών,	Jn. $1^{1ff.}$
ὃς κατὰ πάντα εὐηρέστησεν τῷ πέμψαντι αὐτόν.	Jn. 8^{29} καὶ ὁ πέμψας με μετ' ἐμοῦ ἐστίν· . . . ὅτι ἐγὼ τὰ ἀρεστὰ αὐτῷ ποιῶ πάντοτε. Cf. also with τῷ πέμψαντι αὐτόν, Jn. 4^{34}, $5^{23.24.30.37}$, $6^{38.39.44}$, $7^{16.18.28.33}$, $8^{16.18.26}$, 9^{4}, $12^{44.45.49}$, 13^{20}, 14^{24}, 15^{21}, 16^{5}, 20^{21}.
9. πῶς ἡμεῖς δυνησόμεθα ζῆσαι χωρὶς αὐτοῦ; cf. Trall. 9. οὗ χωρὶς τὸ ἀληθινὸν ζῆν οὐκ ἔχομεν.	Jn. $15^{1ff.}$. Cf. especially *v.* 5 χωρὶς ἐμοῦ.

To the Trallians.

11. Φεύγετε οὖν τὰς κακὰς παραφυάδας τὰς γεννώσας καρπὸν θανατηφόρον, οὗ ἐὰν γεύσηταί τις, παραυτὰ ἀποθνήσκει. οὗτοι γὰρ οὔκ εἰσιν φυτεία πατρός.	Jn. $15^{1.2.6}$ The Father is the husbandman who tends the vine and removes the worthless shoots.

Lightfoot compares Clement Alex. *Paed.* i. 8 καθυλομανεῖ γὰρ μὴ κλαδευομένη ἡ ἄμπελος, οὕτως δὲ καὶ ὁ ἄνθρωπος· καθαίρει δὲ αὐτοῦ τὰς ἐξυβριζούσας παραφυάδας ὁ λόγος, κτλ. The word παραφυάς denotes a side-growth or worthless sucker which detracts from the fertility of the plant. According to Aristotle, *Plant.* i. 4 παραφυάδες δέ εἰσι τὰ ἀπὸ τῆς ῥίζης τοῦ δένδρου βλαστάνοντα. Thus the thought of Ignatius is allied to that of Jn., with the difference that the μὴ φέρον καρπόν of the latter becomes τὰς γεννώσας καρπὸν θανατηφόρον.

In the last clause there is allusion to Mt. 15[13], Πᾶσα φυτεία ἣν οὐκ ἐφύτευσεν ὁ πατήρ μου ὁ οὐράνιος ἐκριζωθήσεται.

11. καὶ ἦν ἂν ὁ καρπὸς αὐτῶν ἄφθαρτος.

Jn. 15[16] ἵνα . . . ὁ καρπὸς ὑμῶν μένῃ.

To the Romans.

3. μεγέθους ἐστὶν ὁ χριστιανισμός, ὅταν μισῆται ὑπὸ κόσμου.

Jn. 15[19] εἰ ἐκ τοῦ κόσμου ἦτε, ὁ κόσμος ἂν τὸ ἴδιον ἐφίλει· ὅτι δὲ ἐκ τοῦ κόσμου οὐκ ἐστέ, ἀλλ' ἐγὼ ἐξελεξάμην ὑμᾶς ἐκ τοῦ κόσμου, διὰ τοῦτο μισεῖ ὑμᾶς ὁ κόσμος.

7. μὴ λαλεῖτε Ἰησοῦν Χριστὸν κόσμον δὲ ἐπιθυμεῖτε.

1 Jn. 2[15] ἐάν τις ἀγαπᾷ τὸν κόσμον, οὐκ ἔστιν ἡ ἀγάπη τοῦ πατρὸς ἐν αὐτῷ.

7. ὕδωρ δὲ ζῶν καὶ λαλοῦν ἐν ἐμοί, ἔσωθέν μοι λέγον κτλ..

Jn. 4[10] ἔδωκεν ἄν σοι ὕδωρ ζῶν.

Jn. 4[14] τὸ ὕδωρ ὃ δώσω αὐτῷ γενήσεται ἐν αὐτῷ πηγὴ ὕδατος ἁλλομένου εἰς ζωὴν αἰώνιον. Cf. also Jn. 7[38].

7. ἄρτον Θεοῦ θέλω, ὅ ἐστιν σὰρξ τοῦ Χριστοῦ . . . καὶ πόμα θέλω τὸ αἷμα αὐτοῦ, ὅ ἐστιν ἀγάπη ἄφθαρτος.

Jn. 6[32.33] ὁ πατήρ μου δίδωσιν ὑμῖν τὸν ἄρτον ἐκ τοῦ οὐρανοῦ τὸν ἀληθινόν· ὁ γὰρ ἄρτος τοῦ Θεοῦ ἐστὶν ὁ καταβαίνων ἐκ τοῦ οὐρανοῦ καὶ ζωὴν διδοὺς τῷ κόσμῳ.

Jn. 6[55] ἡ γὰρ σάρξ μου ἀληθής ἐστι βρῶσις, καὶ τὸ αἷμά μου ἀληθής ἐστι πόσις.

To the Philadelphians.

2. Τέκνα οὖν φωτὸς ἀληθείας,* φεύγετε τὸν μερισμὸν καὶ τὰς κακο-

Jn. 12[36] ὡς τὸ φῶς ἔχετε πιστεύετε εἰς τὸ φῶς, ἵνα υἱοὶ φωτὸς γένησθε.

* Lightfoot's verdict is, 'The reading of the Greek MSS. φωτὸς ἀληθείας "of the light of truth", cannot stand; for definite articles would almost certainly be

διδασκαλίας· ὅπου δὲ ὁ ποιμήν ἐστιν, ἐκεῖ ὡς πρόβατα ἀκολουθεῖτε· πολλοὶ γὰρ λύκοι . . . αἰχμαλωτίζουσιν τοὺς θεοδρόμους.

Jn. 10[4] ὅταν τὰ ἴδια πάντα ἐκβάλῃ, ἔμπροσθεν αὐτῶν πορεύεται, καὶ τὰ πρόβατα αὐτῷ ἀκολουθεῖ.

v.[12] καὶ ὁ λύκος ἁρπάζει αὐτὰ καὶ σκορπίζει.

3. Ἀπέχεσθε τῶν κακῶν βοτανῶν, ἅστινας οὐ γεωργεῖ Ἰησοῦς Χριστός, διὰ τὸ μὴ εἶναι αὐτοὺς φυτείαν πατρός. Cf. on Trall. 11.

Jn. 15[1ff.].

7. τὸ πνεῦμα οὐ πλανᾶται, ἀπὸ Θεοῦ ὄν· οἶδεν γὰρ πόθεν ἔρχεται καὶ ποῦ ὑπάγει, καὶ τὰ κρυπτὰ ἐλέγχει.

Jn. 3[8] τὸ πνεῦμα ὅπου θέλει πνεῖ, καὶ τὴν φωνὴν αὐτοῦ ἀκούεις, ἀλλ' οὐκ οἶδας πόθεν ἔρχεται καὶ ποῦ ὑπάγει· οὕτως ἐστὶν πᾶς ὁ γεγεννημένος ἐκ τοῦ πνεύματος.

Jn. 3[20] καὶ οὐκ ἔρχεται πρὸς τὸ φῶς, ἵνα μὴ ἐλεγχθῇ τὰ ἔργα αὐτοῦ.

8. πιστεύω τῇ χάριτι Ἰησοῦ Χριστοῦ, ὃς λύσει ἀφ' ὑμῶν πάντα δεσμόν.

Jn. 8[32.36] καὶ γνώσεσθε τὴν ἀλήθειαν, καὶ ἡ ἀλήθεια ἐλευθερώσει ὑμᾶς. . . . ἐὰν οὖν ὁ υἱὸς ὑμᾶς ἐλευθερώσῃ, ὄντως ἐλεύθεροι ἔσεσθε.

9. αὐτὸς ὢν θύρα τοῦ πατρός, δι' ἧς εἰσέρχονται Ἀβραὰμ καὶ Ἰσαὰκ καὶ Ἰακὼβ καὶ οἱ προφῆται καὶ οἱ ἀπόστολοι καὶ ἡ ἐκκλησία.

Jn. 10[7.9] ἐγώ εἰμι ἡ θύρα τῶν προβάτων. . . . ἐγώ εἰμι ἡ θύρα· δι' ἐμοῦ ἐάν τις εἰσέλθῃ σωθήσεται.

required. The text might be mended by inserting a *καί*, as the Armenian Version gives "light and truth". On such a point however a version has little weight, since this would be a very obvious expedient for a translator. I am disposed to think that *τέκνα ἀληθείας* was the original reading of Ignatius; and that *φωτός* was first intended as a substitution or a gloss or a parallel, suggested by the familiar scriptural phrase *τέκνα* (*υἱοὶ*) *φωτός*'. It may be remarked, however, that the Aramaic method of expressing '*the true light*' is נְהוֹרָא דִקוּשְׁטָא, Syr. ܢܘܗܪܐ ܕܩܘܫܬܐ '*light of truth*', this latter being used e. g. to translate *τὸ φῶς τὸ ἀληθινόν* in Jn. 1[9]. Thus *φωτὸς ἀληθείας*, which, according to Lightfoot 'is older than any existing authorities', may well be an Aramaism, possibly pointing (like *ὁ ἄρχων τοῦ αἰῶνος τούτου* noted on p. 154) to an acquaintance with the original Aramaic Gospel. For omission of the definite article in rendering such a Semitic phrase into Greek cf. Gen. 24[48] בְּדֶרֶךְ אֱמֶת 'in the true (right) way' (lit. 'in way of truth') = LXX *ἐν ὁδῷ ἀληθείας*, Ps. 118 (119)[30] *ὁδὸν ἀληθείας ᾑρετισάμην*.

To the Smyrnaeans.

1. πεπληροφορημένους εἰς τὸν Κύριον ἡμῶν . . . ἀληθῶς ἐπὶ Ποντίου Πιλάτου καὶ Ἡρώδου τετράρχου καθηλωμένον ὑπὲρ ἡμῶν ἐν σαρκί· . . . ἵνα ἄρῃ σύσσημον εἰς τοὺς αἰῶνας διὰ τῆς ἀναστάσεως εἰς τοὺς ἁγίους καὶ πιστοὺς αὐτοῦ, εἴτε ἐν Ἰουδαίοις εἴτε ἐν ἔθνεσιν, ἐν ἑνὶ σώματι τῆς ἐκκλησίας αὐτοῦ.	Jn. $3^{14.15}$ καὶ καθὼς Μωυσῆς ὕψωσεν τὸν ὄφιν ἐν τῇ ἐρήμῳ, οὕτως ὑψωθῆναι δεῖ τὸν υἱὸν τοῦ ἀνθρώπου, ἵνα πᾶς ὁ πιστεύων ἐν αὐτῷ ἔχῃ ζωὴν αἰώνιον. Jn. 12^{32} κἀγὼ ἂν ὑψωθῶ ἐκ τῆς γῆς, πάντας ἑλκύσω πρὸς ἐμαυτόν. Cf. also Jn. 3^{14}.

The allusion of σύσσημον seems to be to the נֵס 'standard' or 'signal-post' on which the brazen serpent was set, Num. $21^{8.9}$. LXX καὶ θὲς αὐτὸν ἐπὶ σημείου. נֵס is rendered σύσσημον by LXX in Isa. 5^{26}, 49^{22}, 62^{10}. It is so rendered by Aquila in Ps. 60 $(59)^{6}$, Isa. 11^{10}, 33^{23}; by Symmachus in Isa. 11^{10}, 33^{23}; and by Theodotion in Isa. 33^{23}.

2. *Reminiscences of the Odes of Solomon in the Epistles of St. Ignatius.*

The principal passages from which Drs. Rendel Harris and Mingana argue that the Odes were familiar to Ignatius are as follows:

Ode $38^{7.8}$

ܫܪܪܐ ܕܝܢ ܐܙܠ ܗܘܐ ܒܐܘܪܚܐ ܬܪܝܨܬܐ.
ܘܟܠܡܕܡ ܕܠܐ ܝܕܥ ܗܘܝܬ ܡܚܘܐ ܗܘܐ ܠܝ
ܠܟܠܗܘܢ ܣܡܡܢܐ ܕܛܘܥܝܘܬܐ
ܘܠܡܚܘܬܐ ܗܢܘܢ ܕܣܒܪܝܢ ܕܒܣܝܡܘܬܐ ܐܢܝܢ ܕܡܘܬܐ.

'But Truth proceeds in the right path,
And whatever I did not know it made clear to me;
Even all the drugs of error,
And the plagues of death which men think to be sweetness.' *

* In the last line the Syriac construction is somewhat harsh; lit. 'And the plagues which they think to be sweetness, of death'. The separation of 'of death' from 'the plagues' (if not merely an accidental misplacement) may have been dictated by desire to bring it into sharp contrast to 'sweetness', the sense being, 'And the plagues which they think to be sweetness, (though they be the plagues) of death'.

In Trall. 6 Ignatius warns his readers against the teaching of heretics in the following terms: 'For these men do even mingle poison with Jesus Christ, imposing upon others by a show of honesty, like persons administering a deadly drug with honied wine, so that one who knoweth not, fearing nothing, drinketh in death with a baneful delight' (ὥσπερ θανάσιμον φάρμακον διδόντες μετὰ οἰνομέλιτος, ὅπερ ὁ ἀγνοῶν ἀδεῶς λαμβάνει ἐν ἡδονῇ κακῇ τὸ ἀποθανεῖν).

In the view of the editors 'ܚܠܝܘܬܐ *ḥalyūthā* is not merely "sweetness", but something with which the poison is taken, i.e. a sweet drink'. This is substantiated by a passage in which Ephrem states that Bardaisan, in composing his Psalter in imitation of David, 'was administering to the simple bitters in *ḥalyūthā*'. It is a fair inference, then, that the οἰνόμελι of Ignatius corresponds to the Syr. *ḥalyūthā*. Thus both the Ode and Ignatius compare heretical teaching to a poisonous drug concealed in a sweet drink, so that men imbibe it unwittingly. The coincidence in thought can hardly be accidental.

Ode 11[6]

ܘܡ̈ܝܐ ܡܡܲܠܠܐ ܩܪܒܘ ܠܣܦܘܬ̈ܝ

ܡܢ ܡܒܘܥܗ ܕܡܪܝܐ ܕܠܐ ܚܣܡ.

'And speaking waters drew near my lips
From the fountain of the Lord, without stint.'

Ignatius, Rom. 7; 'My lust hath been crucified, and there is no fire of material longing in me, but only water living and speaking in me, saying within me, Come to the Father' (ὕδωρ δὲ ζῶν καὶ λαλοῦν ἐν ἐμοί, ἔσωθέν μοι λέγον· Δεῦρο πρὸς τὸν πατέρα).

In explanation of λαλοῦν, Lightfoot cites Jortin (*Eccles. Hist.* I, pp. 356 f.) as finding an allusion to the heathen superstition that certain waters communicated a prophetic power to the people drinking them. As there was one of these 'speaking' fountains at Daphne (Sozomen, *HE.* v. 19; Evagrius i. 16), the famous suburb of Antioch, Jortin supposes that the image could readily suggest itself to Ignatius. Lightfoot himself is inclined to question the text, and to prefer the interpolator's text ἀλλόμενον (cf. Jn. 4[14]); but the correctness of λαλοῦν is now confirmed by the passage in the Ode, with which we can hardly fail to trace a connexion.

In assessing the character of that connexion, in this and the former passage, Drs. Harris and Mingana remark with justice that 'it is far more likely that Ignatius, writing letters rapidly on his western journey, should quote the Hymn-book of the time, than that the early Hymn-book should have picked up an obscure passage in a letter which had hardly got into circulation at a very early date'.*

Ode $17^{10.11}$

ܘܠܐ ܡܕܡ ܐܬܚܙܝ ܠܝ ܟܕ ܐܚܝܕ
ܡܛܠ ܕܬܪܥܐ ܕܟܠܡܕܡ ܐܢܐ ܐܬܥܒܕܬ ܗܘܝܬ.
ܘܐܙܠܬ ܗܘܝܬ ܥܠ ܟܠܗܘܢ ܐܣܝܪܝ ܠܡܫܪܐ ܐܢܘܢ.

'And nothing appeared closed to me;
Because I was the door of everything:
And I went towards all my bondmen to loose them'.

Cf. Ignatius, Phil. 8, 'Christ Jesus shall loose you from every bond'. This is followed by the statement (9) that 'He is the door of the Father, by which enter Abraham and Isaac and Jacob and the Prophets and the Apostles and the Church'; i.e. Jesus Christ is the door of *everybody*, which is an explanation of 'the *door of everything*' in the Ode.

Ode $41^{1 ff}$.

The connexion of this passage with Ignatius, Rom. 2, has already been noticed on p. 131, n. ‡.

These are the principal parallels between the Odes and the letters of Ignatius which Drs. Harris and Mingana have collected. The few others which they cite are of but slight importance. The case for Ignatius's knowledge of the Odes is, however, considerably strengthened when it is noticed that in Eph. 19 he actually seems to be quoting at length an ode of a similar character. The passage runs as follows:

Καὶ ἔλαθεν τὸν ἄρχοντα τοῦ αἰῶνος τούτου ἡ παρθενία Μαρίας καὶ ὁ τοκετὸς αὐτῆς, ὁμοίως καὶ ὁ θάνατος τοῦ Κυρίου· τρία μυστήρια κραυγῆς, ἅτινα ἐν ἡσυχίᾳ Θεοῦ ἐπράχθη. πῶς οὖν ἐφανερώθη τοῖς αἰῶσιν; ἀστὴρ ἐν οὐρανῷ ἔλαμψεν ὑπὲρ πάντας τοὺς ἀστέρας, καὶ τὸ φῶς αὐτοῦ ἀνεκλάλητον ἦν, καὶ ξενισμὸν παρεῖχεν ἡ καινότης αὐτοῦ· τὰ δὲ λοιπὰ πάντα ἄστρα ἅμα ἡλίῳ

* *op. cit.* ii, p. 43.

καὶ σελήνη χορὸς ἐγένετο τῷ ἀστέρι, αὐτὸς δὲ ἦν ὑπερβάλλων τὸ φῶς αὐτοῦ ὑπὲρ πάντα· ταραχή τε ἦν πόθεν ἡ καινότης ἡ ἀνόμοιος αὐτοῖς. ὅθεν ἐλύετο πᾶσα μαγεία, καὶ πᾶς δεσμὸς ἠφανίζετο κακίας, ἄγνοια καθῃρεῖτο, παλαιὰ βασιλεία διεφθείρετο, Θεοῦ ἀνθρωπίνως φανερουμένου εἰς καινότητα ἀϊδίου ζωῆς. ἀρχὴν δὲ ἐλάμβανεν τὸ παρὰ Θεοῦ ἀπηρτισμένον. ἔνθεν τὰ πάντα συνεκινεῖτο διὰ τὸ μελετᾶσθαι θανάτου κατάλυσιν.*

It seems clear that the description of the Incarnation introduced by the query *πῶς οὖν ἐφανερώθη τοῖς αἰῶσιν;* which is poetical in character and not in Ignatius's usual style, is a hymn which he is quoting. Translated into Syriac it is seen to consist of four stanzas, carefully constructed to consist of 4, 6, 6, 4 lines. The following translation is based, from *ὅθεν ἐλύετο πᾶσα μαγεία*, upon the Syriac version of the letter, in which the earlier part of the poem is not included.

ܟܘܟܒܐ ܒܫܡܝܐ ܢܗܪ
ܝܬܝܪ ܡܢ ܟܘ̈ܟܒܐ ܟܠܗܘܢ:
ܘܢܘܗܪܗ ܕܠܐ ܡܬܡܠܠ ܗܘܐ
ܘܚܕܬܘܬܗ ܡܬܕܡܪܬܐ ܗܘܬ.

ܘܫܪܟܐ ܕܟܘ̈ܟܒܐ ܟܠܗܘܢ
ܥܡ ܫܡܫܐ ܘܣܗܪܐ
ܡܬܟܢܫܝܢ ܗܘܘ ܚܕܪ ܟܘܟܒܐ
ܕܡܢܗܪ ܗܘܐ ܢܘܗܪܗ ܡܢ ܟܠܗܘܢ.
ܘܙܘܥܐ ܗܘܐ ܡܢ ܐܝܟܐ ܚܕܬܘܬܐ
ܗܝ ܕܠܐ ܕܡܝܐ ܠܗܘܢ.

ܡܟܝܠ ܡܫܬܪܝܐ ܚܪܫܘܬܐ
ܘܐܣܘ̈ܪܐ ܕܒܝܫܘܬܐ ܦܣܝܩܝܢ:
ܛܥܝܘܬܐ ܡܣܬܠܩܐ ܗܘܬ
ܘܡܠܟܘܬܐ ܥܬܝܩܬܐ ܐܬܚܒܠܬ:
ܟܕ ܐܬܝܕܥ ܐܠܗܐ ܒܐܢܫܘܬܐ
ܠܚܕܬܘܬܐ ܕܚܝ̈ܐ ܕܠܥܠܡ.

* Following the older punctuation. Lightfoot punctuates *ὅθεν ἐλύετο πᾶσα μαγεία καὶ πᾶς δεσμός, ἠφανίζετο κακίας ἄγνοια, καθῃρεῖτο παλαιὰ βασιλεία, [διεφθείρετο]*, regarding the last verb as a gloss. This, from the poetical point of view, upsets the balance altogether.

ܘܗܘܐ ܫܘܪܝܐ ܠܡܥܒܕ
ܕܒܗ ܐܠܗܐ ܡܫܡܠܐ.
ܡܢ ܗܪܟܐ ܐܬܬܙܝܥܘ ܟܠܡܕܡ
ܕܡܬܚܫܒܐ ܗܘܐ ܚܪܒܗ ܕܡܘܬܐ.

1. A star shone forth in the heaven,
Surpassing all the stars;
And its light was not to be uttered,
And its newness caused amaze.

2. Then all the rest of the stars,
Together with sun and moon,
Joined in concourse round the star;
But its light outshone them all.
Bewildered, they questioned whence came
The new thing, unlike to themselves.

3. Thenceforth was magic annulled,
And bonds of evil dissolved;
Error was swept away,
And the ancient kingdom passed;
When God appeared in the flesh
Unto newness of life without end.

4. Thus was begun the scheme
Perfected in God's design:
Hence all things were perturbed
For that death's destruction was planned.

In this ode the following points of connexion with the thought of the Odes of Solomon may be noticed:

1. Conception of the star shining in the world.

Ode 8[?] 'Let not the Luminary be conquered by darkness;
Nor let Truth flee away from falsehood'.

Ode 41[14] 'And Light dawned from the Word
That was beforetime in Him'.

2. The stars gather round the new star, and express their wonder.

Ode 12[4] 'And the Most High hath given Him to His worlds,
(Worlds) which are the interpreters of His own beauty,
And the repeaters of His praise'.

3. 'And bonds of evil dissolved'.

Ode 17^{3} 'My choking bonds were cut off by His hand'.
Ode 21^{2} 'Because He hath cast off my bonds from me'.
Ode 25^{1} 'I was rescued from my bonds'.
Ode 42^{16} 'And bring me out from the bonds of darkness'.
Ode 17^{11} (Christ speaks)

'And I went towards all my bondsmen to loose them,
That I might not leave any man bound and binding'.

'Error was swept away'.

Ode 7^{21} 'For ignorance hath been destroyed,
Because the knowledge of the Lord hath arrived'.

We have adopted ܛܘܥܝܐ 'error' in our rendering, following the Syriac text. The Greek, however, has *ἄγνοια*, which is exactly ܠܐ ܝܕܥܬܐ (lit. 'not-knowledge') of the Ode. We have both terms in the following passage:

Ode $18^{10.11}$ 'And error (ܛܘܥܝܐ) Thou knowest not,
For neither doth it know Thee.
And ignorance (ܠܐ ܝܕܥܬܐ) appeared like dust,
And like the scum of the sea'.

Ode 38^{6} 'And error fled away before Him,
And would not meet Him'.

With the whole passage cf. Ode $22^{3f.}$ (where Christ is represented as speaking):

'He who scattered My enemies
And My adversaries;
He who gave Me authority over bonds,
That I might loose them;
He that overthrew by My hand the dragon with seven heads,
And set Me at his roots that I might destroy his seed—
Thou wast there and didst help Me;
And in every place Thy name was round about Me'.

Later on in the same Ode we read—

'Thou *didst bring Thy world to corruption*,
That everything might be dissolved and *renewed*,
And on it Thou didst build *Thy kingdom*;
And it became the dwelling-place of the saints'.

This recalls the passage in our Ignatian ode—

> 'And *the ancient kingdom passed* (ܐܒܕ perished);
> When God appeared in the flesh
> Unto *newness* of life without end'.

4. 'Hence all things were perturbed, &c.'

What is covered by the expression 'all things'? It is difficult to think that the whole universe is intended; since, though the verb συνεκινεῖτο = ܐܬܬܙܝܥܘ might mean simply 'were moved' or 'excited', we hardly expect the terror and disquiet of the powers of evil and the joyous excitement of mankind destined to be redeemed to be included under one term. Probably the thought uppermost in the poet's mind is of the power belonging to the ancient kingdom, responsible for the magic, the bonds of evil, and the error mentioned in stanza 3. The somewhat obscure Ode 24 seems to describe a similar state of perturbation caused by our Lord's baptism in the ancient order of things which through this event was condemned to pass away; and this is perhaps pictured as universal, *τὴν τῶν σαλευομένων μετάθεσιν ὡς πεποιημένων, ἵνα μείνῃ τὰ μὴ σαλευόμενα.*

> 'The Dove flew over the head of our Lord the Messiah,
> Because He was her Head;
>
> And she sang over Him,
> And her voice was heard!
>
> And the inhabitants were afraid,
> And the sojourners trembled;
>
> The birds took to flight,
> And all creeping things died in their holes.
>
> And the abysses were opened and closed;
> And they were seeking for the Lord, like (women) in travail:
>
> But He was not given to them for food
> Because He did not belong to them:
>
> And the abysses were submerged in the submersion of the Lord;
> And they perished in the thought in which they had existed from the beginning.

For they travailed from the beginning,
And the end of their travail was life.

And every one of them that was defective perished;
For it was not permitted to them to make a defence for
themselves that they might remain'.

Drs. Harris and Mingana compare a somewhat similar passage at the beginning of Ode 31:

'The abysses were dissolved before the Lord;
And darkness was destroyed by His appearance.

Error went astray
And disappeared from Him,

And (as for) Falsehood, I gave it no path,
And it was submerged by the Truth of the Lord'.

'For that death's destruction was planned'.

Ode 15[9] 'Death hath been destroyed before my face;
And Sheol hath been abolished by my word.
And there hath gone up deathless life in the Lord's
land'.

Thus our Ignatian ode appears throughout to be thoroughly in keeping with conceptions contained in the Odes of Solomon.

3. *Reminiscences of the Johannine literature in the Odes of Solomon.*

The list includes some points of connexion with the Apocalypse.

Ode 1[3] 'For I should not have nown how to love the Lord, if He had not loved me'.	1 Jn. 4[19] 'We love (Him) because He first loved us'.
Ode 1[5] 'And where His rest is, there also am I'.	Jn. 14[3] 'That where I am, there ye may be also'.
Ode 1[8] 'For he that is joined to Him that is immortal, will himself also become immortal; and he that hath pleasure in the Living One, will become living'.	Jn. 14[19] 'Because I live, ye shall live also'.

Ode 1^{10} 'This is the Spirit of the Lord, that doth not lie'.	Cf. 1 Jn. 4^{1-6}.
Ode 7^{4} 'He became like me, that I might receive Him; in fashion was he reckoned like me, that I might put Him on'.	Jn. 1^{14} 'And the Word became flesh, and tabernacled among us'. Jn. 1^{12} 'But as many as received Him, to them gave He power to become the sons of God'.
Ode 8^{22} 'Pray, and continue in the love of the Lord;	Jn. 15^{9} 'Continue ye in My love'.
Ye beloved ones, in the Beloved;	Jn. 15^{9} 'As the Father hath loved Me, so have I loved you'.
And ye that are kept, in Him that lived (again)'.	Jn. 17^{11} 'Keep them in Thy name'. *v.*^{12} 'I have kept them in Thy name'. *v.*^{15} 'That Thou shouldest keep them from the evil (one)'. Jn. 14^{19} 'Because I live'.
Ode 9^{11} 'And all those that have overcome shall be written in His book'.	Apoc. 3^{5} 'He that overcometh . . . I will in no wise blot his name out of the book of life'.
Ode 9^{12} 'For their inscription is the victory, which is yours'.	1 Jn. 5^{4} 'And this is the victory that overcometh the world, even our faith'.
Ode 10^{4} 'I (Christ) took the world captive'.	Jn. 16^{33} 'I have overcome the world'.
Ode 10^{5} 'And the nations were gathered together as one that were scattered abroad'.	Jn. 11^{52} 'That He might gather together into one the children of God that are scattered abroad'.
Ode 10^{6} 'And the traces of the light were set upon their heart; and they walked in My life and were saved; and they became My people for ever and ever'.	Apoc. 21^{24} (Pesh.) 'And the nations that are saved shall walk by the light thereof'. Apoc. 21^{3} 'And they shall be His peoples' (Pesh. 'people'). Apoc. 11^{15} 'The kingdom of the world has become our Lord's

and His Christ's, and He shall reign for ever and ever'.

Ode 17^{10} 'And nothing appeared closed to Me, because I was the door of everything'.

Jn. 10^{9} 'I am the door; by Me if any enter in, he shall be saved'.

Ode $18^{1.6}$ 'O Lord, for the sake of them that are deficient, do not deprive me of the Word . . . Let not the luminary be conquered by the darkness, nor let Truth flee away from falsehood'.

Jn. $1^{1 \text{ff.}}$ 'The Word'.

v. ^{5} 'And the Light shineth in the darkness, and the darkness obscured it not'.

Ode 22^{6} (Christ speaks) 'He that overthrew by My hands the dragon with seven heads, and set Me at his roots that I might destroy his seed'.

Apoc. 12^{3} 'And there was seen another sign in heaven: and, behold, a great red dragon, having seven heads, &c.' Cf. the whole chapter.

Ode $30^{1.2}$ 'Fill ye water for yourselves from the living fountain of the Lord; for it hath been opened to you:

Jn. 4^{10} 'Thou wouldest have asked of Him, and He would have given thee living water'.

v. ^{14} 'The water that I shall give him shall become in him a fount of water for life eternal'.* Cf. Jn. 7^{38} as emended on p. 110.

And come, all ye thirsty, and take a drink, and rest by the fountain of the Lord'.

Jn. 7^{37} 'If any man thirst, let him come unto Me and drink'.

Ode 36^{3} (Christ speaks) 'And although a Son of Man, I was named the Luminary, the Son of God'.

Jn. 1^{9} 'That was the true Light'.

Ode 41^{11} 'And His Word was with us in all our way, even the Saviour who giveth life and doth not reject our souls'.

Jn. $1^{1 \text{ff.}}$ 'The Word'.

Jn. 6^{33} 'That giveth life to the world'.

v. ^{37} 'Him that cometh to Me I will in no wise cast out'.

Ode 41^{14} 'And light dawned

Jn. $1^{4.5}$ 'In Him was light, and

* So Sin. and Cur., omitting 'springing up'.

from the Word, that was beforetime in Him'.	the light was the life of men. And the light shineth in darkness'.
Ode 41[15] 'The Messiah is truly One; and He was known before the foundation of the world'.	Jn. 17[24] 'For Thou lovedst Me before the foundation of the world'.

From the poetical character of the Odes it is obvious that more or less exact quotations could hardly be expected; yet even so, some of the above-noticed coincidences are very remarkable. Ode 8[22] is entirely built up upon thoughts derived from the Last Discourses of Jn. Ode 9[11] is a fairly close representation of Apoc. 3[5]. Ode 10[5.6] is a passage which illustrates very remarkably the poet's use of the Johannine writings. His theme is the gathering of the Gentile nations into the Church; and he seems deliberately to have selected outstanding passages on this subject from Jn. and Apoc., and worked them up in a manner which utilizes their most striking phrases. This appears very clearly through comparison of the Syriac text with the corresponding phrases of Pesh. in Jn. and Apoc.

'And were gathered together as one	the nations	that were scattered abroad;
ܘܐܬܟܢܫܘ ܐܝܟ ܚܕ	ܥܡܡܐ	ܕܡܒܕܪܝܢ ܗܘܘ
ܢܟܢܫ ܠܚܕ	ܥܡܡܐ	ܕܡܒܕܪܝܢ
'He might gather together into one'	'the nations'	'that were scattered abroad'
Jn. 11[52]	Apoc. 21[24]	Jn. 11[52]

and were set the traces	of light	upon their heart,	and they walked in My life
ܘܐܬܬܣܝܡܘ ܥܩܒܬܐ	ܕܢܘܗܪܐ	ܥܠ ܠܒܗܘܢ	ܘܗܠܟܘ ܒܚܝܝ
	ܒܗ ܢܘܗܪܐ		ܘܢܗܠܟܘܢ
	'by the light'		'and they shall walk'
	Apoc. 21[24]		Apoc. 21[24]

and were saved;	and they became My people	for ever and ever'.
ܘܐܬܦܪܩܘ	ܘܗܘܘ ܠܥܡܝ	ܠܥܠܡܥܠܡܝܢ
ܕܐܬܦܪܩܘ	ܘܗܢܘܢ ܥܡܐ ܕܝܠܗ ܢܗܘܘܢ	ܠܥܠܡܐ ܕܥܠܡܐ
'that are saved'	'and they shall be His people'	'for ever and ever'.
Apoc. 21^{21}	Apoc. 21^{3}	Apoc. 11^{15}

We notice incidentally that the text of Pesh. appears to be presupposed in Apoc. 21^{24} (ܕܐܬܦܪܩܘ = τῶν σωζομένων. WH. om.) and Apoc. 21^{3} (ܥܡܐ ܕܝܠܗ = λαὸς αὐτοῦ. WH. λαοὶ αὐτοῦ).

These three lines of evidence taken together form an argument for the early date of the Fourth Gospel which is exceedingly weighty. St. Ignatius, writing in A.D. 110, was thoroughly familiar with the Theology of Jn. and 1 Jn., and therefore (we must surely infer) with the documents themselves. He also appears to have known the Odes of Solomon, and at any rate quotes an ode which is marked by the same lines of thought. Lastly, the Odes of Solomon appear unmistakably to have known not merely Jn. and 1 Jn., but also the Apocalypse. The knowledge of the Apocalypse shown in the Odes is perhaps the most surprising fact of all. If Ignatius knew the Odes, they are carried back, if not to the first century, at any rate to the very beginning of the second. But if the Apocalypse is, as is commonly thought, not earlier than the last years of Domitian's reign, i.e. *c.* A.D. 95, there scarcely seems sufficient time for the book to have influenced the Odes; even when we make full allowance for the facts that intercourse between Ephesus and Antioch was easy, and that the Apocalypse was precisely the kind of work which was likely to gain ready circulation in the east, and to be speedily utilized in time of persecution. This difficulty seems, however, to be resolved by the consideration that the book, if as late as Domitian, is generally admitted to embody much earlier elements; and it may be from these that the reminiscences in the Odes are drawn.

The weakest strand in our threefold cord is undoubtedly that which postulates Ignatius's knowledge of the Odes of Solomon. Though it will probably be admitted, upon the evidence adduced, that Ignatius quotes a hymn like the Odes, and though the evidence that he was interested in hymnology and actually knew some of the Odes is sufficiently striking, it has not been proved that he knew *all* the Odes, or that they are all by one hand, and not (like a modern hymn-book) the work of different authors at various dates. At present, however, the fact which principally concerns us is Ignatius's knowledge of the Fourth Gospel, which seems to be proved to demonstration. The manner in which he utilizes its teaching shows further that his acquaintance with it was not merely superficial, but that he had assimilated it through a familiarity extending over many years. This thoroughly favours the theory of the Antiochene origin of the Gospel.*

* The peculiar character of Ignatius's indebtedness to the thought of the Fourth Gospel is emphasized by Freiherr von der Golz (*Ignatius von Antiochien als Christ und Theologe*, in *Texte und Untersuchungen*, Band xii), and by Dr. Sanday (*Criticism of the Fourth Gospel*, pp. 242 ff.). The former scholar concludes (p. 130) that 'Ignatius must have come under the prolonged influence of a community itself influenced by Johannean thought'. Dr. Sanday says, 'I do not think there can be any doubt that Ignatius had digested and assimilated to an extraordinary degree the teaching which we associate with the name of St. John . . . I had occasion a few years ago to study rather closely the Ignatian letters, and I was so much impressed by it as even to doubt whether there is any other instance of resemblance between a biblical and patristic book, that is really so close. Allowing for a certain crudity of expression in the later writer and remembering that he is a perfervid Syrian and not a Greek, he seems to me to reflect the Johannean teaching with extraordinary fidelity.' The writer concludes by expressing his belief that, to explain the connexion in thought, the alternative lies between falling back upon the tradition that Ignatius was an actual disciple of St. John, or 'had actually had access to the Johannean writings years before the date of his journey to Rome, and that he . . devoted to them no mere cursory reading but a close and careful study which had the deepest effect upon his mind'. Elsewhere in the same work (p. 199) Dr. Sanday remarks, 'I have long thought that it would facilitate our reconstruction of the history of early Christian thought, if we could assume an anticipatory stage of Johannean teaching, localized somewhere in Syria, before the Apostle reached his final home at Ephesus. This would account more easily than any other hypothesis for the traces of this kind of teaching in the *Didaché*, and in Ignatius, as well as in some of the early Gnostic systems.'

INDEX